exploring

DIGITAL
PREPRESS

exploring

DIGITAL PREPRESS

Reid Anderson

THOMSON

™

DELMAR LEARNING

Australia Canada Mexico Singapore Spain United Kingdom United States

Exploring Digital Prepress

Reid Anderson

Vice President, Technology and Trades SBU:
Dave Garza

Editorial Director:
Sandy Clark

Senior Acquisitions Editor:
James Gish

Project Manager:
Jaimie Weiss

Marketing Director:
Debbie Yarnell

Marketing Coordinator:
Mark Pierro

Production Director:
Patty Stephan

Sr. Production Manager:
Larry Main

Sr. Content Project Manager:
Thomas Stover

Editorial Assistant:
Niamh Matthews

Cover Design:
Steven Brower

Cover Production:
David Arsenault

Cover Image:
Chris Navetta

ISBN:1-4180-1236-X

NOTICE TO THE READER

dedication

I dedicate this book to my wife, Irene.
I will be forever grateful for her love, support,
and patience during the writing of this book.

contents

CONTENTS

preface

from analog to digital

GRAPHIC DESIGN GOES ELECTRIC

When Apple launched the first MacIntosh computer in the early 1980s, it forever changed the way designers would approach art. Nearly every designer was quick to embrace the new technology, seeing the endless possibilities to expand their creativity in a digital environment. Within a few years, a new breed of designer soon emerged, a hybrid that was willing to bridge the gap between the traditional analog methods and the new digital art form that was emerging. Along with this technological revolution came changes to the way art and design communication materials were produced. It is now possible to create a graphic communication piece in just over a day. Even a corporate identity program, sales brochure, or annual report can be designed, produced, and printed in a few days. Web sites are launched moments after their internet address is registered. There isn't a person living in civilized culture who hasn't been affected by the change in the speed by which graphic communication is generated.

The people most profoundly affected by the digital revolution have been those who held jobs in printing and publishing. Much of the work that had previously been done by hand now became the job of computer artists. Film strippers and engravers quickly enrolled in training courses to learn the new software. Rubylith acetate, a process by which screens of color were cut out by hand, became obsolete. Typesetters quickly began transforming their shops into service bureaus to keep up with the times (and those who didn't, soon perished). Companies like Adobe created postscript font files and suitcases that could be installed into a computer workstation. Long-standing terms like "mechanical artwork" were replaced by "digital file." Manufacturers of 35 mm cameras also embraced the new technology and began producing digital cameras. Today's prepress technology has grown to the point where digital files can be imaged directly onto the plates required for printing. A few years from now, a prepress professional may ask, "What's negative film?"

Each year, the software industry looks to develop new applications that offer greater flexibility, enhanced features, and faster performance. A freelance designer could end up being cash strapped if they were to stay current on all the latest versions of popular graphics software. Even major design studios do not always purchase the newest edition of popular software programs. Many studios still use older versions of these applications and find it more than adequate for their needs. Some haven't even switched over to the latest operating systems of Mac OS X or Windows NT. In many cases, the studios' existing networks and systems are handling their workflow just fine and they may be reluctant to introduce an unknown variable that may cause unnecessary delays in production. Design studios often live by the saying that goes, "if it isn't broke, then don't fix it."

This is not the case in the education field, where design programs in universities and colleges teach the most current versions, so that you will be prepared to work in a rapidly changing industry. The benefits of this approach will become apparent to you when you are ready to ply your trade in the world. Make sure you make use of this state-of-the-art technology and always take your ideas as far as you can. Many a design student starts working only to find their creativity hampered by deadlines, budget restrictions, and the needs of their clients.

Before the digital revolution, a designer only worried about whether his markers would run dry or if he had enough layout paper. Now you have to be aware of all the technicalities involved in taking a beautiful image created in a software program and ensuring that what you see on your monitor will look the same when it's printed with inks on paper. You will be required to wear a number of hats when you start working. Besides creating stunning visuals, you may have to proofread the copy in your artwork, manage printing and delivery schedules, as well as fix your computer system whenever it crashes. Like a Swiss clockmaker, preparing files for print requires great expertise and precise skills. It's a challenge that has kept many designers from getting a full night's sleep at some point in their careers. So what can you as a designer do? Well, reading this book is a good place to start.

This book will take you on a step-by-step journey through the stages of what happens after a beautiful image is created on the screen. The first chapter presents the different operating systems you will use and shows how they work. You will learn about color models used for prepress in Chapter 2. The next two chapters discuss how to color manage an image, calibrate a monitor, and the easiest way to color correct an image. Chapter 5 discusses image resolution and formats. If you're not sure what kind of software with which to build a document, you'll find out what's going to work out best in Chapter 6. Keep reading and you'll discover the types of fonts in use today and how to manage them on your system.

Chapter 8 shows you when you need to trap and how to apply trapping manually to your files or by using trapping software. You'll learn about PDF technology and how to create a press-quality PDF file in Chapter 9. The next two chapters demonstrate how to preflight files and how to proof your artwork. Finally, the last chapter deals with printing technology and preparing files to send to a prepress service provider.

By the time you finish reading, you will be a prepress expert yourself, ready to take on the challenges of print production without fear. This book provides the means for you to reach an end, which is to produce the highest quality artwork. However, the only true way to learn is by doing, so carry it along with you as a handy reference guide whenever you begin a new project. The information contained in this book is organized in a clear, linear format to make it easier for you as a designer to find that specific area of prepress that will help you complete your work. It will also help you grow as a designer. Someone who understands all the intricacies of prepress production and the printing process can make intelligent choices that will make their work stand out from the crowd.

So read the book carefully and use all the information to your advantage. When designing, think about creating special spot colors, embossed plates, and varnishes that bring extra vibrancy to your artwork. Try combining different printing methods to make your pieces stand out. Consider developing intricate die-cuts for your designs. By utilizing the various special finishes described in the last chapter, you can raise the quality of your work far above the competition. With this new knowledge there is no limit to what you can create.

HOW TO USE THIS TEXT

The following components of this book will help guide you through each chapter and are written to enhance your understanding of the subject.

Objectives

The Learning Objectives appear at the beginning of each chapter. They describe the outcomes and skills the reader should achieve upon comprehension of the learning material.

Tips

Tips are interspersed beside the text and provide the reader with special hints and practical information.

Sidebars

Sidebars appear throughout the text and are useful for describing particular software processes or specific information on a topic related to the chapter.

Summary of the Chapter, Review Questions, and Exercises

Summary, Review Questions, and Exercises are located at the end of each chapter. They help to reinforce the learning material and allow readers to gauge their comprehension of the chapter.

FEATURES

The following lists some highlights of the material found in the text:

- Provides a thorough, yet comprehensive overview of the prepress process that is accessible for both novice and experienced graphic designers
- Teaches the theory behind prepress as well as the terminology associated with print production
- Instructs the reader in step-by-step methods to achieve the maximum quality from the printing process
- Uses practical examples to demonstrate prepress concepts and techniques
- Provides powerful tips and hints that the reader can apply to real-world situations
- Uses an open, fun, and convincing writing style that makes difficult subject matter easy to comprehend
- Objectives define the learning outcomes for each chapter and assist the instructor in preparing lesson plans
- Chapter Summary and Review Questions help to reinforce the learning material presented in each chapter
- Practical and interesting exercises assist students in acquiring the skills necessary to prepare files for print

ABOUT THE AUTHOR

Reid Anderson has been working and teaching in the graphics arts industry for more than a quarter of a century. Along the way, he has won a number of awards for his design work. He is a graduate of the Package Design program at Humber College in Toronto, Ontario. An accomplished educator, he has participated in on-site and on-line program and curriculum development as well as training sessions for both community colleges and private institutions. Mr. Anderson is currently working towards his B.Ed in Adult Education through Brock University. He is a Professor of Graphic Design at Durham College in Oshawa, Ontario, and has served on the Academic Council for Durham College.

ACKNOWLEDGEMENTS

I wish to thank everyone who helped in the development of this project. The people at Delmar who believed in this book and guided me through the process: Jim Gish, Senior Acquisitions Editor, for his enthusiasm and faith in my abilities as a writer. Jamie Wetzel, my Developmental Editor, for her support and patience. I would also like to thank Thomas Stover, Project Editor, and Niamh Mathews, Editorial Assistant.

I owe a debt of gratitude to all the people whose contributions and knowledge of the prepress and printing industry helped me produce the text for this book, including Randy Milligan, Prepress Supervisor at Maracle Press in Oshawa; David Hunter of Pilot Marketing; Ray Larabie, owner of Typodermic; and Peter Linnell of Atlantic Tech Solutions. Your input is deeply appreciated.

A special thanks to my colleagues at Durham College, who are the finest group of people I have had the pleasure of working with. I would also like to thank my wife Irene for her love, support, and never faltering patience through the writing of this book.

Finally, I would like to thank two of my greatest teachers: Wayson Choy my Communications Professor at Humber, and Richard Nicholson, my high school English instructor at Jarvis Collegiate in Toronto. Both were instrumental in helping me develop my writing abilities.

Without the continuing desire to learn, civilization begins to decay.

CHAPTER 1

objectives

- Recognize the differences between traditional and digital prepress
- Explain the color separation process
- Examine different operating systems and find one to suit your needs and budget
- Discover how various operating systems handle different workflows COL

introduction

Before the digital age, all design work went through a time-consuming process before it went to press. These steps could be divided into the creative, production, and film stages. The process began with the concept or thumbnail stage, followed by a presentation to the client. The next stage was to produce camera-ready art. The last step was to send this camera-ready art to film. Most of the work was done by hand, so the turnaround time on projects was considerably longer. If we look at what was required at each stage and how the digital age has changed this process, we can gain a better understanding of today's prepress technology.

THE CREATIVE PROCESS: YESTERDAY AND TODAY

Before designers began to doodle ideas, they first had to understand the needs of their clients. An initial meeting with the client to discover their goals for the communication piece was, and still is, essential. It was up to the sales reps, or "suits" as they are referred to in the industry, to ask questions that address the history or background of the product, such as the target market, their profile and demographics, as well as the sales and marketing goals for the project. The sales reps met regularly with the client and relayed information back to the creative department. This information was used by the design studio to create a strategy brief, which served as a map for the project, keeping the designers focused on satisfying the needs of their client and the marketplace. Once the strategy brief was approved, the creative process of putting ideas on paper began. These first steps have remained intact even in today's electronic age.

A series of sketches or thumbnails were always produced first and then discussed amongst members of the creative department (see figure 1–1). This step has also remained unchanged since the first commercial artwork began appearing in the mid-1800s. The materials required for this stage were fundamental. Any combinations of markers, pencils, pens, and paper will do. Actually, any paper item can be used in a pinch. Many award-winning designs have been created on an art director's napkin over lunch at a local restaurant. Once the ideas were reviewed and revised, rough layouts or renderings were produced using markers on layout paper. Once approved, comprehensives were made and then mounted on art board with a cover stock that was presented to the client.

figure | 1–1 |

A series of thumbnail sketches of a logo design for a computer software company.

Pre-computer Artwork

Once the creative piece was presented and approved with any necessary revisions, the next step was to prepare camera-ready artwork (also called mechanicals) that a printer would use to produce the film to make the plates for the printing press. Camera-ready artwork was basically a white art board with all the elements such as type, images, and line art pasted into position. All the elements were in black so that the filmmaker could shoot and separate the various colors into film for the plates (see figure 1–2). Any text used in the piece had to be done by a typesetter in galleys (long single columns) that were cut and pasted onto the art board. Photographs or illustrations were reproduced in black and white from a photostat camera (see figure 1–3) and were pasted into position on the artwork using tools such as T-squares, set squares, x-acto knives, and rubber cement (see figure 1–4). Once the artwork was completed, it was shown to the client for proofreading, mark up of alterations, and then to "sign-off" on the back of the board. Obtaining a sign-off is still a necessity for every designer or studio as it limits the liability they may incur in case an error is made after the job has been printed (see figure 1–5).

The first set of film negatives (or working film) contained all text, graphics, and photographs. The latter were stripped into position after being converted into

figure | 1–2 |

A typical example of camera-ready artwork with rubylith overlays (used for cutting screens of the colors) placed in position on the art board. Notice the Pantone swatches on the left side.

figure | 1-3 |

A reproduction of a black and white illustration using a photostat camera.

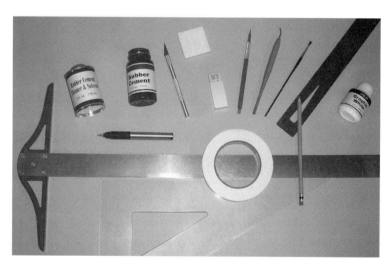

figure | 1-4 |

The materials a graphic artist required to produce mechanical artwork before computers.

halftone negatives from continuous tone images (an example would be a photographic print made from a 35 mm camera). Once the working film was finished, a final set of film separations were usually made for imaging the plates. From there, the plates would go onto the press and the job could be run. A designer would normally attend the beginning of the press run to check for color balance and registration. This is called

ONE Great Design
Studio Inc.

I hearby certify that I have carefully checked and read over this proof and I have found no errors or omissions. By signing this proof, I am releasing One Great Design Studio Inc. from any liability.

_____

Joe Client, ANY Corporation

figure | 1 – 5 |

An example of a sign-off label that would be glued to the back of a digital proof or camera-ready artwork.

a press approval and usually requires a "sign-off" on a proof from the printing press by the designer. This ensured the job looked the same when it was first shown to the client. As you can see, many steps were involved in seeing a project through all these stages (see figure 1 – 6).

ENTER THE DIGITAL AGE

As you've seen, the creative process always begins at the thumbnail stage. It is this initial phase that dictates the direction a project will take. It is often a misconception among graphics students that they can begin designing on the computer using their favorite software program (normally Illustrator). When students choose to work this way, they produce designs that are static, mechanical, and far too formal. They mistakenly believe that Illustrator was created for developing ideas. Although Illustrator is a terrific drawing program, it is not as a substitute for exploring ideas through thumbnail sketches. The same goes for QuarkXPress, InDesign, Photoshop, or any other software. Software is a means used to achieve an end product, but doesn't replace the conceptualization stage in design. By using your hand to draw what your mind conceives, you are allowing ideas to flow freely from your mind onto the printed page.

Software programs are more useful for creating a comprehensive presentation for the client to view, which is the next phase of the creative process. Years ago when designers used markers to do this, the results could be spectacular, but also time consuming. Many hours were often wasted if the rendering did not turn out as planned, or if a cup of coffee

figure | 1 – 6 |

A brochure created for a motorcycle show using traditional tools and materials. You can see the creative and production stages, as well as the final printed piece.

was spilled on the layout the night before the presentation. And, if a client had many revisions, then the layout or mockup had to be recreated from scratch with those changes in the revised layout. Nowadays, a designer can alter artwork for a client in a fraction of the time thanks to the digital nature of the work itself. If there are changes to a design piece, they can quickly be made with a new printout in minutes. And if the client is in a real hurry, almost all software programs allow a file to be saved in a portable document format (PDF) that can be sent back to the client via e-mail.

The process of producing the final artwork used in creating film has also been streamlined. Graphic designers no longer sit at drafting tables using antiquated tools to produce mechanical artwork. They now sit at computerized workstations and send their electronic artwork files across the internet to service providers. Instead of waiting for galleys to come back from a typesetter, designers enter text themselves, or import it from a word processing program. Nowadays, Photostat cameras are obsolete, as scanners can turn any photograph into a pixel-based image to be edited in Photoshop and imported into Quark or Illustrator. Software programs now display colors in almost any model, eliminating the need for color selector books and swatch samples attached to an art board. For these reasons, camera-ready artwork is basically extinct. The phrase now used to describe artwork done on computer is "digital art." And film is no longer done by hand, but created from the digital art files by sending the information they contain to a platesetter that separates the information into the different plates used for printing (see figure 1–7). Each plate represents a different process or spot color in the piece and will be placed onto a cylinder on a press. Let's take a look at how the color separation process works.

From Pixels to Dots

When we scan a photograph into our computer, exactly how does the image we see on our screen get translated onto a sheet of paper from our color printer? The answer is a simple one, yet crucial to understanding the prepress process. As you know, a photograph that is imaged from a 35 mm camera is what we call a continuous tone image. This means there is no separation in any of the colors, so our eye combines the various wavelengths of light that strike the page to form a visual representation of the image

Operator workstation

RIP

Platesetter

figure |1–7|

The stages that digital artwork goes through when it is being output to plates.

(more on how our eyes perceive color in the next chapter). In order to display this continuous tone image on our computer screen through a program like Photoshop, the colors must be broken into small squares of information called pixels (an acronym for picture elements). Pixels can vary both in size and depth (more about bit-depth in Chapter 5). These pixels are displayed on our screen in Photoshop using three channels with differing levels of red, green, and blue. All photos and line art we want to use in our artwork have to be scanned in before they can be displayed on our screen. The exception of course is an image from a digital camera which is already broken into pixels.

In order for these pixels to be represented on paper, they must first be translated into a PostScript language. PostScript is a page-description language invented by Adobe Systems, Inc. in the early 1980s, primarily so output devices could read pixel-based images. When a laser or inkjet printer reads the PostScript language, it replaces the pixels in an image with halftone dots, which are dots arranged in a fixed grid pattern. Actually, all colors we see on our screen, including gray tones, are represented on our paper by dots. Smaller dots that are used to create these areas of color and gray tones on a page are called laser dots. In fact, these laser dots combine to make up the larger halftone dots (see figure 1–8). This process will be discussed in greater detail in Chapter 5.

Let it RIP

This procedure of converting pixels and areas of color into printable halftone and laser dots is called a RIP. It stands for raster image processor. The name says exactly that—images processed into rasters (which means dots). The term is also used to describe the built-in translation device that is in all PostScript-compatible output devices. The

An elliptical halftone dot is actually
made up of smaller laser dots.

figure | 1–8 |

A representation of how laser dots combine to form halftone dots.

amount of time involved in RIPping an electronic file through an output device is dependent on the size of the file (or the amount of PostScript information in your artwork) and also on the resolution of the images contained in the file. Later on, in Chapter 6, we will see why it is important to build your artwork document efficiently and correctly to minimize the time it takes to RIP a file and to prevent costly mistakes.

When electronic files are printed through an imagesetter, halftone and laser dots are imaged onto photographic film. To get an idea of how this device works, think of it as a complex laser printer with much higher resolution capabilities. The size of the halftone dot is determined by the color intensity of the pixel it represents. As mentioned before, the imagesetter creates a halftone dot by constructing it from a number of laser dots. In this way, an imagesetter is really dividing a page into two grids that are superimposed over each other, one grid representing the halftone dots and the other the laser dots.

Going Directly to Plate

Direct-to-plate printing is a faster process from the usual film route, and is rapidly becoming the norm in the industry. This method of creating metal plates for the printing press bypasses the film stage and instead sends the electronic files from the prepress workstation to a platesetter. A laser within the platesetter etches the areas to be printed directly onto the plates, thus saving time and money. Many print and service providers are embracing this method, particularly as the technology has quickly advanced and the purchase price of the platesetter and replacement parts are more reasonable than when they were first introduced. As well, the microdot resolution is much finer in a laser platesetter than in a traditional platemaker, enhancing the printing quality.

You should now have a basic understanding of the color separation process. It sounds complicated, but it really is not. The fine details of knowing at what resolution to scan your images and how to indicate the resolution for the halftone and laser dots will be dealt with in Chapter 5. It is important to ask the manager or prepress specialist at your print plant as many questions as you can think of when first starting out. Also, always proofread your work carefully and when you are absolutely sure it is correct, get someone else to proofread it. A second pair of eyes will usually catch anything you might have missed. Mistakes that are caught at the printing stage are time-consuming, costly, and always avoidable.

CHOOSING THE SYSTEM THAT IS RIGHT FOR YOU

The digital age has placed more demands on the design professional to create high quality work almost overnight. Although designers are called upon to come up with the great idea instantly, it is the production artists who handle the assembly and prepress preparation of digital files who end up feeling the pressure. In order to keep up with the demand for faster turnaround, designers require better performance, more memory, and advanced features from their systems. This causes the developers of hardware and software to compete heavily with each other to meet this demand. New products hit the stores each year, hoping to capture a share of the market. A designer needs to keep up-to-date on the latest trends in software technology. This allows them and the studio in which they work to stay competitive in the marketplace.

There are a number of systems available to you when you become a prepress professional as well as numerous software applications from which to choose. It is important to select a system that is appropriate to the type of work you will be producing. The system and accompanying software that a designer may choose could well be different than someone who is involved in the production of a newspaper publication. Even a prepress service provider who is only producing film or plates may use entirely different software. Let's have a look at the two most popular systems available.

Apples to Oranges: Mac or PC

Fifteen years ago, if you wanted your prepress service provider to do high-end image editing, retouching, or imposition on your files, you had to go to one that used very complex workflow systems. These firms invested hundreds of thousands of dollars in equipment from companies like Agfa, CreoScitex, and Silicon Graphics. The average design studio could not afford such expensive hardware unless they regularly had to produce film for high-end graphics. However, times are changing and even prepress houses are switching to less expensive systems as the power and performance of Mac and PC systems have grown.

It would be difficult to clearly state that one system has the advantage over the other. A MacIntosh computer is used mostly by the design industry. Meanwhile, a PC with a Windows operating system, that has been a mainstay in the business world since computers became readily available, is slowly gaining acceptance in the graphics industry. While PCs are generally less expensive and have a greater number of software and utilities available, graphic applications often run smoother on the Mac OS X system, and the PostScript fonts it uses are more compatible with output devices. Both systems have their good points, so let's take a look at the advantages or disadvantages of each so you can decide which one is right for you.

An Apple a Day...

MacIntosh has taken a huge step toward becoming more PC-like in its interface with the new OS X system. It is Unix-based and has a very different hierarchy for

figure | 1 – 9 |

A typical MacIntosh workstation used by a graphic designer.

saving and storing files than the previous operating system of 9.0. Many designers now prefer it, although a few found a steep learning curve switching between the two. One primary difference between OS X and 9.0 is that most of the system information is stored in a root folder. This has seemingly solved the problem of extension conflicts and frequent system crashes, a nuisance for Mac users in the past. A new feature called the *Dock* makes for easier access to documents and folders. Making changes to how the operating system works is faster, thanks to the *System Preferences* panel. As well, the *Printer Setup Utility* and pre-installed printer drivers available in OS X allow users to switch to a different printer in a blink of a pop-up menu.

There is no mystery why Macs are popular with the graphics industry. Apple leads the way in color matching for designers and desktop publishers. They run graphic applications faster and rendering is also smoother. Apple has also included monitor calibration software into OS X called *Display Calibrator Assistant*, which gives you a couple of ways to calibrate your monitor (see Chapter 3). Files that were created in another platform such as Windows can be easily opened on a Mac. The best news is that Macs do not suffer from the numerous viruses that infect millions of PCs. There are only a few viruses that affect Macs, and most are easy to get rid of.

Perhaps the only misconception that exists among consumers is that Apple computers are more expensive. However, if you look at what comes standard on a Mac it closes the gap in price between the two systems, except for the very low-end PCs. Macs come bundled with software for sending e-mails, surfing the web, creating basic word documents, playing movies or music, and cataloging photographic images. Just these few extras make the price between Macs and PCs comparable. Finally, Macs are easier to fix for the do-it-yourselfer. You can use software like Norton Utilities that fixes most system problems, or the Disk Utility that comes with OS X, which is useful for verifying or repairing disk permissions.

One possible drawback that Apple has is a very small share of the market (less than six percent); which means if you purchase a Mac, you will be in the minority of computer owners in the business world. However, do not be dissuaded by this small obstacle as Apple, for the most part, has a monopoly in the design world. When you talk with designers, they say they find the Mac environment easier to navigate as well as more visually aesthetic. Overall, there are very few disadvantages to owning a computer from Apple (see figure 1–10).

Mac OS X	PC/Wintel
ADVANTAGES	
• OS X environment is easier to navigate through and more aesthetically pleasing	• Numerous vendors make for more competitive pricing
• Faster rendering capabilities with smoother graphics	• Users can custom build their own systems
• Superior color matching	• Software for system, internet, and utilities are both more plentiful and more readily available
• Built-in monitor calibration	
• Not as prone to viruses	
• Better security features such as a built-in firewall	• Have a larger share of home computer and business market
• Uses postscript fonts that are more compatible with imagesetters	• Less expensive for a basic system
	• Same or greater availability of graphics software
• Easier to use multiple printers across a network	• Hardware parts for expanding systems are easier to find
• Repair work can usually be done by user	

figure | 1 – 10 |

This chart compares the advantages of both PC and Apple computers.

> ## Checking Out Your System
>
> If you are not sure what features your CPU has built into it, there is a quick way to check. If you have an Apple with Mac OS X installed, simply go up to the Apple icon in the top menu bar and select *About This Mac*. A window will pop up that shows the processor speed and internal memory. If you want to know more, click on the *More Info* button and the Apple's System Profiler will come up displaying everything that is installed on your system, including internal components, applications, extensions, and networking capabilities (see figure 1–11). Finding the same information on a PC is trickier as Windows has no built-in profiler. A separate application such as MathWorks System Profiler must be downloaded and installed first and then launched from the desktop (see figure 1–12).

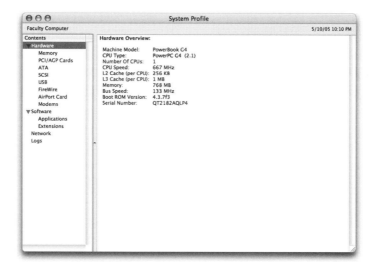

figure | 1–11 |

The Apple System Profiler gives you all the information you need about your MacIntosh.

To PC or Not To PC

The Windows XP environment is quite different from Mac OS X. Although designers who grew up with computers running Windows 95, OS/2, and NT find it an improvement, the novice computer user may still find it a steep learning curve. The price attractiveness of a PC is probably the main reason that some designers choose not to go down the Apple road. There is no doubt that a high-end PC with all the latest extra options costs about the same as its Mac equivalent; however low-end PC systems are definitely cheaper. The greatest advantage that PCs have over Macs is

figure | 1 – 12 |

You can find out what's under your PC's hood with the MathWorks System Profiler.

that there are numerous manufacturers from which to choose for hardware components. Apple clones are extinct these days.

Several years ago, many PC computer buyers found it advantageous to custom build their own computers. These days, most Wintel systems come with all the bells and whistles attached, so there is no need to add components to them. Ethernet cards and PCI slots are abundant in all new models, making it an easily expandable system. Network connectivity that was limited in older low-end versions of Pentium Intel systems has been improved with two FireWire ports now standard. Peripherals are also easier to set up and hook into a PC now that USB ports have replaced parallel ports.

On the down side, PCs are still more susceptible to viruses, spyware, and hackers, although the latest software has definitely improved these security concerns. Still, it may frustrate designers who work in a cross-platform environment that they can easily bring up PC files on a Mac system, but cannot always do the reverse without purchasing a separate piece of software. Microsoft has not addressed this issue with the latest version of Windows, possibly because Apple has so little of the market.

As mentioned before, precise color matching is still an issue with PCs and users can still buy systems with monitors that display only 256 colors, which is definitely inadequate for any serious designer. Lastly, installing printer software and selecting a printer still takes longer in Windows XP. Many designers find they have connectivity problems when switching from one printer to another (i.e. a black and white laser to a color inkjet) when using a PC.

Shopping for Your System

Before you run to your nearest discount computer store, do some research so you know what your needs really are. Start by reading reviews in computer magazines such as *MacWorld*, *PCWorld*, *MacAddict*, etc. They always have comparison reviews for both new models of computers and peripherals, as well as software. Some even include a disk that contains demos of new software for production, networking, internet use, interface design, and utilities. Once you know what you are looking for, find a store that has knowledgeable sales staff. It may be tempting to shop online, but a test drive is worth it. Bring along a USB memory stick with a large Photoshop file and see how long it takes to copy and open on the hard drive. Remember that your system has to last you for three to five years so do not sacrifice performance for a low price.

As a designer entering the creative world, a Mac system would definitely be to your advantage, but PCs are slowly making inroads into the tight-knit design community, so look at all your options and weigh the factors carefully before making a decision.

Processing Speed and Memory

There are other factors to consider when looking for a system. How well your system performs is divided between processor speed and the amount of random access memory (RAM) you have. There are two kinds of memory used by your system. The first is RAM, which runs applications and system extensions. This type of memory is impermanent and is stored on chips in your CPU (central processing unit). The other type of memory is storage and is used for storing files on an internal hard disk drive (HDD) or an external drive (such as a USB drive). Having more RAM will allow your computer to process information more rapidly, while more hard disk space will provide more room for storage of software applications and electronic files. Another type of memory is stored on CDs and DVDs and can only be read from, not written to. It is called ROM or read-only memory.

The internal processor in your CPU also affects how quickly your computer performs certain tasks. The processor is designed to execute different ones simultaneously. Most of the tasks it performs are complex calculations for data operations. Macs use PowerPC processors by Motorola while PCs use Pentium processors made by Intel. If you plan to edit high-end graphics, video, or sound, you will need a processor that is at least 750 MHz.

Generally speaking, more memory and a faster processor for your system is always better, but beware of overbuying and making your CPU too costly. It would be nice

> ▶ ## The Need for Speed
>
> When buying a new system, if you are looking to get the maximum speed for your dollar, then adding more RAM would be your best bet. Without adding more internal memory to your computer, a faster processor will not significantly speed up the processing time. Look for a system that has plenty of open slots so you can add blocks of memory as you need them. Also check out the specifications for the bus speed on the system as well. This is the speed at which your CPU communicates with the rest of your computer. A good bus speed would be at least 250 MHz. Finally, look at the L1 and L2 cache size, which are used by the CPU processor to access a small amount of memory to perform routine functions at full speed. As with processors, when looking at the cache size, larger is always better.

to have a top of the line PowerMac G5 with a 500 Gb hard drive, 1 Gb of RAM, a 2.7 GHz dual-core processor, and three PCI slots. However that is quite an expensive system. An EMac or IMac with at least a 200 Gb hard drive, 512 Mb of RAM, and a 1.6 GHz processor with a built-in LCD screen may serve you just as well. Check to make sure the unit you buy has enough USB slots for all your peripheral equipment such as printers, scanners, digital cameras, etc.

On the PC side of things, a system that runs the latest version of Windows with an Intel Pentium D 930 dual core processor, 1 Gb RAM, and a 200 Gb hard drive should purr along just nicely. Remember, it is not necessary to buy the most expensive system available, as you can easily upgrade to a faster processor or add more memory (RAM or hard disk space) and PCI slots as required. Keep in mind that expandability is the key to making your system last longer, not the final price tag. Many designers have bought expensive systems only to find their options limited when they want to upgrade.

LINUX MEETS PREPRESS

Over the last few years, there has been talk of Linux making its way into the prepress arena as an alternative operating system. Developed in the early 1990s by a university student from Finland named Linus Torvalds, it quickly became available as downloadable freeware on the internet. Despite nearly non-existent marketing and promotional efforts, it has been embraced by individuals and companies worldwide as a viable alternative to Unix.

The appeal of Linux is that it is written in a simple programming language, is cheap to buy, and even runs on older systems with outdated hardware. Many printing plants are using it to replace their existing server software using leftover hardware

► THE *professional* **PROFILE** *Randy Milligan*

MAKING MARACLES HAPPEN

Randy Milligan is prepress supervisor at Maracle Press in Oshawa, Ontario. He oversees 14 people in their prepress production department. As one of the largest printers in the region of Durham, Ontario, Maracle has prospered since its inception and currently employs more than 70 people. Nestled in a quiet community, Maracle first began printing religious material from a church they purchased and converted into a printing plant nearly a century ago. They quickly outgrew the original building and continue to expand with new additions being built even to this day.

Randy Milligan graduated from Sir Sanford Fleming College in 1982 and then began his career working in his family's business. After the business closed, he moved on to Total Graphics in Peterborough, Ontario, until Maracle brought him on board. Most of his day is spent trouble-shooting, assisting clients with preparing files, and ensuring their workflow system runs smoothly. The department has both Mac and PC platforms with a multitude of prepress software. Maracle updates their hardware regularly every two to three years to keep their workflow systems current.

The artwork that arrives from their clients is mostly built either in Quark, InDesign, Photoshop, Illustrator, or Corel Draw. Occasionally, a client sends a file created in an application such as Multi-Ad Creator, Microsoft Publisher, and even Word. "When we get a file created in a word processing program, the text usually reflows," Randy explains, "because they don't always allow you to replace fonts. I usually ask the client to resave it as a PDF file and send it to us again."

A good portion of the production team's time is spent on preparing and repairing PDF files. "PitStop is a savior for a lot of our work," he says, "especially for files with spot colors and missing images or fonts. We can take a client's PDF file, open it up in Pit Stop, fix any errors, and apply our own color profile that is calibrated for our presses." They use Prinergy and PrintReady as imposition programs and will send the final file to one of several digital plotters that come with perfecting capabilities.

Once the job is ready to go to press, the plates are made from the press-ready file using a Fuji or CreoScitex platesetter. "We use an NT server with Unix-based software in combination with an Apple X server to RIP our files to the platesetter," says Milligan. Both Milligan and Maracle Press recognize the value and efficiency of direct-to-plate technology. Production time is significantly decreased, which allows Maracle to stay competitive. He further states, "Five years ago, we used to RIP files to our imagesetter 30 times a day, now we might use it 30 times a year." Another benefit of direct-to-plate printing is that metal plates can be recycled more easily than film. "We don't bother to file our metal plates," concludes Milligan, "It's easier to remake them from the electronic files stored on our database." ◄

that is inadequate for their current workflow. They can purchase additional networking software, like Netatalk, that runs on Linux, which can connect to an Apple system running Mac OS 9.0. Newer operating systems require no special software to connect to a Linux server and many printers find it works more efficiently. In fact, some newspapers are finding Linux a better choice to perform automated layout tasks thanks to a very powerful scripting tool called Python.

Unfortunately, neither Quark nor Adobe have jumped onto the Linux bandwagon, so do not expect to see versions of Quark, Illustrator, or Photoshop for Linux anytime soon. Still, there are some graphics software applications available to the die-hard Linux user who wishes to use this system for digital artwork (more on this in Chapter 6). There is also a version of Acrobat Reader that runs on Linux that a designer could send to a client to proof artwork as a PDF.

As far as environment goes, Linux offers a couple of options. One is a text-based interface, and the other is a graphical interface called the X Windows (also called the K desktop environment or KDE for short). The latter resembles a regular Windows environment, so PC users may find it easier to use (see figure 1 – 13). However, even KDE still relies on some scripting for functionality and most computer novices may find this frustrating.

Unless you are willing to spend hours learning a new operating system, Linux is probably not the best option for your prepress workflow. Obtaining fonts for Linux

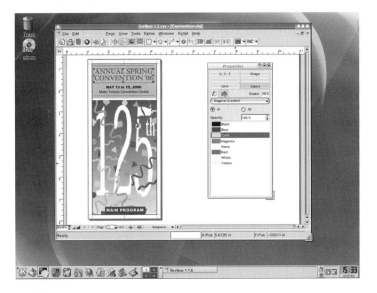

figure | 1 – 13 |

A screen shot of the KDE desktop on a Linux system.

could also prove to be a stumbling block as there are not as many fonts written for this system. Most of them are TrueType fonts, which have proven to be incompatible with the RIP software some imagesetters use (Chapter 7 explains why in more detail).

Although a few printing plants are making the transition into Linux, it will be a few years before it becomes as popular as OS X or Windows. Still, with constant improvement in graphics software, Linux is beginning to gain acceptance in the prepress industry as a viable operating system.

SUMMARY

Whichever hardware and operating system you decide to go with, make sure you choose it wisely. Look at a variety of models and always make sure you can add necessary upgrades down the road. Some salespeople may try to talk you into buying a more expensive system, but keep in mind that you will need to add peripherals like a scanner, color printer, digital camera, as well as software. Factor these costs into the total purchase price so you don't overspend on the computer itself. Typically, you can expect to get five years out of your CPU, and then it will be time to upgrade again to stay current.

Also, consider for what type of workflow you will primarily be using the system. For instance, if you are going to be working on high-end projects such as packaging or advertising, you will want to invest in a more sophisticated system with state-of-the-art technology. On the other hand, if you are going to be doing a lot of one- or two-color work, such as flyers or brochures, you can probably get by with a smaller, less expensive system. When looking at different computers and peripherals, remember the saying, "less is often more." There is no reason to buy an expensive system when a moderately priced one will do.

in review

1. What was the name of the artwork used to make film from before computers were used for digital production?

2. Who set type in galleys before software programs allowed designers to do this?

3. What does the term RIP stand for?

4. What is the name of the process that bypasses the film making stage in printing?

5. Name two advantages of either Mac OS X or the Windows operating system.

6. What is considered an adequate processing speed in a CPU?

7. What is the difference between random access memory (RAM) and hard drive memory?

8. What is the name of the graphical interface used on a Linux operating system?

exercises

1. In order to become familiar with your operating system and what you can do with it, you need to discover what its capabilities are. Turn on your computer and launch your operating system. Using the profiler that comes with your operating system, find out as much as you can about your computer (i.e. how much RAM and hard disk space it has, processing speed, available USB slots, PCI cards installed, if it has FireWire, if it has an internal modem, or DVD burner, etc.). Does it have all the necessities to produce print production material?

2. To help you understand the process of separating colors in your document into plates, it is useful to see how an output device with PostScript capabilities will print each plate. Open an InDesign file that you created using more than two colors. Select Print from the top menu under File. Select a black and white laser printer connected to your computer from the pop-up menu beside Printer. Click on the *Output* section on the left hand side. Now select *Separations* in the pop-up menu where it indicates Color. How many plates are going to be printed out? Notice that you can stop inks from printing by clicking on the printer icons beside each plate name. Try printing out one of the plates. How does the image differ from what you see on screen?

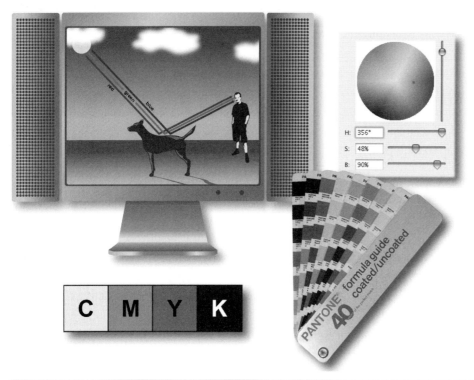

Pantone® Color Selector book courtesy of Pantone® Inc.

CHAPTER 2

objectives

- Explore color systems and discover how they apply to prepress
- Examine the relationship between additive and subtractive colors
- Select and apply colors in software applications that are used in prepress

introduction

Color is something that many people, including designers, take for granted. Yet how often are we conscious of the effect color has on us? We choose certain colors for decorating our homes or offices, the clothes we wear, our hair, and the cars we drive. Even our choice of what foods we like to eat can be based on our preferences for color. How many people would eat a banana if it were blue instead of yellow? Or drink a cup of coffee if it was green and not black? From these examples, we can see why it is important for a designer to show the client a proof with colors that match as closely as possible those that will be on the printed piece. Colors can change dramatically depending on in what mode they are displayed, how they are being printed, and the material on which they are printed. For this reason, color should be considered at each stage of the design process including final production of the artwork. As designers, we need to be aware of matching colors, or we can end up with a final printed piece that is unsatisfactory to both the client and ourselves.

HOW OUR EYES SEE COLOR

To understand color better, it is useful to know how our eye perceives color. We look around and see color everywhere, but how do our eyes translate it into an image our mind recognizes? As wavelengths of light from the sun strike the earth and the objects on it, they are reflected back to our eyes at different frequencies. Some of these wavelengths that reach our planet are out of the range that can be seen by our eyes. For example, we cannot perceive X-rays, microwaves, infrared, or radio waves. When waves of light come in contact with our eyes, small photoreceptors called cones at the back of our eyes interpret small, medium, and long wavelengths and correspondingly translate them into values of red, green, and blue or RGB. This information is then sent as signals along our optic nerves to the brain. As the cones are limited in the amount of color information they can interpret through these varying wavelengths, they will combine values of red, green, and blue to create different hues. Rods interpret the lightness or darkness of a color or its tonal quality. The rods are situated behind the cones at the back of the retina. These rods send the color information along the same pathway to the brain.

After the cones and rods send this data along the optic nerve, our brain combines the information into a seemingly continuous visual image (see figure 2 – 1). For instance,

figure | 2 – 1 |

Wavelengths of light reflecting off objects provide our eyes with color information that our mind translates into an image. See color insert.

if we look at a banana, our eyes are actually combining wavelengths of red and green to make yellow. So an object that is blue, like the ocean, will mostly reflect wavelengths that are in the blue spectrum of light. Any wavelengths that are outside of the blue spectrum (i.e. red or green) will be absorbed into the water and not be reflected back to the eye. This is true of all objects and elements around us. Darker objects tend to absorb color while lighter objects will reflect more color back to the viewer. Also, as the light source diminishes, so does the vibrancy of the color. This is why colors appear more muted and darker in tone in the early evening or morning. To understand how color and light are related, we must take a look at color models that were developed to help understand this relationship.

COLOR MODELS

By the late 1800s, scientists began to study color and developed color systems to describe the nature of color. Alfred Munsell, who was a professor and artist, devised a numerical chart that defined color in terms of hue, value, and chroma (which bears similarity to hue, saturation, and brilliance or the later HSB model). Another scientist, James Maxwell configured a model of color as a triangle with all light comprised of red, green, and blue values. The work of both Munsell and Maxwell eventually paved the way for the development of a standard color system, the CIE model.

The CIE Color System

The CIE chromaticity model is the most traditional method of describing visible colors, and is the basis for color conversion in many graphic software applications. It was developed in 1931 as a standard for industry and science and was named after its creators, the Commission Internationale de L'Eclairage (International Commission of Illumination). It is the international group of experts solely devoted to the study of color.

In the CIE model, the values of color are mathematically plotted along a horizontal (*x*) and vertical (*y*) axis and are meant to accurately represent human color perception (see figure 2–2). From a designer's viewpoint, it is the accuracy of these values that is most useful. They allow colors to be measured and recorded for later use without the loss of quality that can happen with color swatches. In fact, the Info palette in Adobe Photoshop shows the *x* and *y* values of a specific color as well as the RGB and CMYK values. A designer can make use of this feature to more accurately record colors.

Further development of the CIE system in 1971 lead to the creation of the CIE L*a*b* model. This system specifies a color by its location in a three-dimensional color space. The acronym represents three axes used to describe a color. L* stands for the amount of lightness or darkness, a* is the location on a red-green axis, and b* is the position on

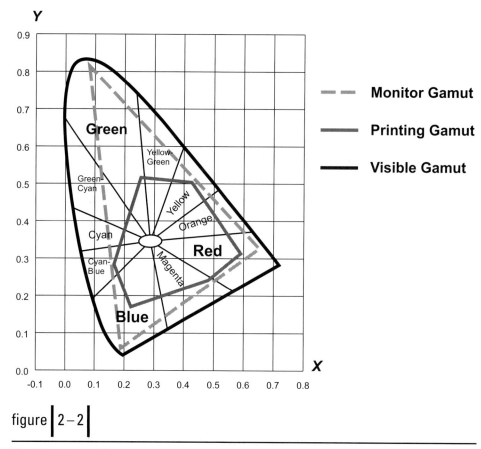

figure | 2–2 |

The CIE color model.

a yellow-blue axis. It is used primarily to translate images from RGB mode into CMYK in most image editing software programs like Adobe Photoshop. Later on, we will see that this translation process does not always produce satisfactory results.

Still, the CIE chromaticity model is the most precise way for designers to manage color in the prepress workflow environment. When used properly, it allows a designer to match colors more precisely on a computer screen.

The HSB Color System

Another model that designers with fine arts training may be familiar with is the Hue, Saturation and Brilliance model (see figure 2–3). In this system, hue is the recognizable quality of the color. As with color, hue is determined by the variance in wavelengths of light. The saturation of a color refers to its purity, or the amount of color that is being used. A fine artist can lessen the saturation of a color by mixing more thinner into her oil-based paint. Similarly, a designer will achieve the same

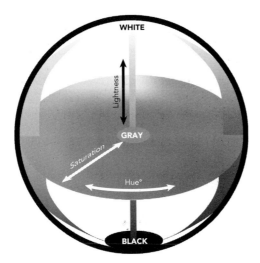

figure | 2–3 |

The HSB model defines color in attributes of hue, saturation, and brilliance. See color insert. (Courtesy X-Rite Incorporated.)

results by decreasing the percentage of a color in her digital artwork. Brilliance is the lightness or darkness that a color has in it. By increasing the intensity of light, a color appears brighter, while decreasing the light will darken a color. An example of this was previously described in the first part of this chapter when discussing how the amount of light at dawn or dusk affects the colors we see during these times.

You can view the HSB model in programs like QuarkXPress, where the color dialogue box allows you to see colors in this model. Although this may be helpful to some fine artists who are transferring their analog art to a digital format, the graphic designer has no way to match the color selected in the HSB system to a printable ink without changing the color mode. This usually results in a mismatch of colors. For this reason, the HSB system is not commonly used in a prepress workflow environment.

Additive Colors

When we look at our computer screen, all colors that appear are the result of a mixing of differentiating values of red, green, and blue by way of phosphors inside our monitor. This is similar to the way our eye mixes these values to see different colors. The reason that RGB colors are called additive colors is because when we want to add to the brilliance of a color, we must increase one or more of the RGB values. So additive colors are those where increasing the values of RGB create brighter colors, while decreasing the values of RGB will create darker colors. Therefore, if we want to achieve a pure white background in Photoshop, we must set each value of RGB to their maximum value of 255. Similarly, if we want pure black, each value is set to 0. In additive colors, black is really the absence of color, as in the HSB model, black is achieved by removing all brilliance or light (see figure 2–4).

Many college or university students who have studied fine arts in high school believe that there are only twelve different colors because they are taught a very basic color model in the form of a color wheel. However, there are infinitely more colors available when designing on a computer. Nearly every color within our range of vision can be captured and displayed by a camera or a scanner. Certain scanners may have limitations on the number of colors they can display depending on whether they can produce images that are 24, 32, or 48 bits in depth (more about bit depth in Chapter 5). Once an image is transferred to a digital format, a designer can display the image on her screen using a program like Photoshop. So how does the software program configure the colors so they can be displayed?

Whenever we scan a continuous tone image and open it up in Photoshop, we are really breaking it apart into black and white values of information that are then represented through the three channels of red, green, and blue. Each channel can display 256 levels of gray, which is why the Info palette in Photoshop has a range of grayscale value from 0 to 255 for RGB. The values of gray in each channel combine together to represent the colors in the image. Given that the number of possible colors is limited only by the number of different values for each color being multiplied by the number of channels, or 256^3, a scanner or digital camera can interpret approximately 16.7 million colors. If we look back at the CIE chart (figure 2–2) we can see this number is very close to the visible gamut (the total number of colors the human eye can recognize).

The challenge for every designer has always been to realize on paper what is seen on screen. A designer who is not prepress wise can spend hours correcting colors in RGB

figure | 2–4 |

Maximum values of RGB produce white in the additive system, while '0' values produce black. See color insert.

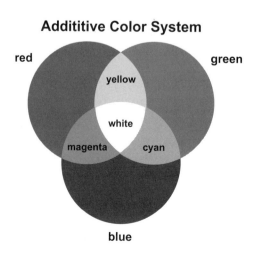

Addititive Color System

mode only to be completely frustrated by the results when she sees the final color proof. "What happened? Where are all the bright colors that I saw on my screen?" she asks in frustration. The answer is a simple one, yet baffling to those who are not familiar with the way screen colors are translated to print.

Additive colors are able to display millions of colors not simply because they are divided into three channels of 256 values. Additive colors are much more luminous and brighter because the light source is directly in front of the viewer's eye. If the number of colors available in an image were dependent on the number of channels, then it would stand to reason that an image in CMYK mode could display more than 4 billion colors (256^4). Unfortunately for the designer, this is not possible with process inks. This difference will become clear as we discover how process colors combine to simulate screen colors.

Subtractive Colors

As mentioned before, additive colors are made up of RGB values projected from a light source inside a monitor. The light source is direct, meaning our eyes receive the light without it reflecting off another object first. This is what gives the colors on our monitor the brightness and vibrancy that we would like to see come off the press. However, the reality is that subtractive colors are never as intense or luminous as the ones we see on our screen. The reasons for this are not that obvious at first, so let's look at how subtractive colors are realized as ink on paper.

Artwork printed in subtractive colors is referred to as four-color process. Whether the image is printed from a four-color press or a color laser or inkjet printer, each color the viewer sees is made of cyan, magenta, yellow, and black dots that the eye mixes together to simulate a continuous tone image. The color white is essentially the absence of ink on the paper, with most of the light being reflected back toward the eye. Meanwhile, areas with ink will absorb a portion of the light. The more ink, then the more light that is absorbed. It is for this reason the system is called subtractive colors. Opposite to the additive model, pure white is achieved by the lack of ink on the paper. In the subtractive model, black is not the absence of color, but the result of full values of cyan, magenta, and yellow being mixed together (see figure 2–5). This works in theory, but not in practice, as we will see later in the chapter. So how does the image we see on our screen become translated into one that will print out on our printer?

As discussed in the previous chapter, when an image is scanned in, it must be broken up into pixels of color. Each pixel also contains smaller bits of color information. In order to see this image in color on paper, it is necessary to translate these pixels into

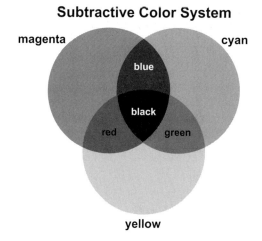

figure | 2 – 5 |

All the subtractive colors combine to form black, while white is the absence of color. Note that combining different subtractive colors also produces red, green, and blue. See color insert.

larger dots (called halftones) that are made up of screen percentages of the four process colors. Each process color must be set to a different angle. The halftone dots are usually so small they cannot be seen; however our eyes are able to assimilate the various overlapping dots of color and compile an image that appears to be a continuous blend of color. The translucent nature of the process inks makes this overlapping possible.

So why is it that process colors cannot simulate all the colors on our screen when printed? There are two reasons for this. First, the source of light is not direct, meaning the wavelengths of light have to strike the page first and then are received by our eyes. With an indirect source of light, much of the strength and intensity of the light is lost by the time it is reflected off the printed surface. Our sun would have to be significantly brighter than it is now for the same number of colors to be available in CMYK as those we can see in RGB. Secondly, the pigments used in process colors are not as pure as sunlight. For these reasons, the number of printable colors available to us in a subtractive system is actually only a few thousand as shown in the CIE Color Chromaticity model (see figure 2 – 2 again). In theory, it should be possible to mix full values of CMY to produce black. Some of the early color printers attempted to do this, and the results were a muddy brown. A black plate is necessary to add depth and definition to an image.

When studying subtractive and additive colors closely, we can see there is a distinct relationship between CMYK and RGB. In order to see process colors on a monitor, the values of red, green, and blue must be combined. On a printed sheet, our eyes combine the halftone dots to perceive the various colors in the image. As light strikes the process

Soft Proofing Process Colors in Photoshop

You can proof what the colors in your image will look like after being converted to CMYK by going to the top menu bar in Photoshop and selecting *View > Proof Setup > Working CMYK* and then turning on the preview by selecting *Proof Colors* (command/control-Y) from the same menu.

colored dots on a page, certain wavelengths of light will be reflected back to our eyes depending on the color of the halftone dot, while others will be absorbed (see figure 2–6). Our eyes then combine the reflected colors together and send this information along the optic nerve to the brain where the illusion of a continuous image is realized.

To see a practical demonstration of how our eyes combine process colors, let's see how a digital artist might produce an illustration of a red apple on a page. By using a combination of yellow and magenta colored inks, the illustrator is able to approximate the redness of an apple (see figure 2–7). If one of the process colors is missing or does not print well, then the apple's color will be off. You must also take into account that colors may not always be exact when a sheet comes off the press. During printing, some inks may print out too heavily or unevenly, causing an image to display a color cast. A press operator may need to adjust the tension on an ink fountain roller to correct this.

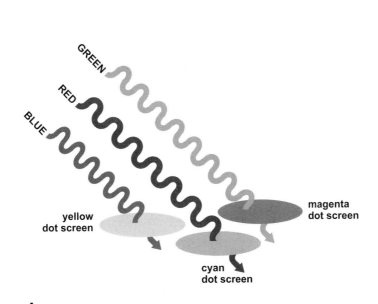

figure | 2–6 |

Process screen dots absorb one wavelength of light and reflect the others back to our eyes. The illustration shows which one of the RGB colors the yellow, cyan, and magenta screen dots absorb. See color insert.

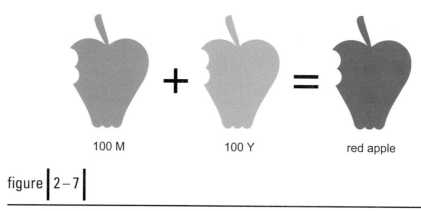

100 M   100 Y   red apple

figure | 2 – 7 |

Screen percentages of yellow and magenta give this illustrated apple its red appearance.

It is the relationship between additive and subtractive colors that is both crucial and frustrating to designers and printers. It is important for a designer to always convert images that are in RGB mode to CMYK before printing outputting film or plates. By converting these colors beforehand, a designer avoids many common problems such as poor color definition, images disappearing from certain plates, and missing color profiles which may affect the image's color as well. She must also be aware that certain colors on the screen may not be accurately represented.

Out-of-gamut Colors

We have already seen that certain colors in RGB cannot be reproduced due to the limitations in the purity of subtractive colors. The colors that appear on a monitor that cannot be realized on paper when changing an RGB image to CMYK mode are called out-of-gamut colors. Those that are within the range of printable inks are said to be within gamut. Special types of inks, like metallic or fluorescent, are other colors that cannot be reproduced by using four-color process.

Those colors we select that cannot be reproduced using process inks will often confound and infuriate us. Luckily most software programs give an out-of-gamut warning if a designer has used them inadvertently. In Photoshop, this warning appears whenever a color is selected where it cannot be accurately represented in CMYK. If a designer selects a color that is out-of-gamut, a small triangular sign with an exclamation mark inside appears at the top of the Color Picker window above the various color models (see figure 2 – 8). To bring a color into gamut, a designer simply clicks on this icon and the color values in RGB will shift to ones that are printable. As noted before, if the image has a lot of bright colors in it when displayed in RGB, this process usually leaves the designer with a rather dull looking image once it is converted to CMYK.

> ## Manually Correcting Out-of-gamut Colors
>
> You can easily correct out-of-gamut colors on an image in Photoshop. First select Gamut Warning (command-shift /control-alt-Y) under View in the menu bar. Any color pixels that do not fall into the CMYK range will be displayed as gray. By opening the Hue/Saturation dialog window and then adjusting the values for hue, saturation, and lightness, you can bring many of the out-of-gamut colors into range. The shift in values for hue should be kept to plus or minus five; however, the shift in values for saturation and lightness can be as high as ten. This method is preferable to letting the software do this function, as many images converted to CMYK from RGB become dull and flat as the software often places too much black in a color after it is translated from RGB to CMYK.

We can still achieve a wide range and depth of color despite the limitations of four-color printing. If we look back at our illustration of the apple, we see that only two process colors were used (see figure 2–7). If we add a third process color (in this case black) to produce the illusion of depth, then more detail is also added (see figure 2–9). Black is mostly used in four-color printing to add detail and definition to an image. Although the number of possible colors becomes greater as more of the process colors are used, there is also an increase in problems such as plates not registering properly on the press and over-saturation of inks.

PANTONE® AND OTHER SPOT COLORS

Occasionally, a client asks a designer to match a color exactly because it is the color of their corporate logo and they want to maintain the integrity of their image. Or a designer may want to add something different to her artwork, making it unique and distinctive. For this reason, the Pantone® color matching system was developed

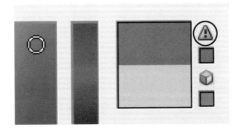

figure | 2–8 |

An out-of-gamut warning icon appears whenever a color is selected that cannot be represented by percentages of CMYK. This applies to Pantone® and special colors as well.

in 1962 to create a standard set of special inks that designers could use for their artwork. As discussed before, most process colors cannot match screen colors and will also vary in intensity depending on the type of material printed on. Unlike four-color process inks that are transluscent, Pantone® inks are opaque premixed and print as solid areas so color matching is precise. There are other color matching systems available for use, namely Trumatch® and Toyo®, however the Pantone® matching system is most commonly used by designers in North America.

Pantone® colors can be selected through color palettes in programs like QuarkXPress, Adobe InDesign, and Illustrator (see figure 2 – 10). Pantone® inks can also be specified to our artwork before sending it to press through the use of a Pantone® Color Selector Guide that shows printed swatches of each color. A Pantone® color selector may be necessary if a designer is using older versions of software that do not carry the latest Pantone® swatches. In this case, she may have to make up a spot color in her document, but indicate to the printer the Pantone® swatch number this color plate is to be printed with.

By looking through a swatch book of Pantone® colors, we can select the color most suitable for the artwork we are creating (see figure 2 – 11). Pantone® colors come in five different finishes of coated, uncoated, matte, metallic, and even process. These finishes represent different finishes that can be achieved depending on the paper you have chosen. When applying Pantone® colors in your artwork, you should always select the Pantone® swatch library that matches the finish and type of paper on which you are printing. In this way, you can more accurately match color when showing proofs to a client. You can even order custom software from Pantone® to calibrate your monitor for precise color matching (more on this in the next chapter).

Pantone® Colors in Photoshop

Photoshop was designed primarily for the editing of images and as a painting program. It is rarely used to create a digital artwork file used for outputting film

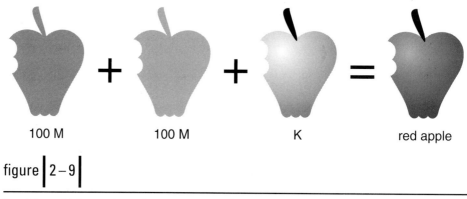

| 100 M | 100 M | K | red apple |

figure | 2 – 9 |

By adding a third or tertiary color, more detail and depth is produced in the apple.

 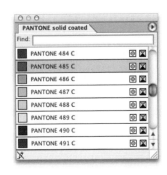

figure | 2 – 10 |

Opening the Pantone® solid coated swatch palette from the swatch libraries in Illustrator allows us to easily apply a Pantone® color to an object.

or plates. For this reason, we seldom select Pantone® colors in a Photoshop file. If you do want to use a Pantone® color in Photoshop, you can easily select them by using the Color Picker and clicking on the Custom Colors in the dialogue box (see figure 2 – 12). However, getting Pantone® colors to print out is more problematic in Photoshop than other software programs. Each image we scan in is automatically saved

figure | 2 – 11 |

The Pantone® Color Selector Guide can help you match Pantone® inks more accurately than selecting them on a screen. (Pantone® is the property of Pantone®, Inc. Reproduced with the permission of Pantone®, Inc.)

figure | 2 – 12 |

Clicking on Custom Colors in the Color Picker window allows us to apply Pantone® colors to an image in Photoshop.

in RGB mode, unless otherwise specified. When converted to CMYK, the spot channel and the information it contains will be lost if you try to save it as a TIFF or EPS file.

If you want to apply a Pantone® color into an image in Photoshop, there are only two ways to do it.

1. Open an RGB image in Photoshop.

2. Change the mode to CMYK.

3. Create a new spot channel by selecting *Spot Channel* under the Channels options.

4. Make sure the image is in multi-channel mode.

5. Choose a Pantone® color from the Custom Color Picker.

6. Choose a channel or select part of the image from a channel and paste it into the new spot channel.

7. Save the file using the desktop color separation file format (DCS 2.0) to retain the spot color information (more on this in Chapter 5).

Color Selection When Creating Special Plates

When creating a plate for a special finish like varnishing or embossing, the spot color should be made up of a single color that is not being used by itself in the document, such as 100 percent cyan as shown in Figures 2–13 and 2–14. By selecting the full value of a process color, and placing the art for the special finish on a separate layer, it is less likely you will mistakenly use it for a normal color in your artwork.

The second is to convert the file to grayscale and then change the image's mode to duotone, selecting a Pantone® color for each channel. The image is then saved in an EPS file format. Using these methods will allow the Pantone® colors to print as a separate plate when it is imaged onto film or plates.

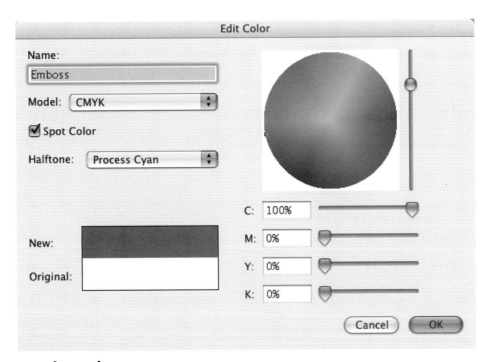

figure 2–13

By selecting New Color in the Colors dialogue window in Quark and clicking on the Spot Color box, you can make spot color plates for special finishes like embossing or varnishing. Renaming the plate as "Emboss" helps you remember what it was intended for.

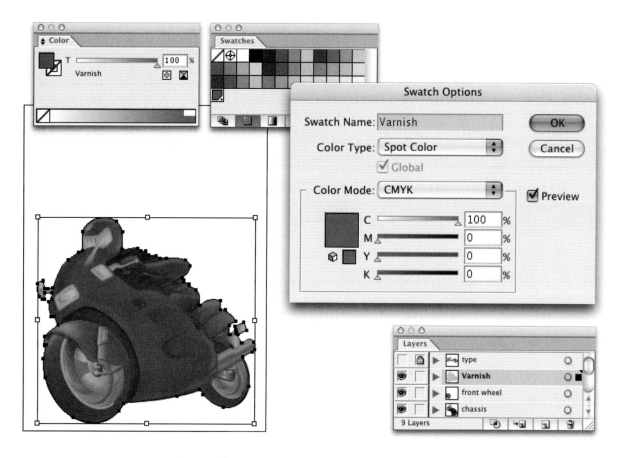

figure | 2 – 14 |

You create a spot color plate for a special finish in Illustrator by opening the Swatch Options from the Swatch palette and selecting Spot Color in the Color Type pop-up menu. Again, the color plate should be named "Varnish" or "Emboss" depending on the finish.

Spot Colors or Special Inks

At times you may want to match a color that is not available through process or Pantone® inks. In this case, you may need to make a spot color in your file, which will then be made into a separate plate for printing that ink. A spot color plate can be made up of any combination of inks. The printer must be supplied with the specific quantities for mixing this ink before the job is sent to press, preferably at the estimating stage. The use of spot colors can also be useful if you want to create a special plate for a varnish or embossing finish in your artwork. As well, you can use gold, silver, bronze, and fluorescent inks to embellish an otherwise dull looking design. A truly innovative designer is one who is able to create outstanding artwork using special inks, processes, and varnishes to enhance her design (more on this in the last chapter).

SUMMARY

Understanding the different color models and how they interrelate can be puzzling. This chapter provides a basic understanding of color systems and how they relate to prepress. For graphic designers, it is necessary to fully understand the interconnected relationship between additive (RGB) and subtractive (CMYK) colors. When a designer makes this connection, she can achieve better results in all stages of the prepress process. Recognizing the color limitations of the project before the design process begins, knowing which color model to select when choosing colors, bringing out-of-gamut colors into printable inks, and selecting the right color profile are all crucial to the production phase of digital artwork. Once the designer appreciates this, she achieves on paper the idea she first envisioned.

▶ *in review*

1. Which three colors do our eyes combine to form an image when wavelengths of light are reflected off an object?

2. Which two color theorists paved the way for the design of the CIE chromaticity system?

3. What is the primary difference between saturation and brilliance in the HSB color system?

4. Where do we normally find additive colors in our work environment?

5. What values of red, green, and blue must be combined to make a pure white?

6. Which colors make up black in a subtractive color system?

7. What color system would we use if we want to print a solid ink in our artwork?

8. Name one special finish that a designer would need to make a spot color plate for.

exercises

1. Try this exercise to help you understand color systems and how they affect printed inks. Create a new document in QuarkXPress and open the **Colors** Dialogue Window under the **Edit** menu. Create a series of new colors using different models by clicking on the *New* button and then choose either the HSB, RGB, or Pantone® Solid Coated model. Try switching the model to CMYK and observe which inks come into the range of color that can be reproduced in four-color process.

2. Open a Photoshop file that is saved in RGB mode. Change the mode to CMYK by going to *Image* > *Mode* > *CMYK*. Create a New Spot Channel in the Channels palette. Click on *Color* under *Ink Characteristics* in the *New Spot Channel* window. Click on the *Custom* button and select the Pantone® Red 032 C color swatch from the *Color Picker* window. Select the magenta channel and copy it onto the pasteboard. Now select the new spot channel and paste the image from the magenta channel into this channel. Change the mode to Multi-channel and delete the magenta channel. What differences do you notice from the original image?

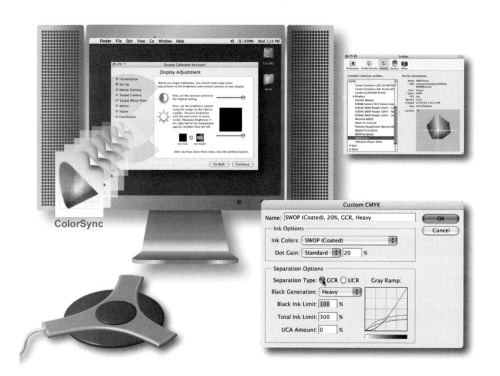

ColorSync

CHAPTER

3

objectives

- Recognize the importance of proper monitor calibration
- Calibrate your monitor using the Apple Display Calibrator assistant
- Calibrate your monitor using Adobe Gamma
- Achieve better printing results from art files with color profiles

introduction

Perhaps the most daunting task a designer will ever face is to perfectly realize on paper the image they see on their screen. As we have seen from the last chapter, the luminous, vibrant colors that appear on our monitor simply do not translate well onto a printed sheet of paper. As designers, it is up to us to achieve optimum results at the printing stage, despite all the obstacles. One way to achieve accurate colors is to know the proper way to calibrate and apply the profiles you create to the various devices attached to your workflow system. There are many types of software available to designers to help accomplish this task. This chapter will outline various methods and explain why calibration is so important.

COLOR CALIBRATION PRINCIPLES

The reason we calibrate devices such as monitors, scanners, and printers is so the colors we use in the output file and the supporting files will be synchronized with each other. This allows you to control the color reproduction throughout the entire print production process and provides optimal results for the images you have used in your digital artwork. You need to assign a color profile for each device you are using. A color profile is simply a data file used by the operating system that defines the working color space or the device's capacity to render color. Profiles then can be divided into three categories: display or monitor profiles, input profiles (for scanners and digital cameras), and output profiles (for printers and presses). The profile you select depends on with what type of media your image will be reproduced. For instance, if you are preparing images for display on a web page, you would apply a different profile then you would for images that are being produced from an inkjet printer.

The best place to begin the calibration process is the screen you look at when you turn on your computer each day.

Calibrating Your Monitor

Monitor calibration is crucial since we need to see on our screen how printed inks will appear under normal interior light conditions. Understanding this principle is essential for any designer who hopes to perform professional quality color correcting. Some clients may not appreciate the time spent on color correcting an image; however, your peers will certainly know if the colors in your images appear unnatural, particularly skin colors. If your monitor is not calibrated properly, then the color of people's faces, eyes, and hair will not be realistic. They could end up looking jaundiced (a yellowish cast to the skin), extremely sun burnt (a magenta cast), or worse, like aliens (i.e. a greenish cast). In addition to people, animals and objects in your images may not be representative of their true colors. This will cause real problems if you are doing artwork that includes food or product photography.

When you first open up your system, you will find that all the colors in your desktop appear very bright and toward the cool end of the spectrum (i.e. with a blue or cyan hue). This is because the default profile that came with your display is one that the manufacturer created for the average user, and is close to the settings that a television screen would use. Since the average user will mostly be surfing the web, writing e-mails or word files, previewing movies, and playing games, a monitor calibrated for daylight or average room conditions would appear too dark and so it is not practical for these sort of activities. Most computer users want a screen that is bright and luminous. The settings that come out of the box are not suitable for correcting colors. In order to calibrate a monitor that is suitable for graphics work, it is necessary to do four things: change the balance between the red, green, and blue phosphors; adjust the brightness and contrast; select a target gamma; and set the white point. If all three are done correctly, the colors in your image appear as they would under normal room light conditions. The two most important factors in this operation are gamma correction and setting the white point.

Gamma Correction

Gamma correction controls the brightness and contrast of an image and also affects the relationship between the red, green, and blue phosphors in our monitor. A gamma correction of 1.8 is standard for a monitor on a MacIntosh computer. A PC monitor will usually be set to a gamma level of 2.2. For this reason, colors on a monitor with an Apple operating system are naturally brighter than the same monitor using another operating system. Setting the gamma level of your monitor too high will make the contrast between light and dark colors too extreme. Similarly, lowering the gamma levels too far will decrease the contrast and make images appear washed out.

Gamma correction settings are based on gamma curves, which are plotted using mathematical calculations that are exponential. There is a separate curve used for each of the RGB colors. The formulas for each curve are rather complex and it is not necessary to understand them for proper monitor calibration. Some kinds of calibration software allow you to adjust these curves. It is not a good idea to attempt to set the target gamma for your monitor manually unless you are an expert. Most monitor calibration software has predetermined correction settings as part of the calibration process. As long as we follow the basic steps within each program, the gamma curves will be correct for our monitor.

Setting the White Point

The white point of your monitor reflects how bright the whites on your screen will be and is measured in degrees kelvin (K). Factory settings for monitors are normally calibrated to a white point of 9300 K, which is too cool for anything but web viewing, playing games, or typing word documents. The normal setting for daylight conditions is 6500 K. This represents how bright a white sheet of paper will appear for mid-day sunlight under very bright conditions (i.e. a cloudless day). For graphics work, the target white point is normally set to 5000 K. This represents how white a sheet of paper will look under normal interior light conditions. In most cases, this setting is acceptable for the standard workflow environment. Some designers though, like me, have found a higher setting between 5000 and 6500 K more ideal for color correction. When using software that allows fine adjustment of the target white point, I have found a setting of 5700 K to be better for color correcting images that will print on a white glossy coated stock. Let's now have a look at how you can properly calibrate your monitor.

Calibrating a Monitor in OS X

If you are using a MacIntosh with OS X installed, you can see what type of profile your system uses by going to the "Dock" and click on the *System Preferences* icon. When the System Preferences window appears, click on the *Displays* icon. This will bring up the Displays window, where you can see all the calibrated displays that come with your system (see figure 3–1). All color profiles that an Apple monitor uses are based on the ColorSync model. The one that your system is currently using is highlighted with blue. Not all the

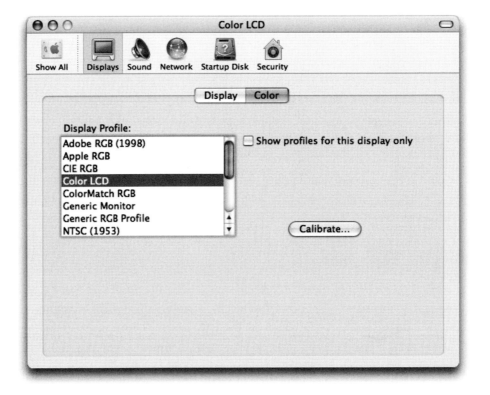

figure |3–1|

The Displays window allows you to choose which profile you want to use with your monitor.

settings in the display window are for the monitor that came with your system. Click on the box in the *Color Display* window where it says, *Show profiles for this display only* if you want to see only the ones that are calibrated for your monitor.

Custom Display Profiles

Although there may be several calibrated settings for monitors you can use with your system, none of them are properly calibrated for normal light conditions. If you are using OS X, you can create a custom profile that is properly calibrated for displaying colors in normal room conditions by using the Display Calibrator Assistant. Open the window for the Display Calibrator Assistant by clicking on the *Calibrate* button in the Displays window (see figure 3–2).

Once the Display Calibrator Assistant window appears, you have a choice whether you want to quickly setup your display or turn on the Expert Mode. The expert method is more precise; however, it involves significantly more steps

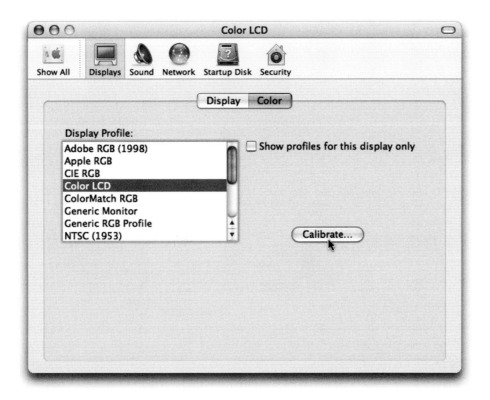

figure | 3–2 |

Clicking on the Calibrate button in the Display window lets you create a custom display profile.

and is difficult to master due to the complexity of the slider tools required to adjust the luminance response curve. For the most part, the quick method will give you a profile that is acceptable for most graphics work. If you are really concerned about matching color for a certain lighting situation or paper stock, then it would be better to use third-party calibration software (more on this later in the chapter).

The Quick Calibration Method

This method is useful for times when you need to calibrate your monitor in a hurry. Although this method does not suit every lighting situation, it is meant to approximate how the colors in your image will appear under certain light conditions. Obviously these conditions may not reflect how our work will be viewed. In that case, we may want a more precise calibration. This method will suffice for most of the calibrations we will perform. Let's go through the different steps and see how the quick method works.

1. Open the Display Calibrator Assistant window by clicking on the *Calibrate* button under the Display window (see figure 3–2 again).

2. When the Display Calibrator Assistant window opens, ensure the Expert Mode box is not selected, and then click on the Continue button (see figure 3–3).

figure | 3–3 |

The Introduction window for the Display Calibrator Assistant. It is a good idea to read the instructions for each step.

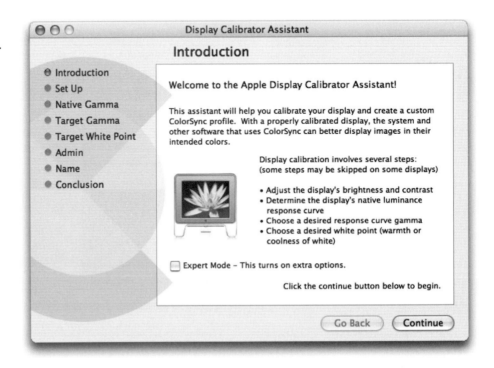

3. The Display Calibrator Adjustment window should appear. If it does not appear, proceed to Step 4. Slide the contrast bar to its maximum setting. Now adjust the brightness by sliding that bar until the gray ellipse is barely visible inside the black square on the right-hand side of the window (figure 3 – 4). The tonal range of the inner ellipse should be about a 90 percent gray compared to the black around it. If you can see a division between the two halves of the ellipse, your screen is set too bright. This stage also sets the black point of your monitor. Click the Continue button.

4. The fourth step is to adjust the gamma settings on your monitor. This will balance the mid-tone values of the screen colors. It is important to be as precise as possible at this stage so the color in your images will be accurate before you begin your color corrections. Simply slide the triangle underneath the gray square until the tonal value of the inside square matches the outside one and the inside square is indistinguishable from the outer square. It helps to squint your eyes or make them slightly out of focus when you do this (figure 3 – 5).

5. Click on the 1.8 Standard Gamma button (figure 3 – 6). This sets the gamma correction to the normal ratio for a MacIntosh display. Gamma correction is necessary to balance the relationship between the numerical values of red, green, and blue and how bright they appear on a screen. Click Continue.

6. In this window, select the target white point you wish to use. For situations where inks will be viewed under normal light conditions in a room with inks printed on white paper, use the D50 setting (figure 3 – 7). This setting is standard for the printing of graphics material. Click Continue.

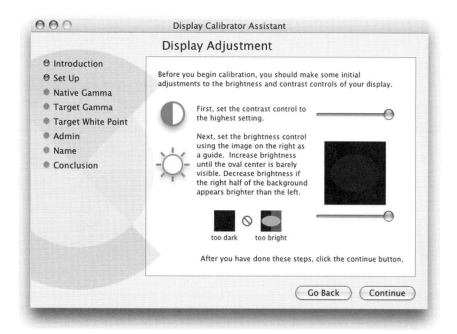

figure | 3 – 4 |

Set the contrast to maximum. Adjust the brightness until the inner circle is barely visible.

Calibrating an LCD Screen

The brightness of colors on an LCD monitor may vary depending on at what angle the screen is tipped. Make sure the screen is set perpendicular (90 degrees) to your eyes. This will allow the light from your display to shine directly into your eyes, rather than indirectly, which could affect the intensity of the light and make the colors appear darker than what they really are. Do not move your head during the calibration process or the measurements could be off. Images on LCD monitors have greater contrast so it may be better to use a CRT screen.

7. When you have finished setting the white point, you must give your custom profile a name (figure 3–8). The name should reflect the conditions for which it will be used. This will help you remember it if you want to use it again. Click Continue.

8. The last window is the conclusion of the calibration. Check the color balance on your screen. If you are satisfied with your calibration, then click the Done button. If you need to edit your calibration, then click on the Go Back button (figure 3–9).

9. If you want to reapply the profile or apply another one, return to the Display window and select the profile you want by clicking on the name (figure 3–10).

Warm Up to Your Monitor

To achieve maximum results of the calibration process, let your monitor warm up for an hour before performing the calibration. It is also a good idea to calibrate your monitor each time you shut your computer down as the balance of the RGB colors can shift each time the monitor becomes illuminated.

Calibrating in OS 9 or Windows

Before Mac OS X came out, Adobe Gamma was a useful tool for calibrating your monitor. It was made by Adobe Systems and was included in later versions of Photoshop. Once installed, it was easily opened in system 9.0 by going under the Apple icon in the top menu bar and selecting Control Panels > Adobe Gamma. In Windows, select Start > Settings > Control Panel and double-click on Adobe Gamma. By opening this control panel, your monitor could be properly calibrated within a few minutes.

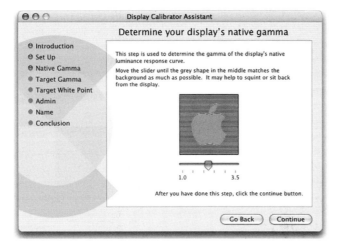

figure | 3 – 5 |

Determine the monitors native gamma by sliding the triangle so the inside and outside of the square are the same.

This method was easier and more precise than the Display Calibration Assistant in OS X. Most designers still find it faster and get a more accurate calibration for their monitor. Unfortunately, Adobe has not developed an upgrade for any versions of OS X yet. So, those who are still using OS 9 or later versions of Windows can still benefit from this handy piece of software.

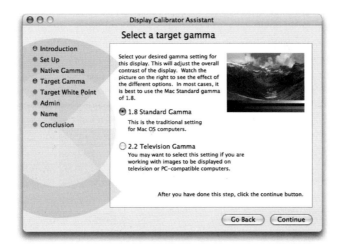

figure | 3 – 6 |

The Standard gamma setting for a MacIntosh system is 1.8.

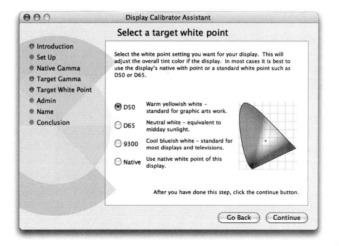

figure | 3 – 7 |

Select the target white point. A setting of D50 is used for most graphics work.

There are two options to choose when you open the Adobe Gamma control panel. You can choose to use the regular control panel settings or the Step-By-Step (Assistant). The latter method takes more time, yet is by far the more reliable of the two (figure 3 – 11).

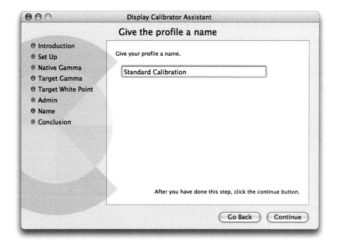

figure | 3 – 8 |

Name the custom profile you have just created.

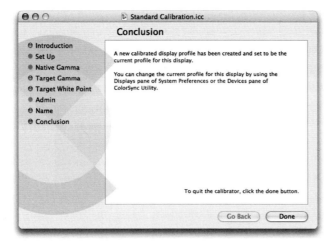

figure | 3 – 9 |

If you are satisfied with the brightness and colors on your screen, then click Done to save the profile.

Try following the steps below to calibrate the monitor if you are using Windows or a Mac with OS 9.0 or an earlier operating system. When you are finished performing a step, click on the *Next* button to move on to the following window.

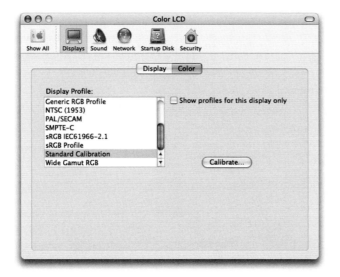

figure | 3 – 10 |

You can view your new profile or apply another one by returning to the Display window.

1. Open the Adobe Gamma control panel by going under the Apple icon in the top menu bar and selecting Control Panels > Adobe Gamma. If you are using a Windows system, then choose Start > Settings > Control Panel. Double-click on Adobe Gamma. Select Step-By-Step Wizard, and then click Next. Type a name for the profile and click Next.

2. Select the type of monitor your system uses by clicking on the load button. If you are not sure of the model, refer to the owner's manual that came with your monitor (figure 3–12).

3. The next step is adjusting the brightness and contrast of your monitor. Set the contrast to the maximum level and then adjust the brightness so the white square you see in your dialogue box is pure white and you are able to discern a lighter gray square inside the black square (figure 3–13).

4. In this step, make sure your phosphors are set to Trinitron. These are the type of phosphors used in monitors made by Apple. If you are not using an Apple monitor, check the owner's manual for your monitor to see what type of phosphors your display uses (figure 3–14).

5. The third step is to adjust the gamma settings for red, green, and blue on your monitor. This will balance the mid-tone values of these three screen colors. It is important to be as precise as possible at this stage so the color in your images will be accurate before you begin your color corrections. Simply slide the triangle underneath each of the three squares until the tonal value

figure │ 3–11 │

Select the Step-By-Step (Assistant) button to begin calibrating your monitor with the Adobe Gamma control panel.

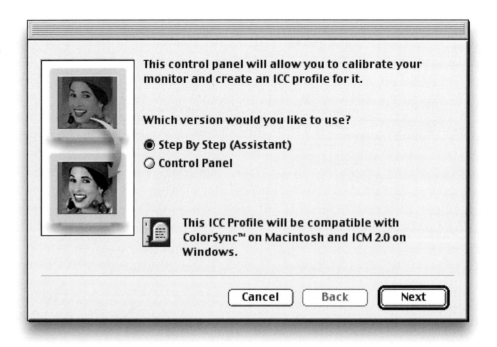

This control panel will allow you to calibrate your monitor and create an ICC profile for it.

Which version would you like to use?

● Step By Step (Assistant)
○ Control Panel

This ICC Profile will be compatible with ColorSync™ on Macintosh and ICM 2.0 on Windows.

[Cancel]   [Back]   [Next]

figure | 3 – 12 |

Load the profile of your monitor before beginning your calibration.

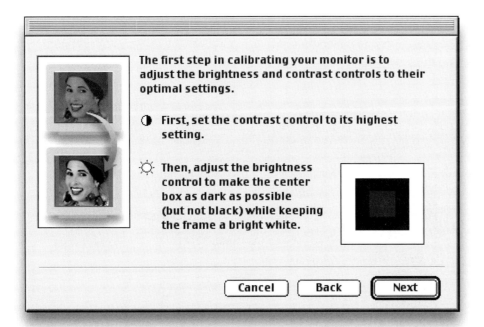

figure | 3 – 13 |

Manually adjust the contrast and brightness of your monitor. The way of adjusting these levels may vary from monitor to monitor.

of the inside square matches the outside one and the inside square is indistinguishable from the outer square. It helps to squint your eyes or make them slightly out of focus when you do this (figure 3 – 15). Leave the gamma setting at 1.8, which is the default for a MacIntosh display or 2.2 if you are using Windows. Click the Next button when you are done.

6. This step is where you measure the white point of your monitor. You can use presets of 5000 K (standard graphics work), 6500 K (daylight conditions), 7500 K, or 9300 K that will give you a brighter and cooler screen. If you want a more precise measurement, you can manually determine the white point by clicking on the Measure button in this window (figure 3 – 16). Click the Measure button now.

7. This window will explain how to manually select your white point (figure 3 – 17). Before you begin, turn off any ambient light in the room. Once you click on the *Next* button, you will see three squares appear on your screen. The square on the left is used to shift your monitor's white point toward the cooler end of the spectrum, while the one on the right will shift it to the warmer end (figure 3 – 18). Try clicking on both squares until the middle one appears to be a perfectly neutral gray. Now click on the center square to commit your choice.

8. Here you can readjust the white point for your monitor if you want. Select Same as Hardware for the adjusted white point if you are happy with the settings. This ensures that the measurements you created for your hardware will remain consistent regardless of changes in room conditions (figure 3 – 19).

9. The final step is to save your settings in a file with a name you will remember and can easily load again (figure 3 – 20). Click on the Before and After button to preview your new calibration. When you are ready to save your calibration, click on the Finish button.

figure | 3 – 14 |

Set your phosphors to Trinitron if you are using an Apple monitor (either a CRT or LCD screen).

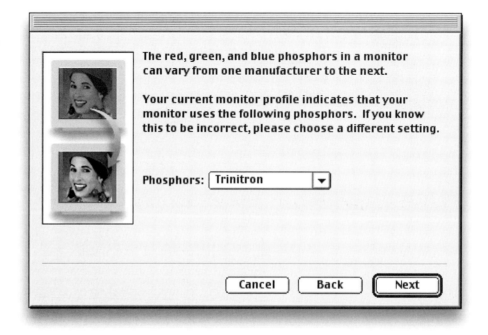

The red, green, and blue phosphors in a monitor can vary from one manufacturer to the next.

Your current monitor profile indicates that your monitor uses the following phosphors. If you know this to be incorrect, please choose a different setting.

Phosphors: Trinitron ▼

Cancel   Back   Next

figure | 3 – 15 |

Adjust the slider bars for red, green, and blue until the inner square disappears.

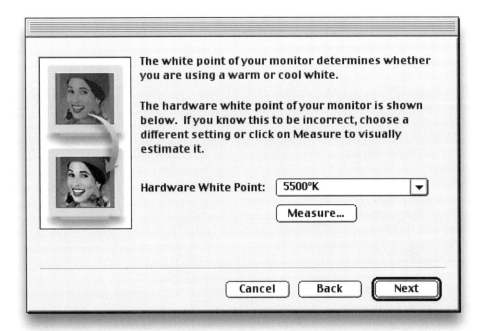

figure | 3 – 16 |

You can choose predetermined settings for your monitor's white point.

The control panel window for Adobe Gamma has similar instructions for each step. You can follow those steps if you prefer that method. Overall, Adobe Gamma is simpler to use than the Expert Mode of Apple's Display Calibration Assistant.

figure | 3–17 |

Read the instructions and turn off all the lights in the room before clicking the Next button.

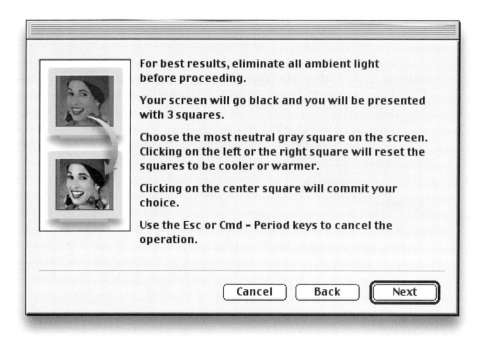

For best results, eliminate all ambient light before proceeding.

Your screen will go black and you will be presented with 3 squares.

Choose the most neutral gray square on the screen. Clicking on the left or the right square will reset the squares to be cooler or warmer.

Clicking on the center square will commit your choice.

Use the Esc or Cmd – Period keys to cancel the operation.

Cancel   Back   Next

figure | 3–18 |

Click on the left and right squares until the middle square is a neutral gray.

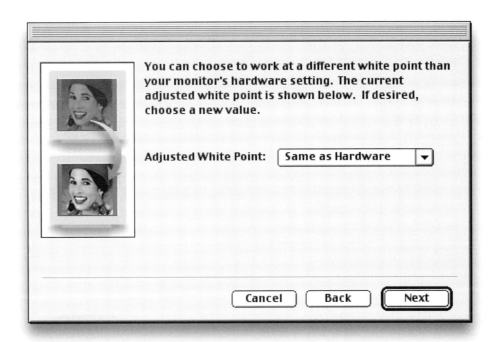

figure | 3 – 19 |

Select Same as Hardware from the pop-up menu unless you want to choose a different white point setting.

figure | 3 – 20 |

Give you new calibration setting a name and then click on the Finish button.

> ## Buying a Monitor
>
> Whether you decide to go with an LCD or CRT monitor, it is important to purchase the highest quality you can afford. Most monitors do not last more than five years or so as the colors begin to dull and darken over time. Consider that a low priced monitor will not provide as clear color definition as a higher priced one that has high-resolution capabilities. Also make sure any calibration software you purchase is made for the type of display you have.

Hopefully, Adobe will release a new version that is compatible for OS X in the near future.

Alternative Software for Calibrating Your Monitor

There are a few other options for calibrating your monitor if you find none of the built-in software on your system is to your liking. A number of third parties manufacture monitor calibration software with more precise color matching. The prices of these packages range from the quite inexpensive (as in shareware) to the very expensive (hundreds of dollars). While it is unnecessary for the average designer to splurge on expensive calibration software, someone doing a great deal of color correcting on high-resolution images may want to look at one of these systems. Let's look at a few of the alternatives.

Third Party Monitor Calibration Systems

There are several more expensive systems if you are really serious about performing any high-end color correcting work. The majority of these software titles are manufactured either by GretagMacbeth, Pantone®, or ColorVision. They all come with a colorimeter device that is placed on top of your screen for more accurate color matching (see figure 3–21). The advantages of using third party software are: more precise measuring of color, better definition in highlight and shadow areas, and more neutral grays in corrected images. Although the quality of the software and devices from these companies is very good, it is not a necessity for the average design professional.

COLOR MANAGEMENT

When the first personal computers began making their way into design studios back in 1985, the term color management was unheard of. Software manufacturers

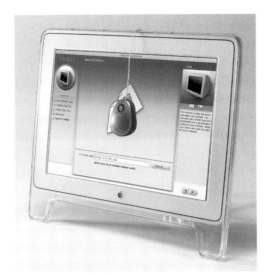

figure | 3 – 21 |

Monitor profiling
software provides precise
color profiling thanks to a
colorimeter.

had not incorporated a standard method of producing color into their applications. This lack of color consistency would lead to frustration among designers
as colors would shift and change depending on the input or output source.
Beginning in 1993, the ICC (International Color Consortium) created a common
standard of color management to address the discrepancies designers were seeing
in color from their monitors, scanners, color printers, and off the press. They
based the standard they developed on the CIE Color System. Each operating
system has a number of profiles that help to synchronize color across various
devices and software applications.

MacIntosh computers use a built-in color profile called ColorSync based on this ICC
standard. Windows operating systems use Image Color Management (ICM), also
based on the ICC standard. Although many designers simply ignore the Missing or
Mismatch Profile window that pops up when an image is opened in Photoshop
using a different color profile, the prepress-wise designer will select a profile that is
congruent with profiles used by other devices connected to her computer.

Color Profiles

By using color profiles effectively, we can maintain color integrity throughout the
workflow environment. Color profiles help us to create consistent color results while
we are working in different software programs and printing to different output
devices. Almost all operating systems come with a built-in library of color profiles.

When you install software for each device you are using, check to see if there is a folder containing the profile(s) for that device. If there is a folder, then open it and install these into the profile folder for the operating system you are using. The profiles for a Mac OS X are located in Library > ColorSync. Additional ones can be added to a folder found under User > Library > ColorSync > Profiles. On a Windows operating system, custom color profiles can be loaded into a folder in Windows/System32/Spool/Drivers/Color.

In a prepress workflow environment, it is important to utilize these built-in profiles to achieve better results when using independent devices. Using these profiles will result in better image quality when proofing artwork from your printer. Another factor to consider is the quality of paper that you are using. Different papers will affect how colors print and their brilliance as some papers have a shinier surface and will reflect more light than others. By choosing a profile that is customized for a specific type of printer and paper stock, you can reproduce colors more accurately. Many print and prepress service providers will provide color profiles calibrated for their own imaging system. If you receive one from your service provider, place it in the appropriate profile folder.

Problems may occur if you provide your own film or plates and apply the wrong color profile for the type of press on which your job is printed. Colors in your images may not appear as they did on your monitor and some detailing may be lost in shaded areas. This loss of detail occurs where the four-process colors overlap each other. For example, if all screens of CMYK are at 100 percent, than the total ink coverage (TIC) is 400 percent. In some images that have a lot of shadows, the screen values of the process inks can be very high in these areas and ink coverage may become oversaturated. This normally occurs when an image contains more than a total of 300 percent of the screen values for all four-process colors. If not compensated for, images can appear muddy and any shadow areas lose detail. The sheets will also take a long time to dry after they come off the press and color may rub off the top of one sheet onto the back of another. The same problem can occur when printing a very dark image to a laser printer. Selecting the correct color profile will eliminate this problem by replacing the saturated areas with black. This process is known as gray component replacement (GCR) or under color removal (UCR).

GCR and UCR

Although GCR and UCR work in a similar manner to replace high densities of CMYK with black, they act differently in how they perform this function. GCR substitutes black in high densities of process inks across the whole tonal range of an image, meaning from the highlights to the shadows. However, you

UCR or GCR? Look at the Subject

If you are trying to decide whether to create a color profile using GCR or UCR, it depends upon the subject matter in your image. Generally speaking, GCR is used for hard mechanical objects such as toys, cars, and tools. UCR works better for images of people, clothes, art, and food. The rule of thumb is that if the subject matter is soft, use UCR to gain better results off the press.

should only use this technique if you know the total ink limit of the press your job will be printed on. UCR replaces only the neutral shadow areas that contain high densities of CMYK inks. Whether a profile uses GCR or UCR depends on how it was characterized when it was created.

Creating and Applying Press Profiles in Photoshop

Photoshop allows you to create a custom profile for press conditions using a characterization of either GCR or UCR. However, you should only use this technique if you know the total ink limit of the press your job will be printed on.

1. Open up a Photoshop document that you plan to use in a document that will be imaged to film or plates.

2. Go to the top menu bar and select Photoshop > Color Settings (command/control-shift K). The Color Settings window appears. Color settings for a CMYK image are matched to the type of printing process used. In this case, the final artwork will be printed on a web offset press, so the U.S. Prepress Default setting is used.

3. In the Settings pop-up menu, select U.S. Prepress Defaults (see figure 3–22).

4. In the working spaces section, select CMYK > Custom CMYK (see figure 3–23). The Custom CMYK window appears.

5. In this window, select either the GCR or UCR button depending on the subject matter in your image (see figure 3–24).

6. If you chose GCR, in the Black Generation pop-up menu, you can specify how much black you want to replace the saturated areas of CMYK. You can choose either light, medium, heavy, or maximum (see figure 3–25). You may notice that the Gray Ramp curves change to show at what total ink limit amount that black will replace the process colors.

7. Now set the Black Ink Limit, Total Ink Limit, and UCA Amount (see figure 3–26). You will need to obtain these settings from your print provider, as each press is different. Typically, the black ink limit is set to 100%, the total ink limit is between 260 and 340, and the UCA (under color addition) is 0%.

Applying Color Profiles in Illustrator

If you are working in Illustrator, go to Edit > Color Settings under the top menu bar. Once you open this dialogue box, you can choose different settings depending on what type of device you are using to print your file. If you planning to match colors in QuarkXPress, you will want to use the standard ColorSync workflow setting for documents that are being imported into QuarkXPress, since Quark uses this profile automatically (see fig. 3–27). You may also wish to use it if you do not have a specific color profile for other output devices connected to your operating system.

You can easily change the color profile you are using in your document while working in either Illustrator or Photoshop. In Illustrator, if you are working in CMYK, then by going under the top menu bar and selecting *Edit > Assign Profile* you can choose a color profile that is calibrated for your printer or for press conditions (see figure 3–28). In Photoshop, choose *Image > Mode > Assign Profile*. You can use a profile calibrated for an output device or even a color profile you have calibrated specifically for your monitor.

figure | 3–22 |

Choose U.S. Prepress Defaults from the pop-up menu in Color Settings for print production.

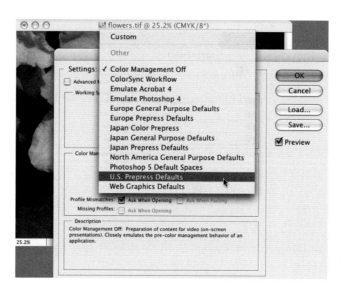

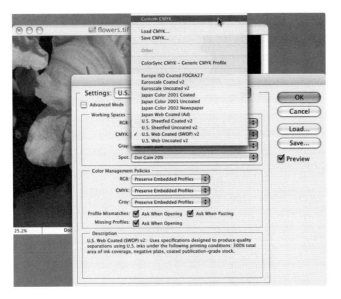

figure | 3 – 23 |

Select Custom CMYK from the pop-up menu to create a custom color profile for a specific press.

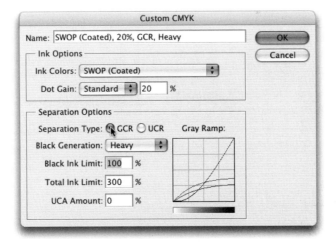

figure | 3 – 24 |

Click on the UCR or GCR button to specify which tonal areas black will replace CMYK.

figure | 3 – 25 |

figure | 3 – 25 |

Select the measure of black that will replace CMYK in your image. The Gray Ramp curves change to reflect the point when black will replace the process colors.

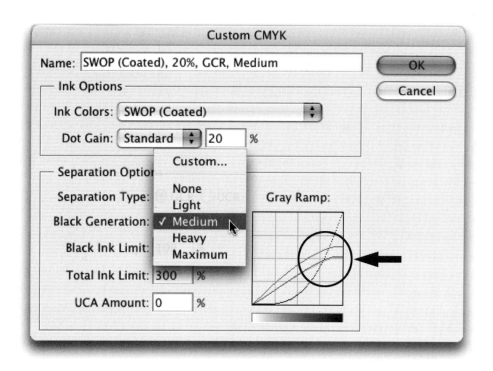

figure | 3 – 26 |

Input values obtained from your print provider for the black ink limit, the total ink limit, and the UCA.

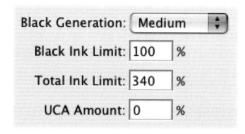

Custom-made Profiles

A number of companies such as Chromix offer services for creating custom color profiles that are specifically calibrated for your output device or for certain types of presses. If you are serious about color management and want the best color definition possible, then you may want to explore this as an option. The process is quite simple:

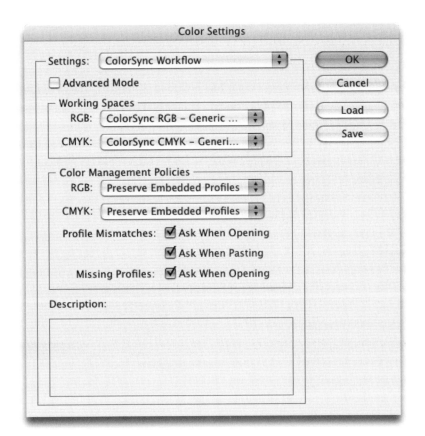

figure | 3 – 27 |

Choose the ColorSync Workflow profile when working in CMYK in Illustrator if you plan to import your files into Quark and you do not have a profile for your output device.

figure | 3 – 28 |

Color profiles can be applied to an image for specific printers or a calibrated monitor.

first download a kit containing target file images. The images are targeted toward either RGB or CMYK and contain color patches that help the service provider match colors from your printer to industry standard targets. Next, print out a test sheet of the target file image that is not color managed. Finally, send it to the service provider with your payment and, *voila*, in a few days you will have a custom-made profile ready to apply to any image.

Use the ColorSync Utility

Want to know what profiles are in your system now? Apple has included a handy piece of software in OS X called the ColorSync Utility. Located in Applications > Utilities, it helps you manage your profiles and view specific data such as location, color space, size, etc. for each one. When you click on a profile in the Profiles section, you can see the information for that profile. You can also view a three-dimensional color gamut model based on various color models. The ColorSync Utility also repairs profiles that are not conforming to the ICC standard.

SUMMARY

Color management is a necessity in any graphic design work that involves photographic images and calibrating a monitor is an important part of this process. You do not need to spend a bundle on expensive profiling software, but you do need to color manage your digital files to achieve the most desirable results. Remember to calibrate your display each time you restart your computer, and apply color profiles that are calibrated for the different output devices and papers on which you will be printing. You will quickly notice the difference proper color management makes in your workflow.

▶ *in review*

1. What is the standard gamma correction on a monitor in a Windows system?

2. Name the calibration software that comes built into the latest Apple operating system.

3. What is the white point setting that is standard for most graphic arts work?

4. How often should you calibrate your monitor?

5. Name a third party manufacturer of monitor calibrating software.

6. What can you do with your eyes that would help you be more accurate when adjusting the gamma settings in Adobe Gamma?

7. What is the name of the company that will build a custom color profile for your printer?

8. What device can you place on your screen to achieve a more accurately calibrated monitor?

▶ *exercise*

1. If your computer has Mac OS X on it, calibrate your monitor for daylight conditions using the Display Calibration Assistant. If you only have OS 9, then use Adobe Gamma. Save the profile you created with a name you will remember. Now open up the Display panel in your System Preferences window. If you are in OS 9, open up your Monitors window in your Control panels. Select a display profile that is set for different light conditions. What differences do you notice?

2. Open a Photoshop file that you saved either in a PSD, EPS, or TIFF format. Open the Assign Profiles... dialogue window from under Mode in the top menu bar. Make sure the image is in RGB mode. Select the profile you created in step one. Do the colors in the image appear darker or lighter? Do the skin tones change at all? Notice that there are profiles for different monitors and peripheral devices.

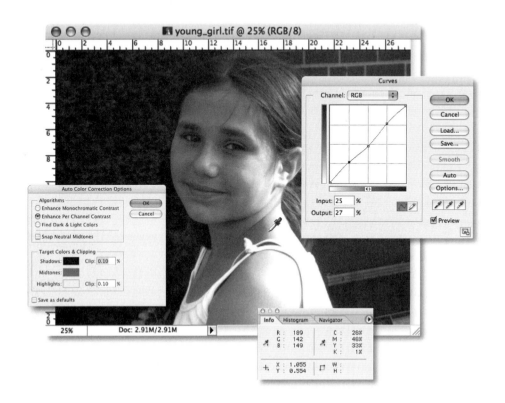

CHAPTER 4

objectives

- Recognize the difference between "high" and "low" key images
- Explore color correcting techniques using levels and curves
- Discover how to sharpen images using the UnSharp Mask command
- Prepare screened images for comprehensive presentations

introduction

If you have ever looked at photographs in a high quality art or photography book, you may wonder how they can achieve such vibrant colors. Photographers and designers have used a variety of techniques and methods to enhance their digital images ever since the first version of Photoshop came out in the late 1980s. Many have learned through trial and error which commands and filters produce the best results. They all know that a poorly corrected image will detract and diminish the quality of even the most elegant and sophisticated design. Ensuring that the colors you see in your onscreen image will translate onto a printed page is crucial to becoming a skillful designer.

These days, a color correction specialist can make a comfortable living. Wages for an artist in this area of design can run as high as $85 an hour or $1,500 per week, which is more than a freelance designer will make when they begin working. Many companies offering computer training have two- or three-day courses in color correction. The costs for these training sessions can be as high as $4,000. Although these seminars and workshops may be worthwhile, it is not necessary for the average designer to enroll in these rather expensive courses unless you are planning to become a specialist who does high-resolution color correcting for top quality printing. You can still have beautiful images to complement your artwork after working through the exercises in this chapter and on the instructional CD.

The Right Mode

Unless you have taken a course in advanced color correction, always color correct your images in RGB mode. It is easier to see results and there is one less channel to correct. Color correcting in CMYK is tricky and best left up to experts. Remember to use your Info palette to help you determine the color balance.

FACTORS AFFECTING COLOR

Many factors affect the quality of a printed photograph besides correcting its color. The different types of inks used in a piece and the paper it is printed on can alter the color balance and brightness of an image. High quality papers will reflect more light, so images will appear brighter on this type of stock. Lower quality papers, such as uncoated stocks, will reflect less light, so a photograph could appear darker when printed on these types of papers. As discussed in the last chapter, this can be compensated for when calibrating your monitor.

Other changes occur when an image is converted to CMYK from RGB mode. You know from reading Chapter 2 that many screen colors cannot be realized on a printed surface. The colors that do not fall into the gamut range are converted to the closest process color, which usually contains a lot of black ink, so it appears dull or gray. An expert in color correction is aware of this and can compensate for this by bringing the out-of-gamut colors into range manually as demonstrated in the last chapter.

Color correcting images involves precise manipulation of an image, so some designers prefer to send the images to a prepress house that has specialists on staff to perform color corrections.

HIGH AND LOW KEY IMAGES

If you look at a photograph, you will notice the image is made up of light, medium, and dark areas of color. These areas can be divided into five tonal ranges: highlights, one-quarter, mid, three-quarter and shadows. These areas do not represent every color within an image, only the average tonal ranges. Measuring in values of CMYK: the highlights are generally between 5 and 15 percent, the one-quarter tones are 15 to 35 percent, while the mid-tones fall in the 35 to 65 percent range, the three-quarter tones are between 65 to 85 percent, and the shadows 85 to 95 percent. A color correction specialist can tell which of these areas needs to be lightened or darkened. The importance of knowing this will become evident when you begin to use curves to color correct a photo.

Whether you use a digital or a traditional 35 mm camera, there are three types of images you will encounter when you start to do your own photography. When you take a photograph that is primarily dark in all tonal areas, you have an image that is called low key (see figure 4–1). If the photo is mainly light in the three tonal ranges, it is called a high key image (see figure 4–2). Photographs that have most of the color information in the mid-tone range are referred to as average key (see figure 4–3). A properly corrected photo will maintain a balance between the different tonal ranges.

It is quite easy to tell if the image you have scanned is low or high key. If the image appears very dark looking with lots of shadows in it, it is low key. However, if the image is very pale or lacking in shadow detail, it is high key. Ideally, a photo should have good contrast between the light and dark tonal ranges, although not to an extreme degree. The highlight areas of the image should not be bleached out so the color is almost pure white, nor should the shadows be so dark that the color in these areas fills in when it is printed. Another way to tell if an image is low or high key is to open the histogram of the image under *Window* in the top menu bar. If the majority of the color is to the left, it is a high key image, as most of the color falls in the one-quarter tones. A histogram of a low key image will show more color to the right, in the three-quarter and shadow tones. The color in an average key image will be centralized in the mid-tone regions of the photo (see figure 4–4).

figure | 4–1 |

A low key image is one where color is mostly in the three-quarter or shadow tones.

Histogram in the Making

Make sure you use the histogram function in Photoshop when trying to determine what type of key your image is. The histogram plots the amount of brightness or darkness among the different tonal ranges, so it helps you achieve better contrast in an image. The histogram can also help you when you are color correcting in individual channels. Keep an eye on the shifts in the distribution of pixels when adjusting a channel's contrast. This will ensure more accurate use of the images' full tonal range and prevent loss of detail.

Adjusting Color Balance

In order to get the best results when printing a four-color image, you need to set the white and black point targets. Not only does this correct the contrast in your image, it also corrects most of the color imbalance or shift that takes place when scanning or shooting a photo. Setting the white and black point targets ensures that you will not lose detail in the highlight and shadow areas of your image.

Using your eyedropper tool and Info palette in Photoshop is the easiest way to tell if the image requires color correcting. Simply drag this tool over the lightest part of the image, preferably a white object. Now look at the Info palette and check the RGB values. The color values for red, green, and blue should not be greater than 245 on average in those highlighted areas and they should also be relatively equal. If they are

figure | 4 – 2 |

A high key image has color mostly in the highlight or one-quarter tones.

> ▶ **Setting Limits**
>
> Check your highlights and shadows with the eyedropper tool after you have set the white and black point targets. You do not want your highlights to be too bright or your shadows too dark. The shadows should have an ink limit that is close to 300 percent if you are printing on a coated stock using an offset press. This means that if you add all the percentages of cyan, magenta, yellow, and black, they should approximately add up to 300. If you want to set a higher ink limit, check with your printer to see what the maximum amount of ink coverage their presses are capable of handling. Your highlights should have at least 5 percent of the four process colors as well (unless they are reflections, in which case they can be nearly pure white).

on average greater than 245, many of the light areas will appear washed out and lacking detail when printed. Now move the eyedropper over the darkest areas. If the RGB values are less than 10 in these areas, then your shadow areas will fill in and lose detail when printed. Once again, these values of RGB should be relatively equal in the shaded parts of your image. If they are not equal in areas you know to be neutral in tone such as white, gray, or black objects, this indicates the image has a color cast.

Using the Curves Command

Nearly all scanners will shift the color balance of an image either too far toward the red or blue spectrum, causing either a reddish or bluish cast in the image after it is

figure | 4–3 |

An average key image is one where color is distributed evenly or concentrated in the mid tones.

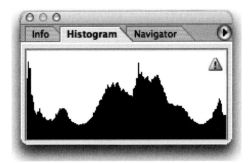

figure | 4 – 4 |

The Histogram palette for an average key image shows the color information concentrated in the mid-tones.

scanned. It can also cause shifts in the light, medium, and dark tonal areas. By adjusting the white and black points of an image using Curves in Photoshop, most of the necessary color correction in an image can be done. By setting the white and black points, you will mostly balance the red, green, and blue colors and adjust the images contrast to lighten shaded areas that are oversaturated with RGB values and deepen highlights that are overexposed and contain very low values of RGB. Remember to leave your image in RGB mode when performing this procedure.

1. Calibrate your monitor as demonstrated in Chapter 3, or open your Displays preferences and select a calibrated profile you previously created.

2. In Photoshop, select the eyedropper tool and make sure the sample size is set to 3 x 3 Average. Make sure the Info palette is open and will not be hidden by the Curves window.

3. Make a duplicate of your image by going under the menu bar to Image > Duplicate. Save a copy of the image to the folder on which you are working.

4. Now you need to set the white and black target points. Select Image > Adjustments > Curves (command/control-M) so that the Curves window appears.

5. Once the Curves window is open, click on the Options button. The Auto Color Corrections window appears (see figure 4–5).

6. Select the Find Dark & Light Colors button. Use this setting for most color corrections. Occasionally, the Enhance Monochromatic Contrast or the Enhance Per Channel Contrast button may produce better results. Select the Snap Neutral Midtones box and click on the Shadows box in the Target Colors & Clipping section (see figure 4–6).

7. In the Color Picker window set the target for the shadows to 10 for red, green, and blue (see figure 4–7). Click OK.

Different Targets for Different Presses

The values for the highlight and shadow target colors in this demonstration are ones most often used for offset printing; however, they may not be applicable to all types of presses. Ask your printer to perform a test of their inks on each press to determine the correct target values. If the highlight and shadow values are not set correctly for a certain press, then the highlight areas may wash out while the shadow areas may fill in. This causes your image to lose definition in these areas. Be sure to use the new values from your printer when adjusting an image's color balance.

8. Now click on the Highlights box in the Target Colors & Clipping section (see figure 4–8).

9. In the Color Picker window, set the target for the highlights to 234 for red, green and blue (see figure 4–9). This will produce a slightly higher value for cyan, which tends to print lighter than magenta or yellow on an offset press. Click OK.

10. Select the Save as defaults box and click OK to return to the Curves window (see figure 4–10).

11. Now click on the Auto button to set the color adjustment and then click OK (figure 4–11).

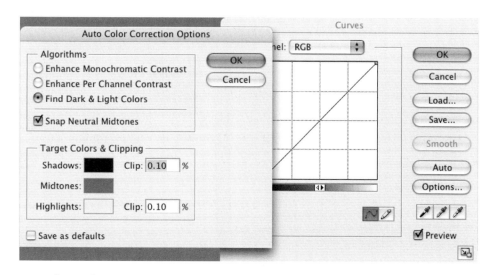

figure |4–5|

Click on the *Options* button to open the *Auto Color Corrections* window.

figure | 4–6 |

Clicking on the Shadow
box opens the Color
Picker window.

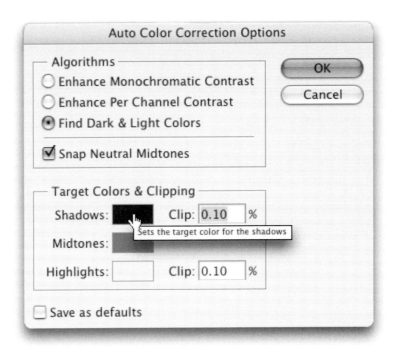

figure | 4–7 |

Set the shadow target
color values as shown.
Click OK.

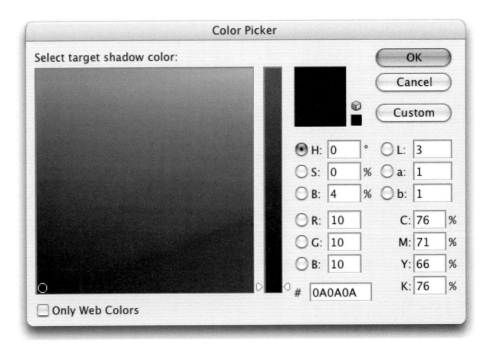

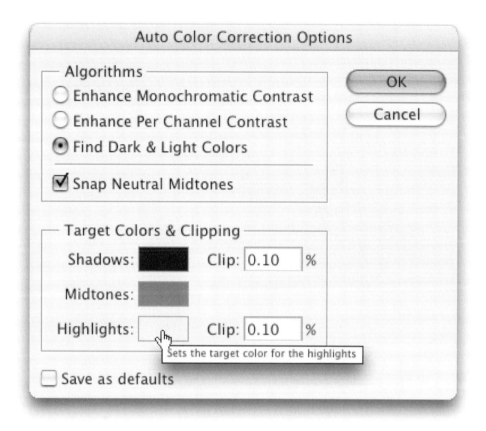

figure | 4 – 8 |

Clicking on the Highlight box reopens the Color Picker window.

12. Open the original image and the corrected one and compare the differences. You should notice a distinct difference in contrast and color balance (figure 4 – 12).

Correcting Color Casts with Curves

I recommend using curves to remove a color cast from an image as it proves to be more reliable than other color correcting tools. The Curves window allows you to increase or decrease values within the various tonal ranges in an image either in the master RGB channel or in each individual channel. It is more flexible than using Variations, which can also ruin an image if overused. Levels are often used for color correcting as well, yet curves are far more precise.

As you have seen, setting the white and black point corrects about 80 percent of the color in an image. Still, at times you may be working with an image that is drastically over or underexposed, or where the colors have severely faded over time. You may also want to fine-tune your color correction to achieve the best possible

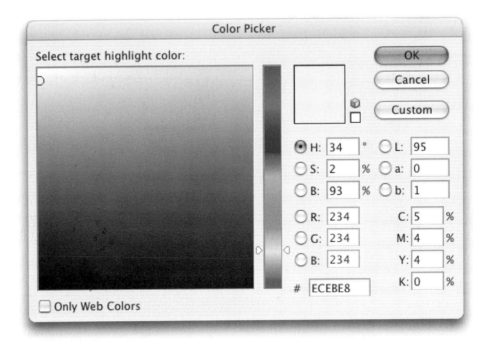

figure | 4 – 9 |

Set the highlight target color values as shown. Click OK.

results. In this case, setting the white and black point may not prove to be sufficient. It may become necessary for you to make small adjustments to your image using the Curves command within the various RGB channels to achieve the results you want. How much you should adjust each curve and what direction they should go is quite complex and would take up most of this book; however, we can look at a few scenarios that will demonstrate some basic rules.

The Curves Window

The Curves window can be daunting to someone not familiar with using curves for color correction. When you first open up the Curves window in Photoshop, you may wonder which direction to move the curves to get the results you want. Examining the different components of the Curves window can help. Select the red channel and open your Curves window by going to the top menu bar and selecting Image > Adjustments > Curves (or command/control-M). You will notice a graph divided into 16 squares, three lines going vertically and horizontally (see figure 4 – 13). A diagonal line travels across the graph. This represents the tonal ranges of the image before changes are made to the curves. In this example, it starts from the white point on the left and ends at the black point on the right. To properly adjust curves, make sure that the left triangle below the graph is selected, this allows you to adjust the curves using percentages instead

figure | 4 – 10 |

Select the *Save as defaults* box so you will not need to reenter the values. Click OK.

of values (see figure 4 – 14). It is much easier for the novice to manipulate curves with percentages, as adjustments you make will be easier to measure and remember using percentages.

Each dividing line between the four sections represents each of the tonal ranges with the highlights and shadows at either edge (see figure 4 – 15). In order to make sure you do not ruin your image, you should always move the curves up or down using points that stay as close as possible to the lines that represent the three tonal ranges. Moving the points up will darken the tones, removing some of the light from that tonal range. Moving the points down will lighten the channel and bring more light into that tonal range. If you move the point you made too far to either side of the dividing line, you may lose or destroy the color information in a channel permanently. You can check to see if your point is exactly on the line by examining the Input box at the bottom of the Channels window. The Output box tells you how much you have moved the point up or down from its original position. These two boxes also let you insert values for the curves manually, instead of using your cursor to move them up or down (see figure 4 – 15 again).

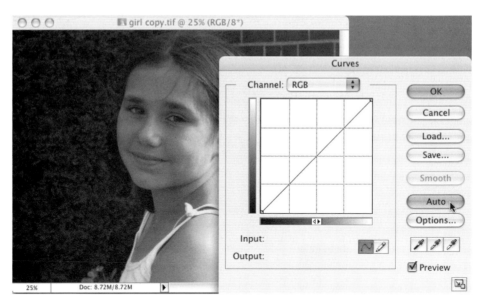

figure | 4 – 11 |

Click on the *Auto* button to adjust the color balance in an image. Click OK to close the *Curves* window.

figure | 4 – 12 |

Open and compare the before and after image to ensure your color corrections are accurate. See color insert.

When color correcting an image, the two most important guidelines to follow are to correct each channel individually: and to make the contrast between the one-quarter, mid, and three-quarter tones distinct enough so that the contrast in each channel resembles a normal black and white photo. Remember to take into account the subject matter though. For instance, if you photographed a red ball on a yellow table, the blue channel would appear very dark, so it would not be a good idea to overly lighten this channel as the color of the objects may not be true.

Playing with Curves

When adjusting curves, there are no set rules and each situation is different. Still, there are some common configurations where the curves settings are similar.

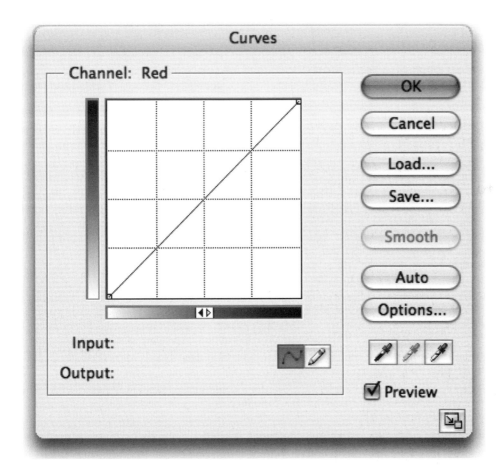

figure | 4 – 13 |

When the Curves window first opens, it shows a graph with 16 squares and a straight diagonal line. This line represents the range of tones in the image before color correction begins.

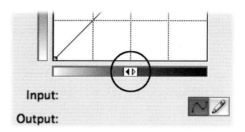

figure |4 – 14|

Click on the left triangle under the graph so you are adjusting the curves using percentages instead of values.

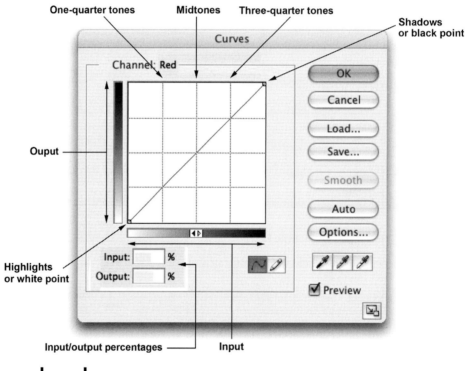

figure |4 – 15|

The Curves window has three dividing lines representing the three tonal ranges.

Frequently, an S curve with steep inclines is used in cases where contrast in the channel is weak and color range between the one- and three-quarter tones is low resulting in a flat image. A gentle valley is used where all of the tonal ranges need to be lightened. In this case, only a single point on the curve is lowered. A sharp slope can be used to darken two of the tonal ranges, with a locking point on the quarter tones and a single point being raised on the three-quarter tones. Twin peaks are useful for

> ## Finding Different Tonal Ranges in an Image
>
> If you want to quickly identify into what range on the tonal scale an area within your image falls, move your cursor into the image window and click on that area. You will notice a marker temporarily appears on the diagonal line in the Curves window. If you want to set the marker to a point on that line, then hold down the command/control key and click on the area again. This comes in handy for the next section when we look at adjusting different tonal ranges using curves to correct color casts.

images in which there is not enough contrast between the mid-tones and other tonal areas (for examples of these, see figure 4 – 16).

Let's take a look at a few typical scenarios where the color and contrast cannot be completely balanced through setting the white and black point. Say we have a photo that is quite old and the colors are no longer 'true' (see figure 4 – 17). The image has faded over time, so the mid- and three-quarter tones are washed-out. Still, if we examine the histogram we can see this is a 'low key' image, as most of the photo has dark shadow areas. As well there is a yellowish cast to the image, caused by prolonged exposure to ultraviolet light. When color correcting an image such as this one, you must go into the individual channels after setting the white and black points and fine-tune the contrast and the color balance manually using curves. If you go through this example step-by-step, you will get a good idea of how you can correct this type of image.

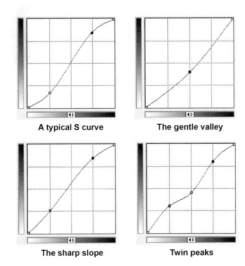

A typical S curve   The gentle valley

The sharp slope   Twin peaks

figure | 4 – 16 |

The most common types of configurations made when using curves.

figure | 4–17 |

This photo has faded over time and taken on a yellowish cast. See color insert.

1. As always, we must calibrate our monitor or select a profile from the Color preferences in our System preferences.

2. Set the white and black point as described earlier in the chapter. Although most of the yellowish cast is gone, there is still some remaining.

3. Closely examine the percentages of CMYK in the skin tones using the Info palette. In this example, you can see that there is a lot more magenta than yellow in the man's face (figure 4–18). Ideally the magenta and yellow values in the skin tones of a Caucasian adult should be nearly equal with the magenta tones slightly higher. The percentage of cyan should be approximately a third of the magenta and yellow values. From the photo's yellowish cast, we can assume that either the red and green channels are overexposed or the blue channel is underexposed.

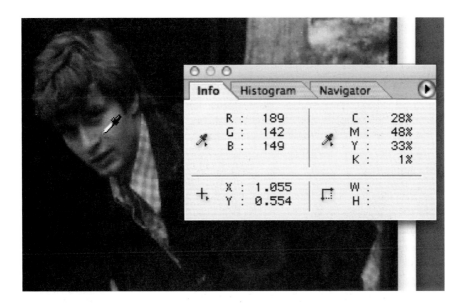

figure | 4 – 18 |

Skin tones are a good way of determining if the color balance in an image is correct.

4. Looking at each channel closely determines which channels are overexposed or under-exposed. When the image is in RGB mode, a channel that is overexposed will appear pale and one that is underexposed will be dark. Here, the red channel is overexposed (figure 4 – 19). In order to properly adjust the contrast in this channel, we must determine which of the three tonal ranges need adjusting. Moving the eyedropper tool around various tonal areas and looking at the values in the Info palette will tell us the red channel is overexposed in the three-quarter tones and requires lightening in the mid- and one-quarter tones. Place a point on the three-quarter line and raise the curve by 3 percent. Now place a point on the mid-tone line and lower it by 3 percent (figure 4 – 20). Click the OK button to close the Curves window for that channel.

5. Now we can examine the other two channels. The green channel is underexposed in the mid- and three-quarter tones (figure 4 – 21). To add yellow into these tonal areas, we can open up the Curves window again and set a fixed point on the one-quarter line, to keep them from lightening. Set a point on the three-quarter tones and move it down until the channel is sufficiently lightened (figure 4 – 22). Click OK when done.

6. The blue channel is underexposed in all three tonal areas (figure 4 – 23). Set a point on the mid-tone line and move it down by 3 percent to lighten both the one-quarter mid- and three-quarter tones (figure 4 – 24).

7. Returning to the master channel and using the eyedropper, we can check the CMYK percentages in the skin tones (figure 4 – 25). The magenta and yellow values should be nearly equal and the cyan values about a third less. View the final color-corrected file and print a copy to your color printer to check that ink coverage is acceptable in the highlight and shadow areas (figure 4 – 26).

figure | 4 – 19 |

The red channel is overexposed in the three-quarter tones.

In cases where you are working with a high key image (figure 4 – 27), you may not have a strong color cast, but the image is rather pale and lacks sufficient contrast. In this instance, you can follow the same steps as before, but add more contrast by deepening the three-quarter tones in each channel.

1. Calibrate your monitor or select a profile from Color preferences in your System preferences.

figure | 4 – 20 |

Raising the curve for the three-quarter tones by 5 percent to darken those areas and remove some of the reddish cast.

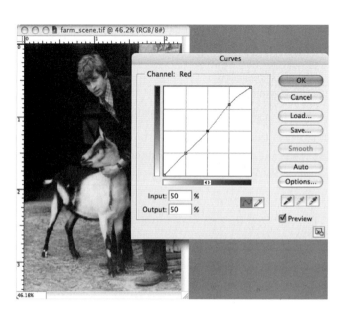

figure | 4 – 21 |

The green channel is underexposed in the mid- and three-quarter tones.

2. Set the highlight and shadow target colors. Although most of the reddish cast is gone, there is still some remaining in the image. Opening up the red channel shows that it is overexposed in the three-quarter tones. This channel is also lacking color in the one-quarter tones, so these tones must be lightened.

3. In the Curves window with the red channel selected, raise the curve on the three-quarter point, and then lower the one-quarter point (figure 4 – 28). This

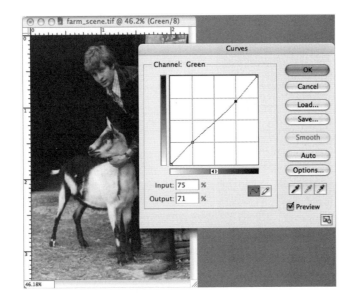

figure | 4 – 22 |

Lower the curve for the mid- and three-quarter tones to lighten this channel overall.

figure | 4 – 23 |

The blue channel is
underexposed in the all
three tonal areas.

will darken the three-quarter tones and lighten the one-quarter tones and
create more contrast.

4. The green channel appears somewhat dark in the mid-tones. Place a fixed point
   on the three-quarter tones to leave them alone and then place a point on the
   mid-tones and lower them (figure 4 – 29).

figure | 4 – 24 |

Setting a point for the
mid-tones and lowering it
adds blue to all three
tonal areas and removes
what is left of the reddish
cast in the photo.

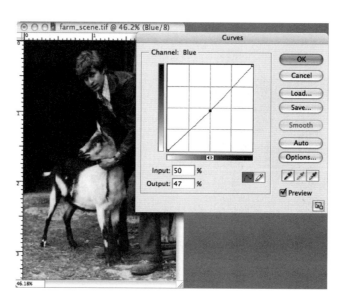

> ### Smooth Curves
>
> When adjusting curves in Photoshop, move the points in small increments, usually a maximum of 5 to 8 percent. Over adjusting the curves will make the channel appear distorted and much of the color information will be lost. It is better to do several small corrections using curves instead of trying to correct everything at once. Your curves should be smooth and gentle, not bumpy and exaggerated. Think of the Appalachians instead of Mount Everest.

5. The blue channel is underexposed, mostly in the mid-tones. Set a point on the mid-tones and lower it by approximately 3 percent (figure 4–30).

6. Print out a color proof of the correction to compare with the original (figure 4–31).

Correcting Skin Tones for Different Races

In the last two examples, you have seen how to adjust skin tones for Caucasian people. However, the skin tones of someone other than a Caucasian can be quite different. People of other races often have higher percentages of yellow and cyan in their skin tones than Caucasians. For instance, someone of African heritage will have less magenta than other races. Looking at a photograph of someone of African descent we can see how adjusting the contrast in the three channels will help to correct their skin tones (see figure 4–32). Observe how the percentages of CMYK vary in the man's skin when the image is properly color corrected.

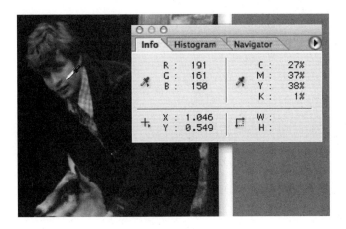

figure | 4–25 |

Check the percentages of CMYK in the skin tone areas to see if the colors are balanced properly.

figure | 4 – 26 |

Print the final file to ensure details in the highlights and shadows are visible, and the color balance is correct. See color insert.

figure | 4 – 27 |

A high key image lacks color in the three-quarter and shadow areas, so there is very little contrast. See color insert.

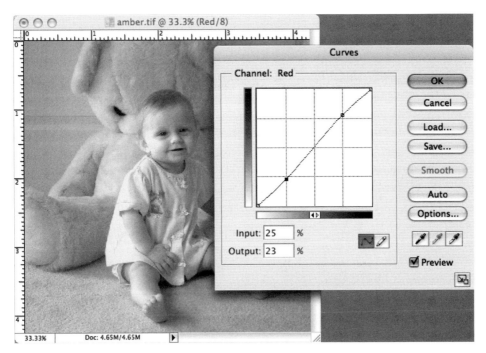

figure |4 – 28|

The curves are shaped to remove color in the mid- and three-quarter tones.

1. Calibrate your monitor.

2. Set the highlight and shadow target colors as in the previous examples.

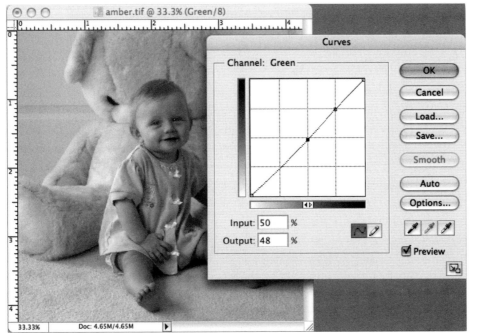

figure |4 – 29|

The curves in the green channel are shaped to bring color into the mid- and one-quarter tones.

figure | 4 – 30 |

The curves in the blue channel are also shaped to bring color into the mid- and one-quarter tones.

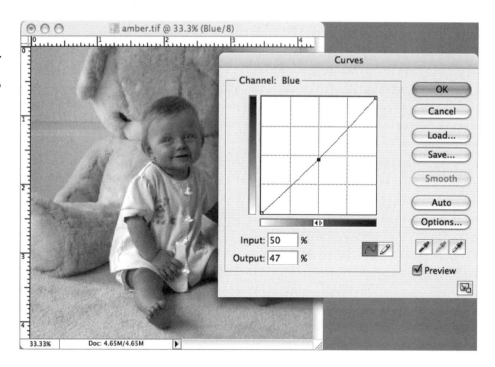

3. The red channel is slightly overexposed in the three-quarter tones, so place a point on that line and darken them. The one-quarter and mid-tones are underexposed, so lighten them (figure 4 – 33).

figure | 4 – 31 |

The final image has better color balance and contrast making it more dynamic. See color insert.

4. The green channel is underexposed in the mid and three-quarter tonal areas, so place a point on the mid-tones and lower it by 5 percent (figure 4–34).

5. Finally, in the blue channel, which is also underexposed in all tonal ranges, it is necessary to lighten overall. Set a point on the three-quarter tones and lower it by 5 percent (figure 4–35).

6. Proof the final corrected image (figure 4–36).

Color correcting for people of Asian descent involves placing a greater percentage of yellow than other races. And like people of African decent, the percentages of the four colors are higher overall. The percentage of yellow should be higher by at least 10 percent. If you follow along with this example (see figure 4–37), you will have a better understanding of how Asian skin tones should appear in a printed piece.

1. Calibrate your monitor.

2. Set the white and black point target colors.

3. In the red channel, which is quite overexposed in all the tonal areas, darken the channel by placing a point at the mid-tones and raising the point by approximately 6 percent (figure 4–38).

4. The green channel is overexposed, so darken it by raising the point on the mid-tone line by 3 percent (figure 4–39).

5. In the blue channel, deepen the three-quarter tones by placing a point on the line and raise it by 3 percent. Place a point on the one-quarter tones and lower them by 2 percent (figure 4–40).

6. In the master channel, adjust the contrast between the one- and three-quarter tones to enhance the image's contrast (figure 4–41).

7. Print a proof the final corrected image (figure 4–42).

At times color correcting may seem to be a painstaking process, but it is absolutely necessary for high quality graphics work. If you are not sure if you are properly correcting each channel, try several different ways until you have found one that looks right. If you get the skin tones in your subject right, you can be pretty sure the rest of the colors in your image will be right. Try not to get discouraged, just keep practicing until you feel confident. Color correcting is like any other skill. The only way to learn is to do it over and over again until it becomes second nature.

Sharpening Your Image

Scanning devices do not always sharpen an image sufficiently even if you have used the sharpening feature in your scanner's software. If you wish to sharpen an image

figure | 4–32 |

This photo is too dark in the one-quarter and mid-tones. This makes the person's features appear flat and not clearly defined. See color insert.

figure | 4–33 |

Darken the three-quarter tones in the red channel.

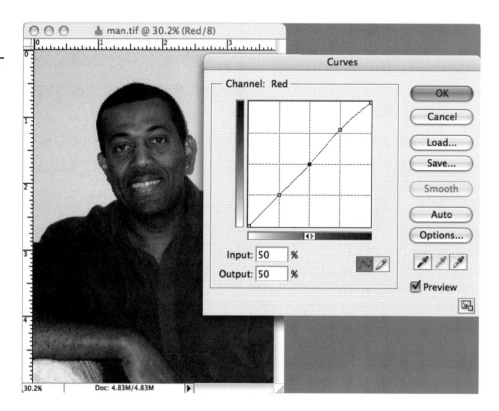

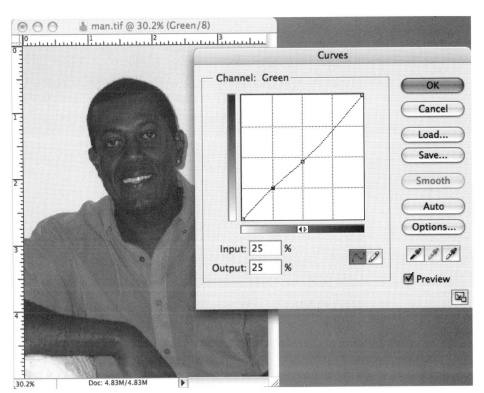

figure | 4 – 34 |

Lighten the mid and three-quarter tones in the green channel.

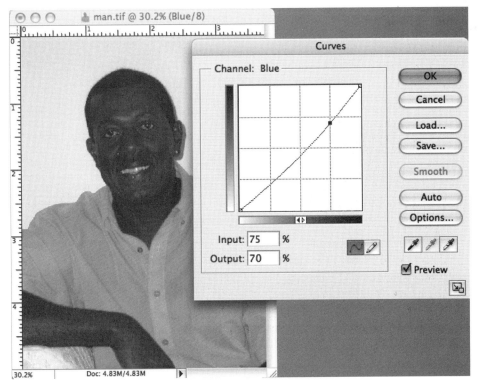

figure | 4 – 35 |

Like the green channel, lighten all the tonal areas in the blue channel.

figure | 4 – 36 |

The final corrected image has better contrast and definition between the shadows and the other tonal areas. Notice the high percentage of yellow in the man's skin. See color insert.

after you have scanned it, then use the Unsharp Mask filter in Photoshop. This filter gives the best results for sharpening an image. Do not use the Sharpen and Sharpen More filters as they do more harm than good and can worsen the quality of your image. Also, be careful not to oversharpen your image as this can cause jagged edges to appear between areas of color, giving your image a surreal appearance.

figure | 4 – 37 |

This photo is an average key image that has a definite reddish cast. See color insert.

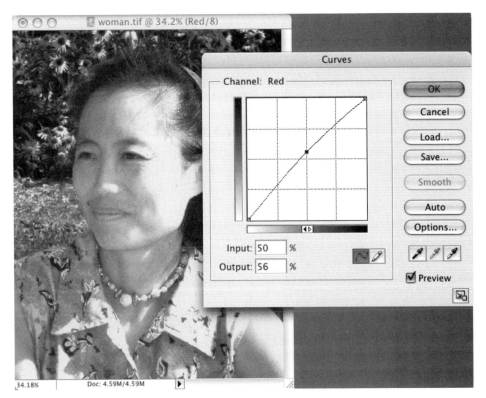

figure | 4 – 38 |

Darken all the tonal areas in the red channel.

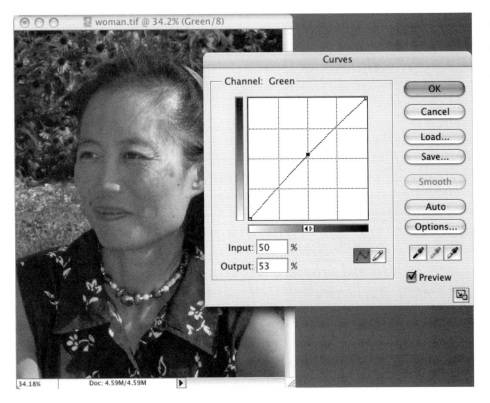

figure | 4 – 39 |

Slightly darken all the tonal areas in the green channel, which is not as overexposed.

figure | 4 – 40 |

Deepen the three-quarter tones and lighten the one-quarter tones in the blue channel.

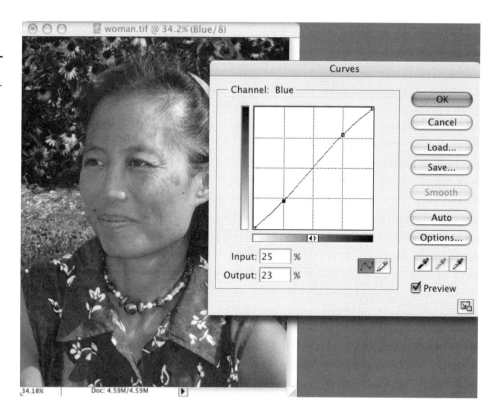

figure | 4 – 41 |

Adjust the contrast between the one- and three-quarter tones.

figure | 4 – 42 |

The final corrected image has a richer tonal quality than the original along with colors that are more realistic. See color insert.

Open up the Unsharp Mask filter by going under Filter in the top menu bar in Photoshop. How much you need to sharpen your image depends on the blurriness of the image, but usually an amount of 100 percent with a radius of 1.0 and a threshold of 0 works for most situations. You can apply the Unsharp mask filter again using lower amounts if you need to fine-tune the sharpness.

Sometimes it is necessary to sharpen one of the RGB channels when color correcting. If you are working with an image that requires a channel to be sharpened, then use the same settings mentioned in the paragraph above. Remember to print out a proof of your image to make sure it has the right amount of sharpness.

Decsreening Images

Although continuous tone images are the most ideal to scan for digital artwork, occasionally we may use a photo from a magazine only for presentation purposes. Since you do not own the copyrights to the image, it will need to be replaced by one to which you own the rights before the job goes to press. An image scanned from a magazine or newspaper will need to be descreened before it can be used in a presentation made to a client. If it is not descreened, the two halftone dot screens will overlap each other, causing noticeable patterns in the image. This is called a moiré pattern. To descreen a photo, apply a Gaussian blur to the image at 100 percent with a radius between 1.5 and 2.0 or until the halftone dots are not noticeable anymore. Then apply an Unsharp Mask using the same settings for the percent and radius with no threshold value. If you have done it correctly, you will end up with a clear image without any halftone dots showing. However, never use this technique for work that is to be printed on a press as the moiré pattern may still appear on the press sheet.

SUMMARY

The credit for every award-winning design can be attributed to the skills a designer has acquired over his career. Design and production go hand-in-hand. If you can understand and apply the principles and methods of correcting color discussed in this chapter, then you are one step ahead of your competition. And once you have practiced these methods, you will be ready to tackle any color correcting challenge with ease and confidence. So cast off those muddy tones. Set sail for the clearest channel. Make way for topnotch photos!

▶ *in review*

1. What should the RGB values be for your target white point?

2. Which filter sharpens your image after it is scanned?

3. What is the difference between a high and a low key image?

4. What is the first operation you should perform before beginning any color correcting work?

5. Is it easier to use percentages or values when adjusting curves?

6. What factors affect the color of an image when it is printed?

7. When do you need to descreen an image?

8. Is it a good idea to exaggerate your curves when color correcting a channel?

▶ *exercises*

1. Open a Photoshop file from the CD and leave it in RGB mode. Make a duplicate of the image. Look at the various channels in the copy and determine which ones are over or underexposed. Use the method from this book to set the white and black points in the curves window. Now compare the channels in the original image. Do you notice any differences?

2. Working with the same file you used for Step 1, adjust the curves settings for each channel. After you have changed the curves for each channel, preview your changes by clicking on the master channel. What happens to the image if you overadjust your curves? What is a comfortable range for adjusting the various tonal ranges in the Curves window?

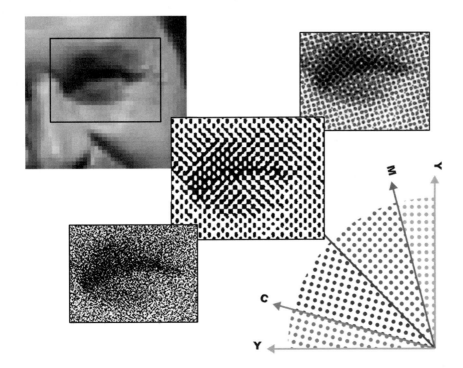

CHAPTER 5

objectives

- Recognize the differences between continuous tone, pixel-based, and bitmap images
- Examine the meaning of the terms ppi, dpi, and lpi, and compare their relationship to one another
- Discover how line screen angles make up halftone images
- Recognize how resolution affects output quality of images
- Examine the various file types used in prepress namely, EPS, TIFF, and DCS formats
- Discover how to create bitmap, duotone, and tritone images

introduction

One area of prepress that is often an enigma to designers is how an image can be transformed from the screen to a printed impression on paper. We know from the first two chapters, that this is a mathematical process and involves several stages. We also know that unless a prepress professional takes several steps to assist this process, the results can be unpredictable. In a prepress workflow, what you see on your screen is not always what you get on paper.

A designer who is trained in a layout or drawing program is probably accustomed to editing elements quickly in those programs. They may treat their images the same way they treat an illustration or text, resizing or rotating them, altering their color or applying masks and filters to them at will in layout programs. While these methods are convenient and may work for presentation purposes, it causes trouble when the file is output to film. If you want to alter the way your image looks, you have to perform the changes in the program in which it was created. To understand why this is necessary, it is essential to learn how images are constructed in image-editing programs.

Image-editing Programs

Image-editing programs and painting programs like Photoshop or Fractal Painter allow the designer to create images using a pixel-by-pixel arrangement. Pixels are small units of color that make up the image you see on your monitor. The word pixel is an acronym for picture element. The size of these pixels is determined by the resolution used in the image.

Image-editing programs are ideal for creating digital art where a sense of texture or depth is important. They also allow the user to colorize certain areas or objects, combine parts of different photographs, and add their own content into the composition. Unlike other types of software programs, they require greater amounts of memory to produce a file. To help understand their complexity, let's go through the process of transferring a continuous tone photograph into a pixel-based image.

A continuous tone photograph is basically an image that has been reproduced onto photographic paper through a film processor. All the colors in the image blend together and there is no separation between them. In order to transfer this image into a digital format, you must use a scanning device. After launching your scanning software, you select what resolution at which you want your image to be scanned. When you examine the window of your scanning software, you can select in how many pixels per inch (ppi) you want your image to be scanned (see figure 5–1). The number of pixels contained within each square inch will determine the resolution of the image. Do not be fooled if your scanning software uses the term dpi. All input and output devices describe resolution using dpi. Once the image is scanned, the resolution of an image on our screen is defined in pixels per inch.

Once you have scanned the image, a digital file for it is created on your hard drive. Opening this file in Photoshop will display it on your monitor by using three channels of red, green, and blue to make up all the colors within the image. When trying to imagine how pixels make up a photographic image on your screen, think of the image being composed of small squares of color, almost like tiles on a bathroom wall. The pixels in a digital image are plotted using a horizontal and vertical grid system. And like the tiles in your bathroom, once an image has been created, it cannot be easily altered, without reconstructing it from scratch.

Files created in image-editing and painting programs are referred to as resolution dependent due to the configuration of these pixels. This means that the size of the image cannot be significantly altered without some difference in quality. For instance, if the image is enlarged in size, so are the pixels, making them more noticeable. An image where the pixels are easily observed is referred to as a pixelated image (see figure 5–2). This can be seen most frequently in images that are down-loaded from web pages on the internet. Most photos you see on web sites are

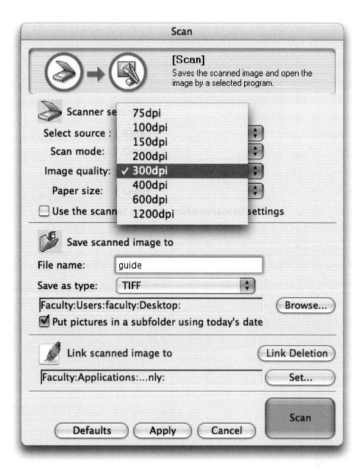

figure | 5 – 1 |

You can select the resolution quality of your image when you first scan it into your computer. Remember, if you want to change the resolution later on, you must rescan the image.

displayed in low resolution, typically 72 ppi. Images of this quality are not acceptable for a prepress workflow environment, as we will soon see.

Bits and Bytes

Pixels can also vary in another way besides size, and that is in bit-depth. Every pixel is broken into smaller pieces of information called bits. There is a minimum of 1 bit per pixel to a maximum of 64 bits per pixel for a four-color image. Each bit can be one of two colors, so each pixel in an image with a bit-depth of one has two color possibilities (either black or white). A one-bit image is also called a bitmap image (see figure 5 – 3). If an image has a bit-depth of two, then each pixel has four possible color combinations (or 2^2). The number of color possibilities increases exponentially with the number of bits. Each channel we view in an image in Photoshop can contain

figure | 5 – 2 |

An image from a web page has a resolution that is too low and not satisfactory for prepress workflow situations.

either 8 or 16 bits. However, output devices do not read images saved in 16 bits per channel, due to the fact that they are not capable of producing more than 256 levels of any one color. An 8-bit channel in an RGB image has exactly 256 levels of gray. Therefore, when saving an image in Photoshop, we need to make sure each channel has only 8 bits (see figure 5 – 4). When we add all the channels together, an RGB image will be 24 bits, while a CMYK image will be 32 bits. If we could use 16 bits per channel, a CMYK image would be 64 bits. This would not produce better results at the printing stage, yet the file size would be larger.

Increases in resolution and bit-depth ultimately lead to larger file sizes, so more bytes of information are required for each file. One way a designer can keep their

figure | 5 – 3 |

A bitmap image contains a single bit that is either white or black. This format is mostly used for line art such as maps.

Photoshop file sizes to a minimum is to use a resolution that is appropriate for the intended use. For example, web sites use images that are scanned and saved at a lower resolution than ones used for print production. Most web pages contain images saved at a low resolution; whereas an image that we plan to use in a magazine layout will need to be scanned in at a much higher resolution, usually a minimum of 250 ppi. The reason for this depends not only on the medium, but the nature of printed inks. A look at how screen resolution affects output resolution will help you to understand this difference better.

Output Resolution: dpi and lpi

As you know, you use pixels per inch to describe the resolution of an image on your screen; however, different terms are used to describe the resolution of an image or object once it is printed on a page. If you look closely at a printed sheet of paper, you can see that it contains both laser and halftone dots. As discussed in the first chapter, these two grid systems overlap each other, with the smaller laser dots making up the

figure | 5 – 4 |

Photoshop documents must be saved with 8 bits per channel to avoid printing errors.

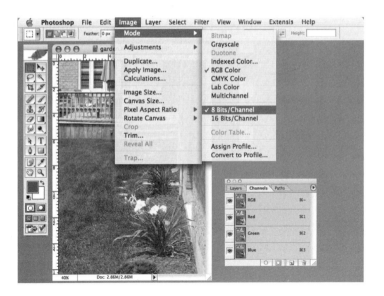

larger halftone dots. At this point, you may be wondering if it matters at what resolution you scan your images if you know what resolution your printer is capable of outputting at as well as the line screen frequency it uses. The answer is yes. As we will see, there is a definite relationship between the resolution you see on your screen and the one that eventually translates onto the printed page.

Laser Dots

We use the terms dots per inch (dpi) to measure the resolution of the laser dots generated by an output device. The laser dots make up that part of our artwork where elements such as text, illustrations, areas of color, or texture appear. The type of output device we are using determines the number of laser dots within a linear inch, or the print resolution. All output devices print within a certain range of resolution, with more complex devices having greater range. For instance, most laser printers can print anywhere from 600 to 1200 dpi. Imagesetters and platesetters have the capability to image film and plates between 1200 to 4500 dpi. The resolution you select for printing depends upon the complexity of the output device, how smooth you want your graphics to look, and the paper stock on which it is being printed. If you were printing a magazine on medium clay coated paper, you would ask the service provider to image the film using a resolution of 2500 dpi. If you were printing on very high quality art paper, you would ask for a finer laser dot screen, perhaps 3600 dpi or more.

Halftone Dots

Every photographic image we use in our artwork must be interpreted on paper using halftone dots. The halftone dot grid is described in terms of number of lines per inch or lpi. This grid is also referred to as line screen frequency. As with laser dots, the resolution of the halftone grid is dependent upon the printer itself, how sharp you want your images to be, and the quality of the paper on which it is being printed. As the quality of paper gets better, a finer halftone grid can be used. A line screen frequency of 100 lpi is now standard for newsprint and other uncoated paper stocks. A medium quality stock, such as you see used in a magazine, can hold an image where the line screen frequency is between 133 and 150 lpi. A halftone screen of 200 lpi is only used on fine quality art paper (see figure 5–5).

There is an interconnected relationship between dpi and lpi, since the laser dots make up the halftone dots. In fact, the number of laser dots per inch will determine how many levels of gray will be rendered by the halftone dots. Output devices are capable of producing a maximum output level of 256 of any one color. The number of levels of gray that can be reproduced when the image is output is determined by the ratio of dpi to lpi. The ratio between dpi and lpi cannot be greater than 16:1. Therefore, the size of the halftone dot in the line screen frequency depends on the resolution of the output device. An increase in the output resolution will not result in better image quality unless the lpi is also increased. However, only very high quality coated stocks are capable of producing an image with a line screen frequency of more than 150 lpi. This is because the dot gain is too great in coarser papers.

As you know, determining what line screen frequency to use really depends on what type of paper you will be using, as certain papers absorb more ink than others (more on this later in the chapter). Say you are planning to print a job on a medium quality clay-coated stock. You would need to select a maximum line screen frequency of 150 lpi. If you wanted the quality of your images to reproduce well, then your output resolution must not exceed a 16:1 ratio. Therefore, you would need to ask your service provider to output your files at 2400 dpi (see figure 5–6). Similarly, if you plan to print on newsprint using a line screen frequency of 80 lpi, then your output resolution would need to be at least 1280 dpi.

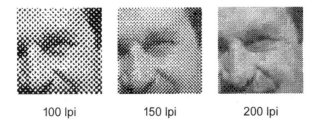

100 lpi   150 lpi   200 lpi

figure | 5–5 |

An image printed at three different line screen frequencies (100 LPI, 150 LPI, and 200 LPI).

The halftone dot itself can be a number of shapes from round, elliptical, square, cross, diamond, and even a custom shape. They will also vary in size depending on the density of color they are representing. For example, lighter colors will produce smaller halftone dots while darker areas of color will produce larger ones. However, the halftone grid pattern remains constant, so the distance between each dot is always the same. So how do all those halftone dots produce an image that the eye can recognize? This is a good question that can best be answered by examining how the different colors of halftone dots are configured in relation to one another.

Traditional Screen Angles

Most halftone images that you will use in your work will be made up of more than one color. When an image is converted to CMYK, each of the four process colors must be set to a specific screen angle when printed onto paper. If two colors have the same angle, they will produce a moiré pattern on press that will adversely affect the quality of the image. The screen angle for each color is not randomly set but is actually mathematically configured so that each color halftone dot slightly overlaps the other. If we have a look at the halftone dots under a magnifying glass, we can see a distinct configuration to the dots (see figure 5–7). We call this design a Rosette pattern since the configuration resembles a floral shape. Almost all film and plates are imaged using this process, which is called traditional screening or AM screening. The

Inches

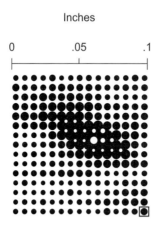
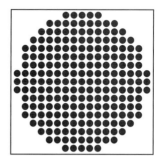

A photographic image made up of halftone dots. There are fifteen lines or dots per 1/10 of an inch, making 150 lines per inch.

A close up view of a halftone dot from the image on the right. Here sixteen laser dots make up one halftone dot, so there are 2400 dots per inch.

figure | 5–6 |

Laser dots (at a resolution of 2400 dpi) combine to form halftone dots in an image that uses a screen frequency of 150 lpi.

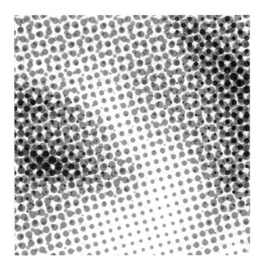

figure |5 – 7|

Halftone dots in CMYK form a rosette pattern in traditional (AM) screening. (See color insert.)

AM stands for amplitude modulation. The angles for each of the four process colors are as follows: cyan is 15°, magenta is 75°, yellow is 0°, and black is 45° (see figure 5–8). If a monotone or grayscale image is being used in your document, then the screen angle for the one color should always be set to 45°.

Angles for Traditional (AM) screening

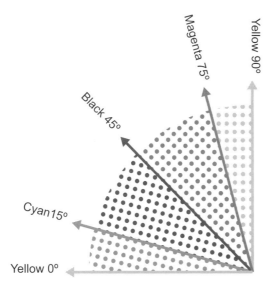

figure |5 – 8|

Screen angles for the four process colors in traditional (AM) screening.

Nontraditional or FM Screen Angles

Recently, designers are asking service providers to use a more precise method of screening halftones called stochastic or FM screening, which stands for frequency modulation. This process mathematically plots much smaller halftone dots in a seemingly random pattern. The configuration of the dots resembles the interference pattern you see on your TV when the signal is lost. Each dot is the same size, although smaller than in traditional screening. However, the spacing between the dots varies. The result is a smoother, more detailed image in the printing stage (see figure 5–9). Although this technology has been around for quite a while, it is being implemented more frequently into software for RIPping files through an imagesetter or platesetter. FM screening also avoids the problem of moiré patterns developing during printing.

Dot Gain

Quite simply, dot gain is the amount of ink saturation when laser or halftone dots are printed onto paper. As a dot is impressed onto the surface of the paper, a certain amount of ink will soak in and spread, enlarging the dot. How much each dot enlarges depends upon the printing method and the paper or substrate being printed on. For printing on newsprint, the dot gain can be as high as 35 percent. Most uncoated stocks produce a dot gain around 25 percent. A clay-coated stock usually has a dot gain between 15 and 20 percent. As a prepress professional, you need to know the dot gain of various papers on certain

figure | 5–9 |

Stochastic or FM screening produces a smoother, finer halftone image. (See color insert.)

> ## ▶ A Designer's Best Friend
>
> As a designer working in a prepress environment, if you choose one supplier with which to build a strong relationship, make it the prepress specialist at the printing plant you plan to use. Whenever you are unsure about specifications you need for preparing artwork for their presses, pick up the phone and call to get the right information. Become familiar with their workflow environment and with what systems and software they usually deal. Take a tour of their operation and get to know what type of presses they have and what their capabilities are. Make sure the prepress supervisor has all your phone numbers (work, home, cell, etc.) in case they are running a job for you in the middle of the night and there is a problem. Press time is very expensive, so take steps to make sure your job runs smoothly.

presses, or the quality of your graphics can be adversely affected. Imagine you are printing on a rough surface such as newsprint. Unknowingly, you indicate to the service provider that you want your film to be imaged at 2400 dpi with a line screen frequency of 150 lpi. When you see the press proofs you are horrified to see that your sharp, clean graphics and images have gone all muddy and flat. The reason is that the resolution you specified for your laser and halftone dots was too fine for the stock on which you chose to print. The dot gain of the paper is so great that the dots have bled into each other, so they are no longer distinct enough for the eye to discern the distance between them. Remember, halftone dots fool the eye into believing it is seeing a continuous tone image. If the dots are too close together, then the image cannot be clearly interpreted. If you are unsure what the resolution of your film should be then ask the print or prepress specialist who works at the company you have contracted to print your job.

Scanning for Prepress

The relationship between pixels and halftone dots makes it necessary to scan our photos in such a way that the size of each pixel is at least 50 percent of the size of a halftone dot. If the size of the pixels in our image equals the size of a halftone dot, then we are ascribing one pixel per line, or a ratio of 1:1. This is insufficient and will produce an image that is of low quality and has a jagged appearance. A proper ratio for measuring pixels against line screen frequency is at least 2 ppi:1 lpi. This will allow for greater sharpness and better definition and prevent the image from looking pixelated. Therefore, if you plan to use a line screen frequency of 150 lpi, it would be necessary to scan your images in at least 300 ppi.

It is helpful to fix your images as much as possible in the scanning stage. Many scanners come with software that allows you to scale, rotate, crop, and perform some color corrections before you begin to scan. This can save time later on, and avoid you having to perform a lot of color correcting. If you know that your scanner tends to give your images a reddish cast, you can adjust the curves settings in your scanner software to compensate for this (see figure 5 – 10). You can also sharpen your images before scanning them using the same software.

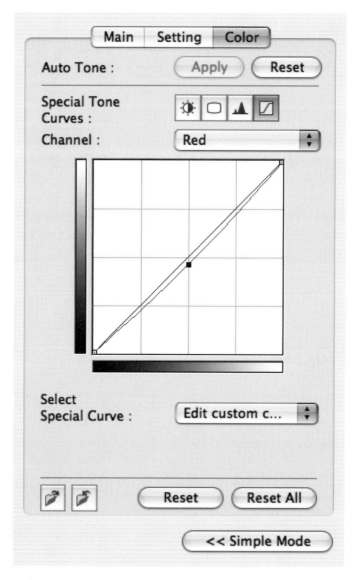

figure | 5 – 10 |

Adjusting curves in your scanning software may save time color correcting photos later on.

Caring for Your Scanner

In order to get the maximum life out of your scanner, it is necessary to take steps to ensure a long life. Clean the glass under the cover with a solution that does not contain ammonium or other harsh chemicals. Using abrasive materials will leave scratch marks on the glass. Also use a soft cloth when cleaning. Cloths that are specially made for lenses on 35 mm cameras are best. These can also be used to wipe off photographs before placing them on the scanner bed. Avoid tissues and handy-wipes, as they tend to leave white powder on the glass. Finally, never place artwork on the glass that has media such as paint, charcoal, and crayons on it. It would be better to take a digital photograph of the artwork for reproduction.

Image File Formats for Prepress

Although there are many file formats available in which to save Photoshop images, most of the formats are made for importing into multi-media applications or for use on web sites. Only a few of the formats are correct for prepress workflow situations. In some cases, you can still import files saved in these formats into your layout documents however, the results will be unsatisfactory. This is due to the way these formats were written and how they save the color information in the file. Let's take a look at some common formats that are suitable for prepress.

TIFF

Back in the mid-1980s, Aldus Corporation was looking to develop a file format that could import images into PageMaker, a page layout program it had recently launched. Their programmers came up with the tagged image file format, also known as TIFF. As one of the earliest file formats for importing images into layout documents, it has become a standard in the prepress environment. TIFF is a raw pixel storage format and uses a compression system known as LZW, which stands for its creators, namely Lempel, Ziv, and Welch. This system allows information to be condensed without degradation of image quality and is called lossless compression. While it was a useful method of compressing files when floppy disks were around and computers had limited hard drive space, it is impractical for use today as it may cause some imagesetters using PostScript Level 1 and 2 to crash. It is a good idea to turn the LZW compression off before outputting your files to film.

One advantage that designers have found with the TIFF format is they can colorize and even edit the color in the image after importing it into their layout document. While this may be a quick way to add color to a grayscale image when producing a presentation, it is not recommended for print production. It is always better to make alterations to your supporting files in the program in which they were created. TIFF files are generally larger in size than those created for the web or multi-media; however, they are also smaller than other formats used in prepress. Another advantage is that TIFF files are not written in PostScript language, so they can be printed off of any type of printer. Some prepress experts argue that the color definition and quality is not as good in TIFF files compared to other formats. For most designers, however, a TIFF file is the most versatile.

EPS

Adobe Systems first developed the Postscript language in the early 1980s. By using this language, their programmers realized they were able to create a file format that could be imported into a layout program. From this, the encapsulated postscript format known as EPS evolved. Originally intended for saving vector-based graphics for importing into layout programs, the format was adapted for pixel-based images as well. In the EPS format, each file has two components: a PostScript description language that can be translated by an output device and 8-bit PICT preview. The language is basically locked within the file, hence the name "encapsulated." This PostScript language cannot be altered without returning to the native program to edit the file. For this reason, EPS files can only be edited in their native programs like Photoshop and Illustrator.

One advantage that EPS files do have is better color definition than TIFF files. Many prepress houses prefer this format for Photoshop files. Also, the complexity of the Postscript language allows for more features to be saved within an EPS file, namely clipping paths and duotones. A disadvantage is that the EPS file sizes are larger, and cannot be compressed, so more memory is required to store them on your hard drive. It remains the most widely used format for importing images into layout documents.

DCS

One format that is becoming more common in the design world is DCS. It stands for desktop color separation, and is also called EPS5. It was developed by Quark Inc. to allow pre-separated files to be imported into a Quark document. This format saves the various channels as single files with a separate preview file. Therefore, in a four-color process image, there would be five files. Prepress professionals maintain that DCS files have superior color integrity compared to other formats. Service providers often prefer these files as they claim they RIP through imagesetters more quickly since they are already separated into color plates. A drawback is that like EPS files, they are larger than other files and there are also more of them.

No Layers Allowed

When saving your Photoshop files for print production, make sure you flatten the layers first. This will avoid any possible problems with hidden or adjustment layers not printing out properly. You can always save a copy of your original with the layers not flattened if you wish to edit the file. Likewise, do not save your Photoshop files using transparency layers, as this may also cause Postscript errors when your service provider prints your document.

You now have an understanding of all file formats used for prepress. If you save your image files either as TIFF, EPS, or DCS format, you can't go wrong. Even so, there are always those designers who break the rules, and want to use file formats that give less than satisfactory results.

Image File Formats Not for Prepress

Although most designers are aware there are only three image formats available for prepress, there are still a few who insist on using ones that are not. Be warned that if you use these formats, you will not be happy with the final results from the press and neither will your client. To help get the point across, let's have a look at a few formats that are used for other types of media, and see why they cannot be used for print production.

PSD Format

The native Photoshop format is ideal for saving large working files of images with many layers or transparent layers, but does not output well through to film or plates. And now that QuarkXPress 6.5 and InDesign 3.0 allow native files to be imported directly into documents made with these programs, many designers are doing exactly that. It is not a good habit to get into and causes many problems when the RIP attempts to separate the image. Use it for saving images with which you are currently working, but resave them in one of the formats recommended for output.

JPEG Format

The JPEG format was developed by a group of photographers and scientists called the Joint Photographers Experts Group, so the name is an acronym for its creators. It uses a method of compressing information that is called lossy. This means that much of the original color data in the file has been eliminated after it has been saved in this format. This renders the file unacceptable in the prepress workflow environment. You may wonder why your digital camera or some stock photography sites save

> ## Saving Images on a Digital Camera
>
> If possible, try to save images from your digital camera in a TIFF or raw file format. This will give you better results and prevent loss of most of the color information. If your camera does not give you this option, then save the files in JPEG format with the least amount of compression. After you perform the necessary color corrections on a JPEG file from a digital camera or a stock photography site, then make sure you resave the file in a format suitable for prepress.

images using the JPEG format. This is because JPEG files are smaller due to their compressibility, so storing, downloading, and transferring these files is faster.

Although JPEG is currently not a proper prepress format, because of its lossy compression, there is a new version of JPEG that may soon be acceptable for prepress. The new format is called JPEG2000, or J2 for short, and offers enhanced color definition using lossless compression through a wavelet coding system. Manufacturers of digital cameras are currently integrating J2 technology into their equipment. The prepress industry is also keeping their eyes on new developments in an area of JPEG2000 called JPM, which promises to offer many of the same benefits in direct-to-plate imaging and archiving that PDF technology currently does.

PICT, GIF, BMP, and PNG

If you are not sure for what these terms stand, here is the scoop: PICT stands for picture file format and BMP is short for bitmap graphics. Meanwhile, GIF and PNG are acronyms for graphics interchange format and portable network graphics, respectively. These formats offer low-resolution quality with a limited palette range (usually 256 colors). They are useful for displaying images on web pages and in audio/visual applications like PowerPoint or Flash, but are of no value for use in prepress. These formats cannot save files in CMYK mode and imagesetters will not properly convert them when they are RIPped through to film. If you receive a file from a client using this format, it is best to ask them to rescan it and send it either as a TIFF or EPS file.

Creating Bitmap Images, Duotones, and Tritones

Not all projects a designer works on are four-color process with special inks and finishes. Ideally, that would be nice; however in many cases the client does not have a large enough budget to accommodate this type of work. At times, the client may only be able to afford one or two colors. In that case, you may be limited in terms of what you can do with your images. Despite the limitations, there are a number of creative ways to spice up your images, rather than just printing them monochromatically in grayscale mode.

Bitmap and Custom Halftone Screens

Occasionally, we receive an image from a client that is of such poor quality that no amount of correction will make it look good. Or perhaps it is a full-color image that simply does not translate well to grayscale mode, where there is little contrast between the lighter and darker tones. In these cases, it makes sense to alter the image so that it looks more like a vector graphic than a photograph. Luckily, Photoshop allows us to do this rather easily. By following the few simple steps below, we can change a flat, low key image into a dynamic graphic.

1. Look for an image where there is little contrast between the light and dark areas, or where the image has faded due to age (figure 5–11).

2. Once the image is opened in Photoshop, change the mode to grayscale by going under Image in the top menu bar and scroll down to Mode (figure 5–12).

figure |5 – 11|

A poor quality photo makes an ideal subject for a bitmap graphic.

3. Now repeat step two, except this time, change the mode to bitmap.

4. In the bitmap window that pops up, set the resolution to approximately 300 ppi. Set the method in the pop-up menu to halftone screen angle. (**Note:** You can also use a pattern or diffusion dither, a 50% threshold, or even a custom pattern.) Click the OK button when you are done (figure 5 – 13).

5. Set the halftone frequency to a relatively low value between 25 and 50. Setting the screen frequency too high will cause the image to lose definition, as darker tones tend to fill in when the image is printed. Now set the angle of the screen to 45°. You can select from a number of shapes to use for your halftone screen. Try experimenting with different ones to see the effects. For now, set the halftone screen to Line. Click the OK button when done (figure 5 – 14).

6. Change the mode back to grayscale and print your bitmap image out to a laser printer to ensure it looks the way you want. Since the resolution on your screen is only 72 ppi, the halftones will not look the same on your monitor as when they are printed on paper (figure 5 – 15).

Duotones and Tritones

Another way to enhance an image in a project where you are limited to only two or three colors is to create a duotone or tritone image. There are a number of ways to do this and the results will vary depending on the method. The simplest method is to import a

figure | 5 – 12 |

Change the mode to grayscale if it has not already been done.

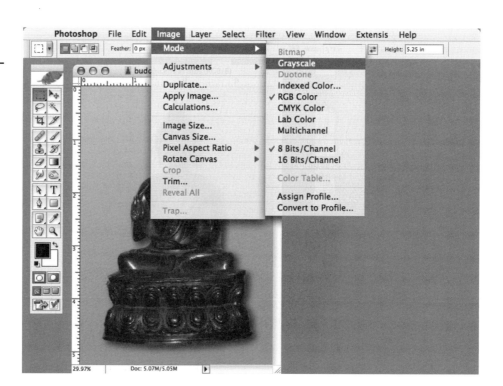

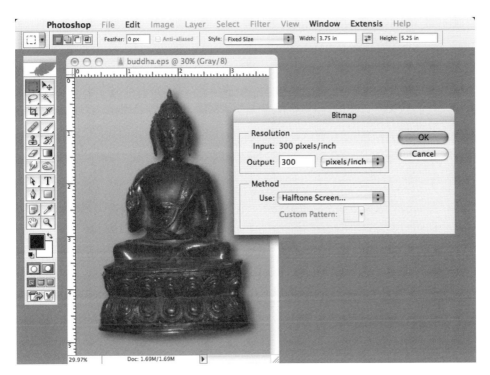

figure | 5 – 13 |

Set the resolution within press quality range in the bitmap window. Choose what type of screen pattern you want your bitmap to be made up of.

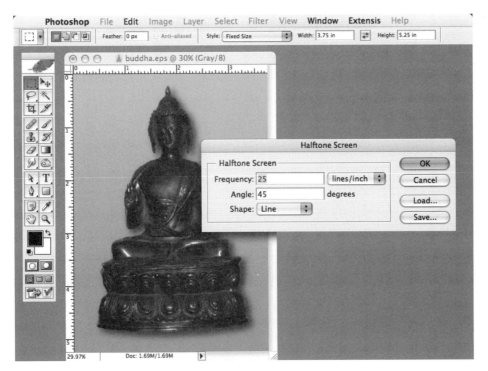

figure | 5 – 14 |

Set the screen angle for your bitmap (if you selected a halftone pattern) as well as the halftone dot shape.

figure | 5 – 15 |

Change the mode back to grayscale and preview your bitmap image.

grayscale image into QuarkXPress or InDesign and apply a color to the background, behind the image. Although this method is fast and fine for a presentation to a client, it tends to produce an image that is not clear or sharp enough for print production.

Another way is to use the Mode function under Image in the top menu bar in Photoshop. Follow the steps below to create a multicolor image that you can use in your document.

1. First, convert the image into grayscale mode, like you did in the previous section.

2. Once the image is in grayscale, repeat the steps again and select Duotone ... from the menu. A window pops up that allows you to apply colors to the image (figure 5 – 16).

3. You can select monotone, duotone, tritone, or quadtone from the pop-up menu (figure 5 – 17).

figure | 5 – 16 |

You can change your grayscale image into a multicolor one by selecting either duotone or tritone in the pop-up menu.

4. You can control the amount of each color in the image by using the transfer function buttons at the left side of the window. By clicking on these buttons, a window for the transfer curves appears on the screen. You can adjust the curves up or down to increase or decrease the quantity of each color in the three tonal ranges (figure 5 – 18).

figure | 5 – 17 |

Select a mode for the number of colors you want in your image.

figure | 5–18 |

Use the transfer curves to adjust the intensity of each color throughout the image.

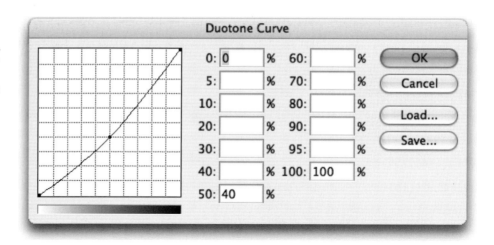

SUMMARY

This chapter has covered a number of topics relating to the use of digital images in the prepress workflow environment. Although much more can be said with regards to using Photoshop to create digital artwork, there are many resources and textbooks available for you to explore this subject further. Understanding how the resolution of the image on your monitor relates to the resolution of the graphics on a printed piece is crucial to producing high quality artwork.

▶ *in review*

1. Who developed the EPS file format?

2. What does the term ppi stand for?

3. Name three file formats for prepress.

4. How many colors make up a duotone image in Photoshop?

5. In what format should you save images from a digital camera?

6. How many bits are in a CMYK image saved with 8 bits per channel?

7. When you create a clipping path in Photoshop, what file format would you save it in?

8. What is JPEG an acronym for?

▶ *exercises*

1. Now it's time to see how different modes of color affect the output quality of an image. Open a Photoshop file that was saved in RGB mode. Save the file in a number of different formats with different resolutions. Print the various files out to a color printer. Which formats and resolutions gave you the best results? Do you know why?

2. Using the transfer function allows you to balance the various colors in a multi-tone image. Open a Photoshop file that was saved in grayscale mode. Try creating a duotone image by first changing it to duotone mode and then selecting two Pantone® colors from the Color Picker window. Now use the transfer function buttons to increase or decrease the intensity of each color. Look at the result on your screen. Are the colors you selected suitable for the image? What colors would yield better results?

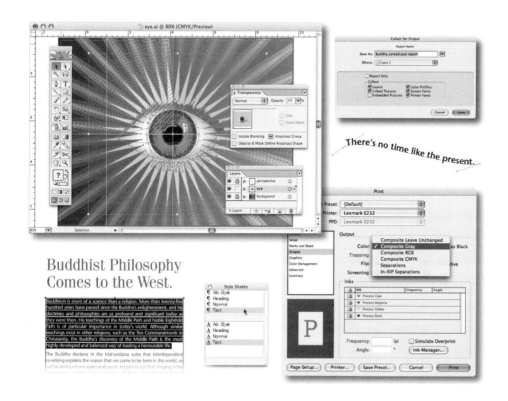

There's no time like the present.

CHAPTER 6

objectives

- Recognize how vector-based applications fit into the prepress workflow
- Discover why QuarkXPress, InDesign, and other layout programs are ideal for most artwork documents
- Discover why Adobe Illustrator, FreeHand, and other drawing programs are used only for supporting documents
- Prepare artwork documents properly for output to film or plates
- Examine the steps necessary to ensure your files will print out correctly

introduction

When programmers write graphics software applications, they do so with a specific purpose in mind. Most software applications operate so they can perform a particular task or interact better with peripheral devices. Because these applications are written in this way, you can choose the one that most suits your needs. For instance, if you want to create a document that contains multiple pages with special inks, you will choose an application that has built-in functions that allow you to select these options. Then again, if you wish to create artwork that basically looks as if it was sketched out by hand, you would select software that came with drawing tools that could simulate this look. Knowing which software to use for the type of document you want to build is the key to being an effective graphic designer.

Making Sure Your Software is Adequate

Before buying software for your system, ask yourself what type of work you will primarily be doing and how the final piece is being imaged (i.e. onto film, paper, directly to plate, etc.). Always purchase the latest version of software titles. It is better to buy directly from the manufacturer rather than a third party. Manufacturers offer better technical support if you have installation or functionality problems. It is easier to get patches or upgrades from them. Avoid buying from discount software sites on the internet. The majority of titles are older versions and tech support for the software is usually non-existent. Try to obtain a CD or DVD with a software license included with the package. This will save you download time if you ever need to reinstall the application. Finally, make sure the software you purchase will run on your current operating system.

GETTING STARTED WITH SOFTWARE

If you are serious about being a graphic designer, then you need to invest heavily in software that will allow you to achieve the best possible results. The Creative Suite package of InDesign, Illustrator, and Photoshop is invaluable to anyone involved in print production. In addition, the latest version of QuarkXPress and Acrobat Reader is also a necessity. Microsoft Office is an ideal compilation package that allows you to write letters, send e-mails, produce spreadsheets, and create slide shows. If you plan to make your system functional, it would be useful to install software that will allow you to manage fonts, repair and maintain your operating system, and transfer files to your service provider.

There are other options available depending on what your needs are; however, keep in mind that by choosing less popular brands you may run into problems with technical support, compatibility with your operating system, and even a discontinued software application. Imagine investing hundreds of dollars into a product only to find out the company is no longer making it when you go to upgrade to a new version a few years later. It is a good idea to regularly read reviews of new software in computer graphics publications to keep up-to-date on current trends in the industry.

All graphics software used for print production can be divided into three categories: page layout, drawing or illustration, and image-editing or painting. You have already gained understanding of how pixel-based programs work from the last chapter, so let's discover what makes page layout and drawing programs work.

VECTOR-BASED GRAPHICS

In all layout and drawing programs, objects are created using vector lines that are connected by plotted points. These points are mathematically plotted along an x and *y* axis. Vector-based artwork is also known as object-oriented artwork. The most advantageous aspect of creating graphics this way is that, unlike images in Photoshop, all the objects in these files are resolution independent. This means you can enlarge or reduce the artwork that is vector based to whatever size you want without any loss in quality. For example, if you were producing a transit ad for a client where the final size was 18″ × 30″, you could reduce your page size by one-third to 6″ × 10″ in your layout document and simply enlarge it by 300 percent at the output stage. However, any images in those files would need to be re-imaged using the native application.

In addition to objects being resized, they can also be manipulated in every other way. The vector lines and points are re-plotted each time an object is changed. This makes vector-based programs ideal for artwork where there are many alterations. In most cases, the lines are straight; however, they can also bend through the use of Bezier curves (more on these later in the chapter). Color can also be ascribed to the inside of an object or line, as well as color tints and gradients (see figure 6 – 1).

The text you create in your document is also plotted using points and vector lines. This lets you set text as large or as small as you want. And since the type you set is

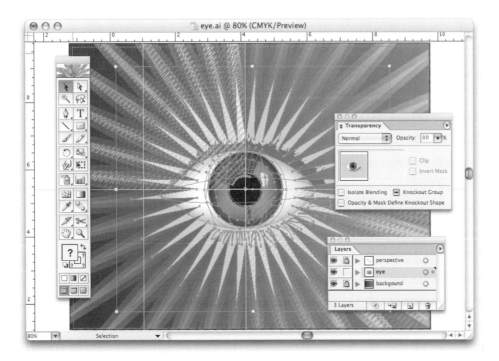

figure | 6 – 1 |

Vector graphics are made of points connected by vector lines. They can be filled with solid colors, tints of color, gradient blends, and can be made transparent as this illustration demonstrates.

object-oriented too, you can modify it in a number of ways as well as adjust the spacing between the letters.

Although layout and drawing programs are based upon the same principle, they have very different features, which make each one practical for a specific phase of the production of digital artwork. To learn which type of program is best suited for which phase, let's compare page layout and drawing programs and see how they differ.

Page Layout Programs

If you plan on becoming a graphic designer, then you will definitely be using layout programs like QuarkXPress, InDesign, or PageMaker for the majority of your work. These programs allow you to create a number of large graphic documents that can be any size, contain large amounts of body text, import images and illustrations alongside this text, and use a wide variety of color models. Each one of these programs contains tools to allow the user to create and apply style sheets, so text can be styled and altered quickly. One of the other benefits of layout programs is that a number of master page formats can be designed and applied to individual pages throughout an entire document. Layout programs were also written so they communicate more easily with output devices, so you have more options on how you want your document to print.

For these reasons, you need to build your output file (this is the file that is RIPped through an imagesetter onto film or plates in a layout program). Aside from the production of complex packaging, every other type of document you create will be produced in this type of program. To understand the significance of layout programs in the prepress workflow environment, let's review the two most popular ones and see how they benefit our work.

QuarkXPress

Quark is considered to be the premiere page layout program. The first version of QuarkXPress was released in 1987. It soon became the standard for prepress workflow systems. Quark allows you to create up to 127 master pages and 2000 document pages, which is ideal for producing large catalogs, reports, or brochures. It lets you create both character and paragraph style sheets that can be linked together through the Edit Style Sheets window. The Style Sheets window palette makes the formatting of large amounts of text as easy as clicking a button (see figure 6 – 2). Quark also has advanced text-editing capabilities so making changes to copy is fast and simple.

Quark lets you choose from a large selection of color models when applying colors to objects (see figure 6 – 3). You can also create Multi-Inks by combining shades of two solid Pantone® inks in the Edit Colors window.

Buddhist Philosophy Comes to the West.

Buddhism is more of a science than a religion. More than twenty-five hundred years have passed since the Buddha's enlightenment, and his doctrines and philosophies are as profound and significant today as they were then. His teachings of the Middle Path and Noble Eightfold Path is of particular importance in today's world. Although similar teachings exist in other religions, such as the Ten Commandments in Christianity, the Buddha's discovery of the Middle Path is the most highly developed and balanced way of leading a honourable life.

The Buddha declares in the Mahanidana sutta that interdependent co-arising explains the reason that we come to be born in this world, as well as being reborn again and again. He points out that clinging is the prerequisite condition for becoming, which in turn is the prerequisite

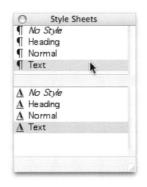

figure | 6 – 2 |

By selecting text in Quark and clicking on a paragraph or character style sheet, a document can be quickly formatted.

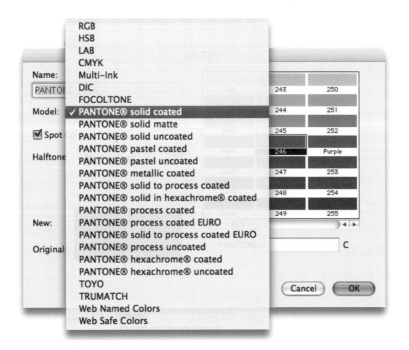

figure | 6 – 3 |

You can select from many different color models in Quark.

1. Open a Quark document that contains at least two Pantone colors.

2. Open the Colors window by selecting Edit > Colors.

3. Click on the New tab and then choose Multi-Ink from the pop-up menu beside Model.

4. In the box on the right look under Ink and select a solid Pantone® color.

5. Now look under Shade and choose a shade of the Pantone® color that will be mixed with the second Pantone® color.

6. Repeat again for the second Pantone® color (see figure 6-4). Be careful not to mix Pantone® and process inks as they may not print exactly as you see on your screen.

Overcoming the Quirks in Quark

To get the most out of QuarkXPress, you must learn the majority of key commands for the program. Key commands are shortcuts that allow you to perform certain functions by pressing keys instead of moving your cursor and selecting them from the menu bar. Illustrator and Photoshop users may find that many of the commands they are familiar with are different in Quark. To get used to using key commands, make up a sheet of the ones you use most frequently, print it out, and place it near your CPU for a quick reference guide. You will quickly find that your ability to use Quark effectively will increase dramatically.

This technique is very valuable when you have limited number of colors with which to print, such as a two- or three-color piece of artwork.

You can also trap colors against each other in the Edit Color window (the principles of trapping are explained further in Chapter 8). Select a color and then choose how it will trap against other colors you are using by clicking on the Edit Trap button (see figure 6–5). Select each color and then set the trapping for it by clicking on the

figure | 6 – 4 |

By selecting Multi-Ink from the color models, you can add more color to a two-color project.

> ## Make Use of the Usage Window
>
> Before you print out from Quark, always open the Usage window by going under Utilities in the top menu bar. Select Usage and click on the Font tab to make sure you are not missing any fonts in your document. If they are missing, they are not installed on your system (figure 6–7). Also, check to make sure the images in your document are not missing or modified by clicking on the Pictures tab. Clicking on the More Information box gives you all the specs on your image, namely where it's located on your system, file size and dimension, color depth, and mode in which it is saved (figure 6–8).

pop-up menu where it says Trap. Or you can trap item-by-item in the Trap Information palette.

Yet despite all these features, perhaps the single reason that Quark is so popular with prepress professionals is the way it interacts with output devices. You can choose to print out your document as a composite or turn on separations, which prints out a page for each color in your document. Quark allows you to specify the output resolution of your document, the line screen frequency, the screen angle of each color, and to turn colors on or off for printing (see figure 6–6). These features were specifically designed for making film and plates, but you can also use them for proofing black and white separations in Quark.

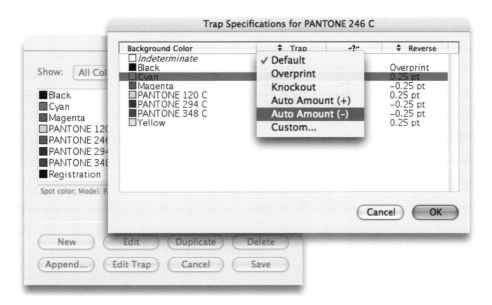

figure |6–5|

Quark lets you trap a color against other colors in the Edit Trap window.

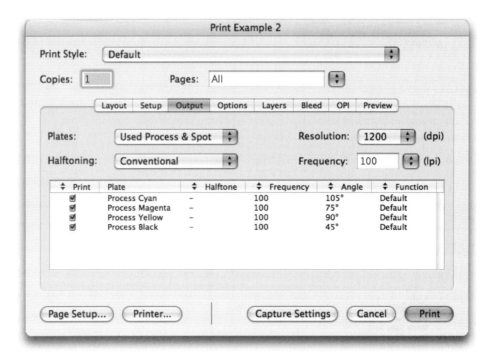

figure | 6 – 6 |

You can alter the way your document will print out using the options in the Output section of Quark's print window.

Finally, when you are ready to send your Quark files off for film, make sure you perform a Collect for Output. This step is the most crucial part of prepress process. It ensures that your Quark file, all your supporting files, fonts, and even color profiles will be sent together for imaging to film. Without performing a Collect for Output, you may get a call from your service provider asking you where an image is, or worse, telling you a font has defaulted to Courier in your final film. To make sure this does not happen, perform the following steps:

1. Go under the File menu and select Collect for Output.

2. When the Collect for Output window appears, select the desktop as the destination and click on the New Folder button (figure 6 – 9).

3. Name the output folder and then click OK.

4. Select the Layout, Linked Pictures, Color Profiles, Screen, and Printer Fonts buttons (figure 6 – 10). Now click on the Save button.

5. You will get a warning message regarding copying licensed fonts. If you are sure your fonts can be copied, click OK (figure 6 – 11).

6. Open the folder when you are done and check to make sure the original document is there with folders for the pictures, fonts, and profiles (figure 6–12). Since many service bureaus do not open the report document that is generated in a Collect for Output, most designers trash it before copying the files to a CD.

7. Now you are ready to copy the folder onto a CD or USB drive to send to your prepress service provider.

Perhaps one drawback of Quark for most students is the steep learning curve to becoming proficient in using it. There is no doubt, it is a complex program and will take the novice a few years to master. Still, once you become comfortable working in

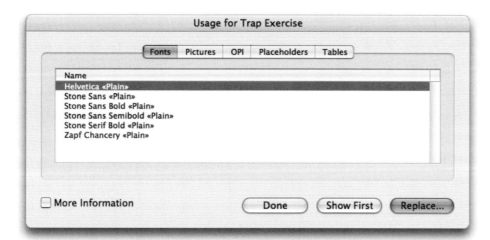

figure | 6 – 7 |

Check the status of your fonts under Usage in the Utilities menu.

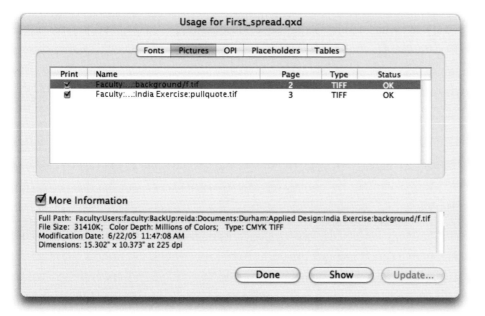

figure | 6 – 8 |

Make sure your pictures are updated and are not missing before you print.

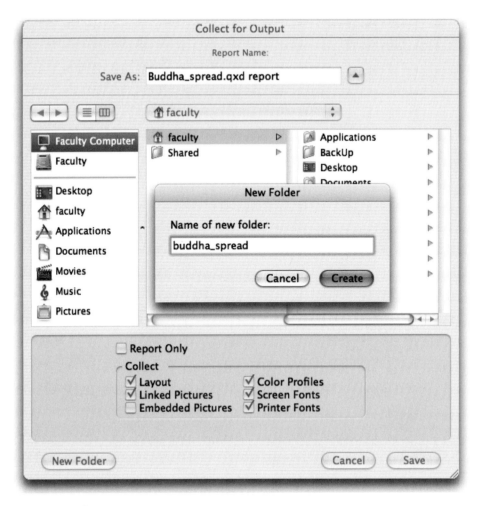

figure |6–9|

Select a destination for your output folder and then click on New Folder.

Quark, you will find you can format a large document in no time at all. The best way to learn Quark is to use it on a daily basis for as much of your work as you can. When you see the benefits to your workflow, you will see why QuarkXPress has remained so popular with prepress professionals.

InDesign

Several years ago, Adobe decided to launch its own page layout program that would compliment its other graphics programs like Illustrator and Photoshop. InDesign has created a lot of interest in the design and printing world. In fact, many designers who have been trained on other Adobe software prefer it. It also helps that InDesign behaves in a very similar fashion in terms of functionality, tools, and key commands

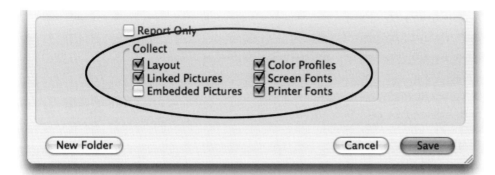

figure | 6 – 10 |

Select a button to collect each component of your Quark document.

figure | 6 – 11 |

Make sure the license agreement for your fonts allows you to copy and distribute them to third parties.

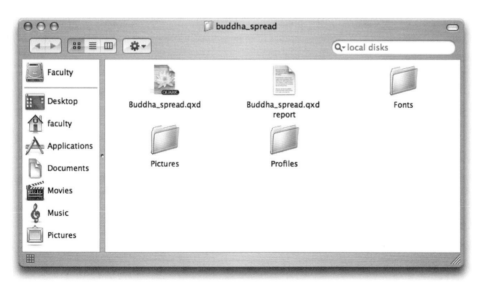

figure | 6 – 12 |

Ensure all your pictures, fonts, and profiles are collected before sending the folder out for film.

to other Adobe products. Recently, Adobe has capitalized on this by bundling all three programs together in the Creative Suite package.

Basically, InDesign can do nearly everything Quark can. It has master pages and style sheets, the same color models as Quark, gradient fills, and even links for imported images. It also has a few features that Quark does not have. One feature you will find helpful for preparing a file for output is the Separations Preview palette (see figure 6 – 13). By opening this window (*Window > Output Preview > Separations*) and selecting Separations from the pop-up menu, you can preview every color you have used in your artwork. Simply click the eye button to the left of the color to turn the preview on or off.

Another feature of InDesign that is not found in Quark is the Object Library. It comes in handy if you plan on using an image or graphic repeatedly throughout your layout. The Object Library can save you a lot of time importing and placing the same image over and over again. Open a New Library from under New in the File menu. Once a new library has opened, you can use a drag and drop approach to place images into the Library palette (see figure 6 – 14).

InDesign rivals Quark for options in the Output section of its Print window. In this window, you can choose color Composite CMYK or RGB, Composite Gray, or Separations and In-RIP Separations from the pop-up menu (see figure 6 – 15). You can turn inks on or off as well by clicking on the printer icon to the left side of each color. Line screen frequency and angle can also be specified in the Output section of the Print window.

By using the PreFlight command in InDesign, you can quickly check your document for errors or problems (more on this in Chapter 10). Like Quark, InDesign has a feature that allows you to collect all the pictures, fonts, and the output file in a folder. By selecting Package under File in the top menu bar, you can ensure you have all the necessary elements when you send your file for output (see figure 6 – 16). This is one function that most drawing programs do not offer. That is another good reason to build your output documents in a layout program.

InDesign has imitated Quark in another way, as it has a built-in trapping engine that automatically traps a document when separations are turned on. When you are outputting a document, you can select this feature in the Output section of the Print window (see figure 6 – 17). Unfortunately, you normally have to create trapping

figure | 6 – 13 |

The Separations Preview palette provides you with an advance look at what the plates for your project will look like.

Buddhist Philosophy Comes to the West.

After more than twenty-five hundred years since the Buddha's enlightenment, the doctrines and philosophies he realized are as profound and significant today as they were then. His teachings of the Middle Path and Noble Eightfold Path is of particular importance in a world that is eroding in moral values and ethics. Although similar teachings exist in other religions, such as the Ten Commandments in Christianity, the

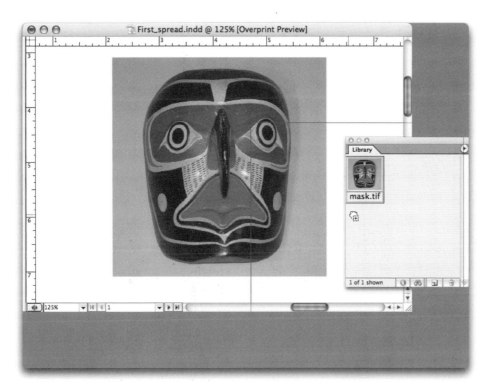

figure | 6 – 14 |

The Library palette speeds up placing recurring images and graphic elements in your document.

presets and change the settings in the Ink Manager window for the trapping to be properly applied. This can be time consuming if you are using many colors. The Ink Manager window lets you specify ink densities and trap sequences (see figure 6 – 18). Ink density is the measurement of how much light is absorbed or reflected in a solid patch of ink. The trap sequence is the order in which the inks will be printed on a press. However, changes to the default settings are best left to someone who is familiar enough with the type of press on which the job will be printed. If you do want to alter these settings, you need to obtain the correct information from your prepress service provider. It may be easier to let your provider do the trapping using their RIP software.

Overall, InDesign offers greater compatibility with other Adobe products, a faster learning curve for those already familiar with Illustrator and Photoshop, and output capabilities that are close to those of QuarkXPress. If you plan on purchasing the Creative Suite package from Adobe, then you will find InDesign a solid addition to your graphics software collection.

Drawing Programs

As you have seen, some software programs are designed to perform certain tasks better than others. Page layout programs were specifically written so they could

figure | 6 – 15 |

Make changes to how
your document will print
out in the Output section
of InDesign's print
window.

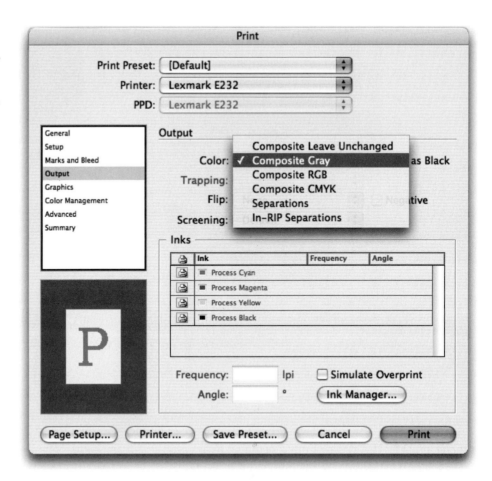

produce files for output. On the other hand, drawing programs were written with specific tools and functions that could produce sophisticated illustrations that are not possible in a layout or image-editing program. Because of this, files created in drawing programs are referred to as support documents.

Drawing programs offer advanced features such as precise pen and path editing tools, smoother and more complex gradients and blends, transparency filters, paint brush effects, and even some image-editing features (although it is better to use Photoshop for this). They also have superior capabilities for manipulating and customizing text, such as setting text on a path or inside objects, adding blends and gradients to text, and setting vertical type. Let's have a look at one of the most popular drawing programs and see how it works to produce artwork.

Adobe Illustrator

As one of the first drawing programs available, Illustrator has become a staple for graphic designers and illustrators. It remains tremendously popular thanks to

Create Package Folder

Save As: First_spread Folder

Where: Preflight

☑ Copy Fonts (roman only)
☑ Copy Linked Graphics
☑ Update Graphic Links In Package
☐ Use Document Hyphenation Exceptions Only
☑ Include Fonts and Links From Hidden Layers
☐ View Report

Instructions...

Cancel   Save

figure | 6 – 16 |

The Package command collects your fonts and linked graphics in InDesign and places them in a separate folder.

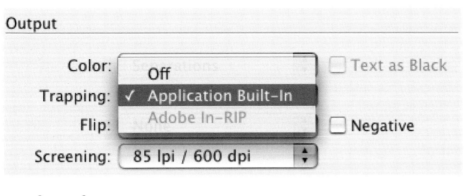

figure | 6 – 17 |

A built-in trapping engine automatically traps InDesign documents.

upgrades that offer enhanced tools and features. In addition to illustrations, the accomplished user can generate superb graphics in the form of charts, graphs, logos, and maps. And there are lots of filters and effects to assist you in the process.

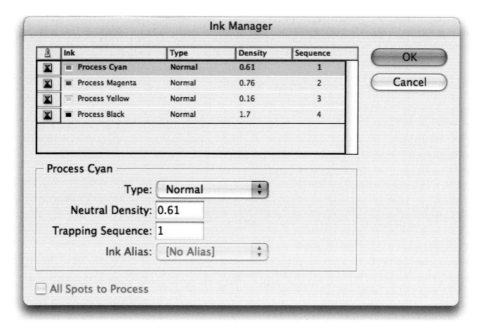

The Ink Manager window gives you the option of editing the trap sequences and densities of different inks.

However, it is the various pen tools and their properties that make Illustrator so ideal for creating object-oriented artwork.

Like layout programs, drawing programs are vector-based. Although both employ the same principles to create digital artwork, they do it in a way that is much more complex. Rather than simply drawing simple geometric objects, Illustrator allows you to bend and manipulate vector lines to any shape. It accomplishes this by way of a function of the pen tool called a Bezier curve. It is named after its inventor, Pierre Bezier (1910 to 1999), a mathematician whose curve formula also helped to develop digital font technologies. When you apply Bezier curves to an anchor point, Illustrator places a control bar with two direction points on each end, in line with that point. These direction points can be moved so that the intrinsic direction of the line (also called a path) between the two points is altered (see figure 6 – 19). The connector bar operates like a seesaw. If one end point is moved up or down, then the other point moves in the opposite direction. However, the connector bar can be divided using the convert anchor point tool in Illustrator. This allows the direction of the vector line to be altered on one side of the anchor point (see figure 6 – 20). Lastly, the direction points on the control bar can be moved away from the anchor point to give a more pronounced curve.

Importing Spot Colors into Your Layout Document

If you are using Pantone® or spot colors in your Illustrator artwork, then you should import it into Quark or InDesign when you first create your layout document. By importing artwork with spot colors, both InDesign and Quark will automatically add them to the color palette in your document. This also avoids having two colors in your palette with the same name as various software programs often name colors slightly differently.

There are many benefits to using Bezier curves. Obviously, they allow you to draw any shape of object you want, making them ideal for illustration work. You can easily cut apart objects with Bezier curves and unite them with segments of other objects. In addition to these features, text can also be placed on a vector line using the Type on a Path tool (see figure 6–21). This gives you the ability to create interesting type treatments and flow text around objects and images. Although later versions of Quark and InDesign include Bezier curve tools along with the regular pen tools, they are most effectively used in Illustrator.

Some of the best features Illustrator has going for it is the Color and Swatches window palette and its extensive Swatch Libraries. These allow you to choose from a variety of color models and alter the colors quickly. If you are working in CMYK, the slider bars in the color palette allow you to mix values of the four process colors quickly and to

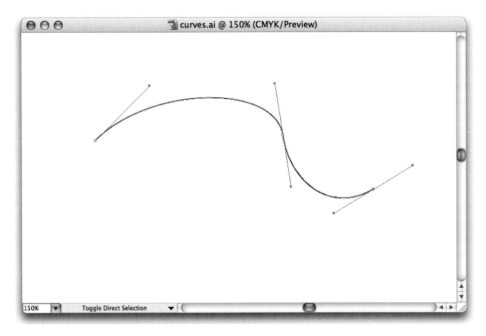

figure | 6–19 |

Using Bezier curves in your Illustrator document allows the vector lines to bend.

Type in Illustrator

You may be tempted at some point in time to create a special type treatment in Illustrator. This works well for logos or even headlines; however, Illustrator should not be used for large amounts of text. Avoid setting any text smaller than 20 points and more than 10 words in length. All small body copy should be set in your page layout program. This rule applies to Photoshop as well. Any type you create in Photoshop is made up of pixels and, if small enough, will show jagged edges when output to film. Remember to convert your text into objects (command-shift/control-alt-O) in Illustrator, especially if you plan to stretch or manipulate the type. Converting your text into objects will also stop your fonts from defaulting when you output your document, as Quark does not collect fonts used in EPS files.

create a swatch from that newly created process color (see figure 6–22). However, it is a good idea to delete the preset color swatches and start with a fresh palette when you open a new document. If you want to convert a process color to a spot color, then by double-clicking on the swatch, you can open your swatch options and select the new mode from the pop-up menu where it says Color Type (see figure 6–23). Also, colors from different models can be added to the swatch palette by opening the Swatch Libraries under Window in the top menu bar (see figure 6–24).

figure | 6 – 20 |

The convert-point direction tool gives you the flexibility of altering the direction of a line on the other side of a plotted point.

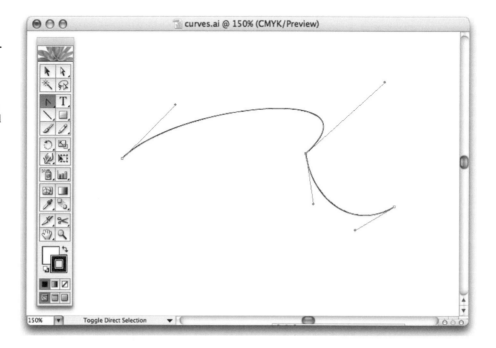

Naming Swatch Colors in Illustrator

Make sure to name the swatch color you create in Illustrator. If you do not name the new swatch, then Illustrator will give it a default name like *New Color Swatch 1*. Each subsequent swatch you create will have the same name with the next sequential number at the end (i.e. *New Color Swatch 2*). It is best to name the swatch with the percentage of colors you have used (an example would be 30C/100M/80Y/10K). If you are using spot or Pantone® colors, then make sure they match the Pantone® swatch number. This makes the colors easier to select if you want to edit them later on.

Although Illustrator has the same output features as InDesign, some prepress artists prefer to save the file in EPS format and import it into a layout program like QuarkXPress. If the file is particularly large, it will RIP through an output device faster in a program like Quark. One potential problem this method may pose at the film stage is that if the Illustrator file contains placed images, and is saved as an EPS file to be placed in Quark, then the RIP in the RIP software may not read the placed images. As a rule, RIPs do not have the capability of reading embedded (also called nested) files. Embedding a file happens when you import an image into a document, then save that document and import it into another application. The RIP may not read the nested image because the information contained in an EPS file is locked

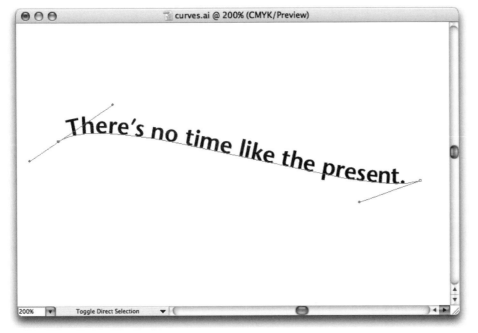

figure | 6 – 21 |

You can create unique type treatments by using the Type on a Path tool.

figure | 6 – 22 |

Slider bars in the color palette window allow you to quickly create a color swatch.

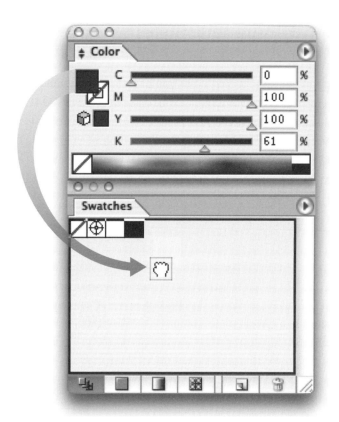

figure | 6 – 23 |

Double-click on a swatch to open up its options and create a spot color using the pop-up menu.

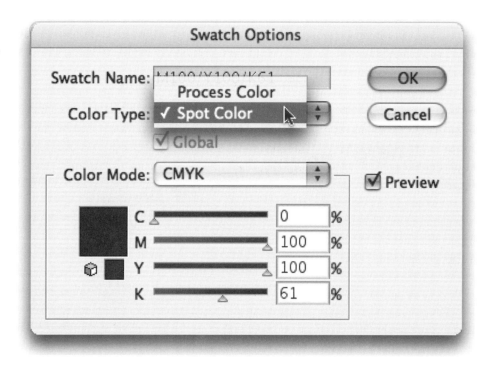

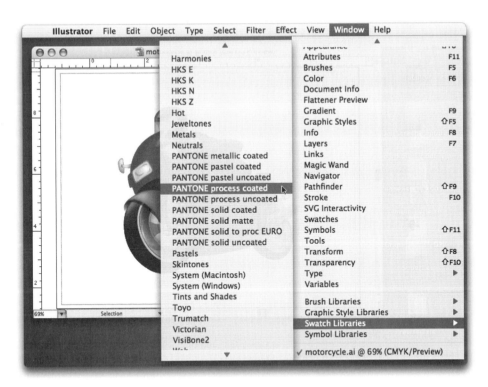

figure | 6 – 24 |

By opening the Swatch Libraries, you can create a color from one of many models.

away due to the way an encapsulated postscript file is written. You may recall this from part of the last chapter that dealt with image file formats.

As you can see, Illustrator lives up to its name as an awesome drawing program. Its tools produce wonderful artwork for all types of graphic arts work. Still, Illustrator was intended to be a support program for other applications, not for outputting film. It is not a program capable of handling large amounts of text and always produces a single page document. Illustrator does not have style sheets and you cannot create preformatted master pages in it. As a student, you may find it a fun program and try to use it to do all of your work. This is a mistake that you will find difficult to overcome when you start working in the industry. Get in the habit of using Illustrator for drawing and Quark or InDesign for page layouts and you will find your transition into the working world a lot smoother.

Hybrid Programs

There are a few programs that do not fall into one single category. In some cases they function as both a layout and drawing program, and even have limited image-editing capabilities. These types of programs are useful for design studios that may handle projects crossing over a number of different disciplines such as corporate, advertising, packaging, sales promotion, etc. There is one that rivals Quark and InDesign as a layout program and has drawing tools that are similar to Illustrator.

Macromedia FreeHand

FreeHand was originally developed as a drawing program and has been around as long as Adobe Illustrator. It was first released back in the mid-1980s by Aldus Corporation. In fact, Aldus developed the TIFF image format specifically to work with its new software applications, namely FreeHand and PageMaker. Many designers in the early 1990s started out using FreeHand, mainly because it had preset gradient fills which Illustrator did not have until version 5.0 came out. Today it is available from Adobe Systems Inc. There have been rumors of it being discontinued, but Adobe insists it will continue to support and develop this popular program.

It is both a drawing and layout program with very similar tools to Illustrator, yet matches Quark in offering more functionality. FreeHand allows the user to create multiple-page documents like Quark. It also permits the user to replace colors and change color modes more quickly. Another similarity to Quark is that FreeHand interacts more precisely with output devices. One feature it has, which is not found in other production programs, is the ability to alter the size of a document from page to page within a single file.

One part of the graphics industry where FreeHand seems to have gained popularity is in studios that specialize in package design. The aforementioned ability to interact with output devices, as well as ease in replacing low-resolution images with high-resolution ones, makes it a wiser choice than Illustrator for this discipline. Still, the pen tools in FreeHand differ somewhat from Illustrator, so someone trained in the latter may find them difficult to work with. All in all, there is no reason not to give FreeHand a test drive when selecting software for your system.

There are other applications for creating page layouts and illustrations which are rarely used by designers in the industry. These programs are often bought by home office publishers and independent marketers who can get by on simple, easy-to-use, low-end software. You can investigate these on your own, but a word of caution, "You get what you pay for." Try downloading a demo version first, before laying out a few hundred dollars for a program you may rarely use.

Layout Applications for Linux

If you are adventurous enough to create a partition on your computer, and install one of the many versions of Linux, there is a layout program called Scribus, which was written specifically for this operating system. The latest version of Scribus can do everything Quark and InDesign can including print process color separations, create press-quality PDF files, apply ICC color management, and import images. The color management profile that Scribus uses is called littlecms and is said to be superior to ColorSync. Another area that Scribus leaps over other layout programs is that it can create PDF files more easily and also can incorporate interconnectivity and Java scripting into them. Actually, Mac OS X users can install Scribus onto their systems without running Linux with the addition of a couple of pieces of system software called Ghostscript and Fink.

As far as creating vector-based artwork goes, Linux users can use Inkscape, an application that possesses a user-friendly interface and a multitude of shortcuts that makes creating illustrations easy. Artwork created in Inkscape can be imported into Scribus using the svg (scalable vector graphics) format. Illustrator also gives you the option of saving files in this format, although not many PC or Mac applications support it.

If you are looking to edit images in a Linux environment, then an application called GIMP, which is an acronym for Gnu Image Manipulation Program, will help you out. GIMP can resize, crop, and rotate images like Photoshop, although it uses linear interpolation instead of bicubic, the latter being superior. However, GIMP can apply color profiles to your images using littlecms. And the tools are similar to those found in Photoshop, which will delight users of this program.

Learning graphics software for Linux may be a steep learning curve for most designers; however, the costs are very attractive. Nearly all the applications are free and there is a wealth of technical support available as all information is copyrighted under a free software foundation license called the GNU project. If you have a little computer programming experience, then you can easily create a partition on your computer, install Linux, and try these programs out.

SUMMARY

Becoming a prepress expert requires both theoretical and practical knowledge. This chapter has demonstrated how to utilize the different types of software to improve the production quality of your artwork. Each studio or agency has its own method and particular equipment to manage its prepress workflow. They purchase software based on their needs and the type of work they will be producing. As you begin working in the graphics industry, you will discover which software works best for you.

▶ *in review*

1. What program lets you preview color separations before you output your document?

2. How many master pages can you make in a QuarkXPress document?

3. How are vector-based graphics configured?

4. What feature of the pen tool in Illustrator that lets you bend or a curve a path?

5. Name one software program that is both a layout and drawing program.

6. In Quark, what window allows you to change the line screen frequency with which your images will print?

7. Name one feature in InDesign that is not available in other graphics software.

8. What feature of Quark lets you easily gather all your files into one folder? What is this called in InDesign?

▶ *exercises*

1. Try this simple exercise to quickly create Pantone® color swatches in InDesign. Open a new Illustrator document. Create a simple geometric shape using one of the preset box tools such as the Star tool. Now open the Pantone Solid Coated Swatch Library. Select a color and apply it to the object you just created. Now save the file in EPS format. Open a new letter-size InDesign document. Place the EPS file in the document. Look at the Color palette in InDesign. What do you notice?

2. This exercise will help you understand how artwork documents are separated into four-color process. Open an InDesign file that you created using four process colors. Go to the top menu bar and select Window > Output Preview > Separations. In the window that appears, select Separations from the pop-up menu. Notice that you preview the different process plates by clicking on the printer icons beside each plate name. Try selecting two or more plates at a time.

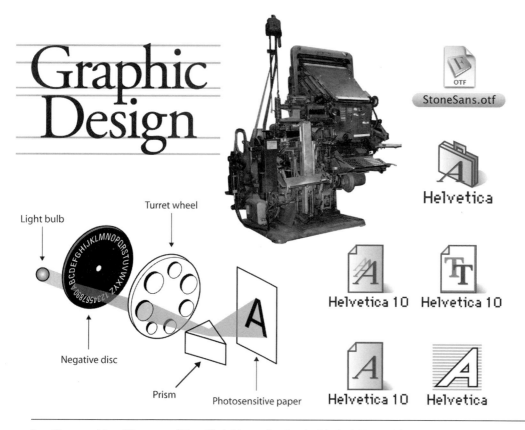

InterType machine. (Courtesy of Don Black Linecasting Service Limited, Toronto.)

objectives

- Discover how typography evolved and when fonts were first developed
- Explain the difference between Postscript, TrueType, and OpenType fonts
- Determine how to load and manage fonts on your system using Font Reserve
- Display the fonts on your system using FontBook

introduction

Although there are a myriad of fonts a designer can use, available either by purchasing a CD or downloading them from the internet, many of them are not in a format suitable for prepress. Improper use of fonts is one of the most common causes of output problems at print providers and service providers. This chapter will help you understand font management as well as explain different types of fonts and their components.

Even though fonts can be loaded into an operating system by storing them in a font folder inside the system folder, it is more effective to load them when you need them using font management software. With some guidance, a designer can simplify the loading and collecting of fonts, as well as avoid outputting film with substituted or default fonts, causing expensive delays. In order to appreciate the importance of fonts, knowing how typography began would be helpful.

WHAT IS TYPOGRAPHY?

All verbal or non-verbal communication that takes place in our society is based upon alphabets, symbols, gestures, or numerals. Graphic communication takes place when a visual message or idea is transferred from one person to another. Typography, which is part of graphic communication, is the assembling of letterforms into words that are the symbolic expression of thoughts. In order for these thoughts to be clearly interpreted, the letterforms must be legible.

The Make Up of a Font

A font of type refers to all the characters, numbers, punctuation, accents, and symbols that make up a typestyle. Imagine if you typed out all of these in one style of a typeface on your keyboard. How many characters would you have? In fact, you could have up to 256 different characters. In the example on this page (see figure 7 – 1), you are looking at a font. In this case it is ITC Fenice Regular. A font can be any typeface you select but not more than one style or point size. So ITC Fenice Italic would be a separate font.

Properties of Type

The earliest typestyles were based on handwriting done by scribes using a reed pen. The strokes of the letters had thick and thin parts, so they resembled the stroke made with the pen as the hand turned. Serifs were added at the end of the stroke to imitate the short stroke the pen made when lifted off the page, hence the name serif type-styles (see figure 7 – 2). However, later typestyles like Garamond and Jenson were actually based on Roman letter styles. They still maintained the serifs from the earlier ones. These typestyles helped to create standard letterforms that made public notices easier for the common person to read.

Up until the beginning of the twentieth century, all typestyles based on Roman letters had serifs, with the exception of script styles. However, in the early 1900s sans serif fonts began to appear (see figure 7 – 3). By the 1920s, typestyles like Futura and Helvetica were being used more and more frequently as designers wanted a more functional look to their designs. Today's typestyles fall into five categories: serif, sans serif, script, decorative (also known as display), and pictorial (essentially dingbat and symbol fonts).

EARLY TYPESETTING METHODS

You could say that typography is as old as the beginning of civilization. Although the characters used in early times do not look like they do today, they certainly

ITC Fenice Regular

AÆBCDEFGHIJKL
NOŒØPQRSTUVWXYZ
aæbcdefghijklmn
oœøpqrstuvwxyz
0123456789+¢£¥µß#
ÁáÂâÄäÅåÂâÃãÀàÇçÉéÈèËëÊê
ÍíÎìÏïÎîìÑñÓóÒòÖöÔôÕõ
ÚúÙùÜüÛûŸÿ
.,„:;'""""‴′…!?¡¿–-÷~*
&§†¶@•›‹·»«
®©™[({})]`´˜¨ˆ˙˚–˜˘ ˇ
              ˏ ˎ
<>+±=‡fifl ƒ
‰°ªº\/

figure | 7 – 1 |

A typical font with all the possible characters, numbers, accents, and punctuation displayed.

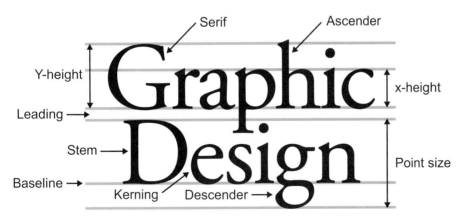

figure | 7 – 2 |

The various properties of type.

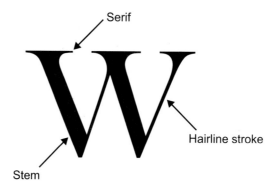

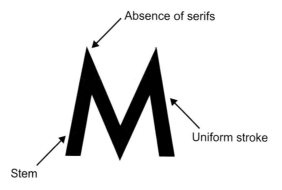

figure | 7 – 3 |

A comparison between a serif and a sans serif letter typestyle.

communicated a visual message. You may not think of the hieroglyphics that the Egyptians used on their pyramids as typography, but there are some similarities. Even Chinese characters, which are based on symbols, can look slightly different depending on the typestyle that is applied to them. Still, most of the world uses characters that were adopted during the spread of the Roman Empire through Europe. Let's now take a look at how the art of typography came about.

Movable Type

In the middle of the fifteenth century, a goldsmith named Johannes Gutenberg invented a printing press with replaceable wooden, and later on, metal letters that were carved or formed out of blocks. Because the Gutenberg press had inter-changeable letters, printed materials became available for the masses. The church and state no longer held the monopoly on written manuscripts. This also led to better education, as more people learned to read and write with the books that were produced at that time.

Guttenberg's invention required each letter block to first be placed by hand on a composing stick (see figure 7 – 4) and then set line-by-line into a galley tray. A way of measuring each block of type was devised using points and picas. There are 72 points in an inch and 12 points in a pica. You probably have already figured out there are 6 picas in an inch. The point size of a block of type was determined by measuring the distance from the top of the ascender to the bottom of the descender.

The space between the lines of letters was created with the use of bars of lead, and so became known as leading. Kerning of the letters relied on the typesetter to file the edges of the letter blocks down. The letters were then locked into a metal frame and inked. Finally, paper was pressed or rolled onto the surface of the letters. This method was quite time consuming, yet far quicker than hand lettering each piece of paper. Eventually, the principle behind Gutenberg's press was adopted for letterpress printing.

Linotype and Other Typesetting Machines

Typesetting methods remained unchanged and in the hands of individual compositors until the end of the nineteenth century when a mechanical typesetting method called Linotype was invented. The machine itself resembles an oversized typewriter (see figure 7 – 5). Imprints of letters were punched into a brass matrix or block. Once a few lines of matrices were put together, they were transferred to a mold-making

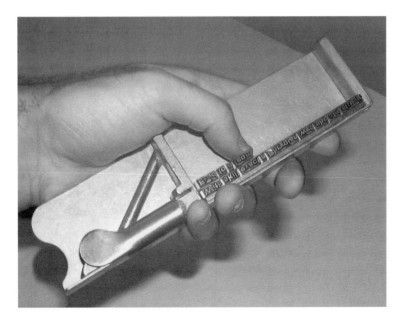

figure | 7 – 4 |

A composing stick allowed the typesetter to set lines of type to transfer onto a press. (Courtesy of Matt Kirschenbaum, University of Maryland.)

figure | 7 – 5 |

An InterType machine, which is based on the LinoType model. (Courtesy of Don Black Linecasting Service Limited, Toronto.)

instrument. From that point, soft metal alloys that had been preheated were injected into the matrice to form a cast, which would then be inked and pressed onto paper. Afterward, the cast made of the soft metal alloy could be melted down and reused again. This method of casting type was also known as hot type.

In the early part of the twentieth century, other typesetting machines were invented namely the Monotype and the Typograph. However, Linotoype was by far the most popular up until the 1960s.

Photocomposition

By the mid-1960s, computers became more compact and economical and subsequently more available to the business world. They made their way into the graphic arts industry through a new typesetting method called photocomposition. In this process, a typesetting firm would print out galleys of type from hard copy provided by the client. The characters were keyed in by the typesetter into a computer and stored in a data file. As each line or paragraph was keyed in, the typesetter would place a coded language beside the text to indicate to the imaging device what typeface, style, alignment, and size it would be set in. Once all the copy was input, the fonts were imaged onto paper by way of an optical process. Light was shone through a negative film disk that contained all the characters of a particular font, which then was projected through a turret lens and finally through a prism onto photographic paper (see figure 7–6). The prism could be adjusted to vary the size of the type, as well as slant it, condense, or expand it. Once all the text was imaged onto the paper, it was run through a developer. At this point, a proofreader would check the copy for errors and then the galleys were sent back to the design studio.

The machines themselves resembled today's computers, only larger. There was a monitor, CPU, and keyboard along with a phototypesetting processor that printed the galleys onto photosensitive paper. This method was far faster than Linotype, and changes could be made quickly without a new cast being made each time. Although

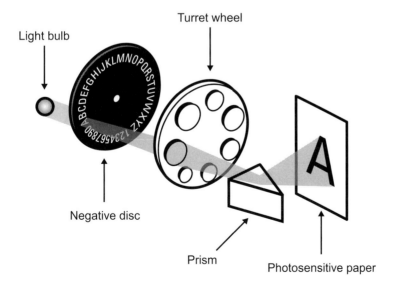

figure |7–6|

The inner workings of a photocomposition typesetting device.

the time involved in setting type was greatly reduced, some type purists did not embrace the photocomposition method. A few stalwart designers would not even consider allowing the text for their artwork to be set on a computer and would only order from typesetters who had linotype or monotype machines.

Digital Typesetting

The mid-1980s saw the advent of computerized artwork and the beginning of the desktop publishing industry. Typesetting became nearly obsolete as designers now input copy directly into graphics software that was imaged through a digital process onto film or paper. The nature of typography changed as well. Fonts of typefaces were no longer imaged optically, but broken up into a dot pattern on a computer screen. The font file itself contained bitmap renderings of each character that were used to create the screen image. Early fonts could not be scaled up or down, so they had to be used at whatever size of type they were written to. Also, the text on the screen looked jagged, as there was only the metrics data in the font from which to read. The quality of the type was measured by how many dots per square inch (dpi) the output device printed at. If it was a dot-matrix printer, the quality was poor, to say the least. Not every designer had a Postscript printer back then.

Benefits of Digital Type

Digital type technology improved quickly and soon this new method of setting type became revolutionary because of the speed that type could be imaged and also because it was far more cost effective. Working in layout programs, a designer could set text quickly in a number of fonts, styles, and formats. Laser proofs of the text could be printed and proofed almost immediately. Designers no longer needed to character count their copy and spend time trying to figure out what size their type needed to be in order to fit into a specific area. This was one of the most time-consuming aspects of ordering type. The type itself along with photos and other elements could be imaged together on an output device, eliminating the need for galleys to be pasted into position on an art board. This process has not significantly changed since it began. Today's graphic designers have it easy compared to those designers who had to use more traditional typesetting methods.

INSTALLING FONTS ON YOUR COMPUTER

Where your fonts are installed depends upon what operating system you are using. If you are on a MacIntosh with a version of OS X, fonts are found in five different locations:

- Users/[user folder – local or remote]/Library/Fonts
- Library/Fonts
- Network/Library/Fonts
- System/Library/Fonts
- System Folder/Fonts (used by systems with older versions of Mac OS also running on them).

In OS 9.0, the font folder is always located in System Folder/Fonts. For Windows, go to the C drive and look in the Windows folder to find the Fonts folder. Installing or moving your fonts in the aforementioned places is the quickest way to get them to work on your system, although not the most efficient. Using the font folder in your system folder will activate all fonts placed in there, but will also slow down the operating speed of your system if you have a lot of different fonts as it has to load all the fonts into the RAM.

Different Fonts for Different Systems

If you work across different operating platforms, you know that not all fonts will work on all systems. Font conflicts arise when you work on a computer at school or work and try to open the file at home on another computer with a different operating system. Some applications will give you a warning message that says some of the fonts used in your document are missing. This dilemma has plagued designers for years and caused no end of headaches for the studios and suppliers with which they deal. There is a solution which you will discover soon. For now, have a look at various types of fonts and find out their advantages and disadvantages.

PostScript Fonts

Adobe Systems developed the first PostScript fonts in 1984. Adobe launched these fonts along with the new PostScript language they had just finished developing. Their intention was that PostScript fonts would become popular with designers when they were printing to complex output devices. The new fonts took off and became the mainstay for every serious computer graphic artist. PostScript fonts are popular in the graphics industry because of their compatibility with laser printers and imagesetters.

PostScript fonts have two basic components, a screen and printer font for each typestyle (see figure 7 – 7). The screen font contains the bitmap metrics data that is read by the software program. This allows them to be resized and manipulated in a variety of ways on your screen. Prior to OS X, usually all the screen fonts were placed

Postscript Fonts

Helvetica 10

Screen font icon

Helvetica

Printer font icon

figure | 7 – 7 |

The icons for screen and printer fonts used by the Mac OS 9.0 system.

Helvetica

Suitcase folder

figure | 7 – 8 |

The icon for a suitcase folder in OS 9.0, which contains a number of screen fonts.

together in a suitcase folder, especially if there are more than a few of them (see figure 7 – 8). The suitcase allowed all fonts within a family to be grouped together in the type menu of nearly all graphics software programs.

The printer font is made up of characters created by outline vectors that are read by the software program and are downloaded to the printer when the electronic file is RIPped through the output device. A PostScript translator located in the printer reads the data and uses it to image the text onto paper, film, or plates. It is necessary to have both the screen and printer font installed in your system; otherwise the fonts will not display or print properly. Remember to send both these components to your print provider when outputting film or plates. The Collect for Output feature in Quark allows you to select both when collecting the various elements that you will send out (see figure 7 – 9).

Postscript fonts are available from a number of vendors. You can purchase them for both Mac and PC platforms; however, they are not interchangeable. It is also possible

> ## May I See Your License?
>
> Recently, font foundries have cracked down on illegal copying of fonts. However, it is acceptable to send your fonts to a print provider as long as you have purchased the license for them. Most foundries allow their fonts to be copied for this purpose. Still, read the fine print on your license before you send the fonts to them. Some of them do not allow copying or distribution of their fonts for any reason. Still, many foundries offer free fonts that have no licensing restrictions on them. Search around for these, but only download Postscript or OpenType fonts.

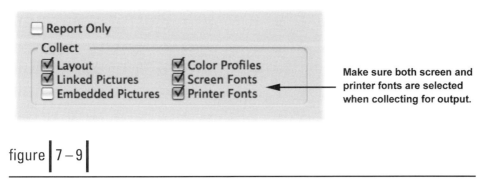

figure | 7 – 9 |

Make sure you collect both screen and printer fonts when collecting for output.

to create a Postscript font or edit one using font creation programs like FontLab or Fontographer. You can create specialized fonts for logotypes and wordmarks, or for a particular client. Be careful not to give the typefaces you create names that are the same or similar to ones you have on your system. If you do, you may end up with conflicts and even software crashes.

TrueType Fonts

When Apple launched System 7.0 years ago, they decided to create a font format that would challenge Adobe's hold on the type market. Their answer was the TrueType font. These fonts are configured using outline vectors as well, but have only one component instead of two (see figure 7–10). They use a variation of the Bezier curve principle that requires fewer points in a curve than PostScript printer fonts. However, TrueType never became popular in the Mac world due to Adobe lifting the hold on the Type1 licensing. Type1 is the original font format developed for Postscript fonts. Eventually, when Apple and Microsoft got together, TrueType became the standard font format on PCs. Now, TrueType fonts can be found on a Mac using OS 9.0 in the system font folder. They are used by OS 9.0 and have

Leave the Big City Fonts Behind

You may be tempted to use one of the system fonts in your artwork. This is not a good idea, as these fonts are TrueType and not PostScript. The text probably will not print out and if it does the kerning and spacing of your text will be poor. If you want to use these fonts, presumably to show the world what a clever designer you are by breaking the rules, there are PostScript versions of these fonts available. Download and use these instead.

names like Chicago, Charcoal, Courier, Geneva, and Monaco. Even typefaces like Times and Helvetica can be TrueType, so check your fonts before using them.

In newer versions of OS X like Panther, default fonts used by the system are located in System/Library/Fonts. These fonts differ from those in OS 9 in that there are more of them and they have different names. However, they are also TrueType fonts and should not be used for output. Download Postscript or OpenType versions of these instead and install them into the font folder located in your User folder. Removal or additions of default fonts is not recommended as it can interfere with the operation of the system and displays.

If you are working on a PC, you may encounter a problem when you send your documents out for film or plates, since most PCs come with TrueType fonts installed. Unfortunately, for PC users, early levels of PostScript development are not able to translate TrueType fonts. Even today, some older RIPs do not always read these fonts and substitute them with Courier. If the PostScript translator in these devices only supports PostScript Level 1 or 2, then they will not reproduce correctly. However, the most recent version, PostScript Level 3, reads TrueType fonts. You can ask your service provider if they support PostScript Level 3 if you are using TrueType fonts.

Helvetica 10   Helvetica 10

Truetype font icons

figure | 7 – 10 |

TrueType font icons for a Mac and a PC.

Don't Mix Fonts

It is better to stick with one type of font on your computer. Many TrueType and Postscript fonts have the same name. This can cause font conflicts on your system. It can also lead to trouble when you output your film at a print provider. Say you have used Helvetica in both a TrueType font and a PostScript font. The kerning and tracking will appear differently in your film work. For the same reason, it is better to buy a family of fonts from one manufacturer rather than from many different ones. Finally, organize your fonts in one folder so you can load them easily into your system (more on this later on in the chapter).

Multiple Master Fonts

When you are downloading fonts for your system, you may occasionally come across a font with a name that has the extension .mm after it. These are Multiple Master (MM) fonts and they are based upon the same outline vector principle as Postscript fonts. They also have a screen and printer font. However, like TrueType fonts, they do not print on all output devices. Imagesetters with Postscript Level 1 cannot read MM fonts. Once again, check with your service provider if you are using these fonts on your system. As far as using them on a PC, they can run on Windows 3.0 and later versions. However, if you are using a Mac with OS X on it, forget using these fonts. Many designers had to remove these fonts when they upgraded to this new system a few years ago.

OpenType Fonts

In the late 1990s, Microsoft and Adobe finally buried the hatchet and developed a font format that could be used cross platform on both Mac and Windows systems. OpenType fonts (OTF) are written in Unicode and use a single file that contains the outline, metrics, and Postscript data (see figure 7 – 11). The benefit to those designers

StoneSans.otf

figure | 7 – 11 |

An example of an OpenType font in OS X.

who work cross platform is tremendous. It also saves prepress service providers time and money, as they no longer have to search for compatible fonts for files they receive that were created on other operating systems.

OpenType technology allows you to easily manage your fonts as there is only a single file to worry about. Also, more typographic options are available in OpenType fonts such as a greater number of special characters and glyphs and better language support. Adobe software like Illustrator and InDesign allows you to alter these, so you can have more than the standard 256 characters that are in other font formats. In Illustrator there is an OpenType palette that allows you to apply type modifications like ligatures, swashes, alternate characters, ordinals, and fractions (see figure 7 – 12). InDesign has a menu bar for OpenType when you select text that allows you to perform the same instances, but also lets you create character styles and save them for reloading later (see figure 7 – 13).

Although OpenType technology may seem like an enormous breakthrough, not all designers are happy. Some who own type foundries are not pleased that some of their font creation and editing programs do not easily produce OpenType fonts. In fact, a few type designers have had to hire outside artists to create OpenType versions of fonts they have designed. Still, OpenType has been embraced in many educational

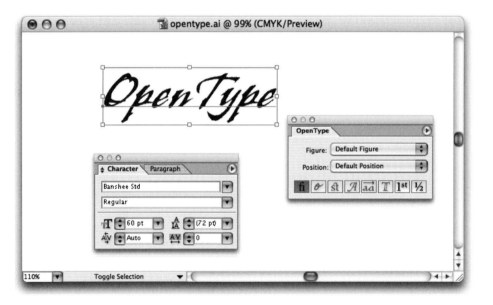

figure | 7 – 12 |

The OpenType palette in Illustrator allows you to use a variety of typographic controls on these types of fonts.

> ## Avoid Applying Styles to Text
>
> When selecting a style for a typeface in your document, always select the font itself, instead of applying styles to the plain typeface. For instance, if you want to select Garamond Bold Italic, then look under your font menu in the top menu bar rather than clicking the bold and italic buttons in your text or measurement palette (see figure 7–14). The reason designers avoid using these buttons is because imagesetters will not read the styles that are used on them. All text that has these styles applied will be imaged as plain text and you will have to reprint your film again.

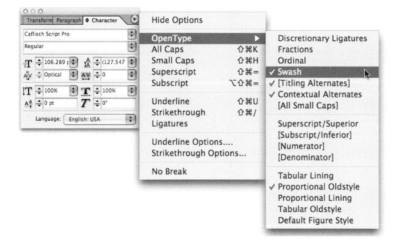

figure | 7 – 13 |

A pop-up menu is located in the Character window of InDesign. This lets you select alternate styles for your font as well as creating New Character Styles.

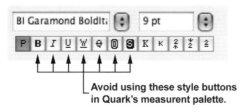

Avoid using these style buttons
in Quark's measurent palette.

figure | 7 – 14 |

The style buttons in Quark are tempting, but will not work when film or plates are imaged.

THE *professional* PROFILE *Ray Larabie*

A FONDNESS FOR FONTS

Ray Larabie started his career in the video game industry after studying classical animation at Sheridan College. He always had a keen interest in type from an early age when his grandmother brought home sheets of Letraset from her workplace. Taking inspiration from dry transfer lettering, Ray started to create his own fonts and launched his own website in 1995. By offering a new font for free each week, his site quickly grew in popularity. By 2000, he had more than 400 fonts available for download from larabiefonts. com. His success led him to launch Typodermic, a secondary web site. His fonts are also available from a number of font distributors like MyFonts.

Ray lists Morris Fuller Benton as one of the prominent type designers who have influenced his work. "Franklin Gothic and Alternate Gothic and many of his other designs are still considered cool a century later," he states, "that's staying power." Ray uses FontLab to create his fonts, switching from Fontographer in 1999. The changeover has been very worthwhile, cutting down the time to design a font by one-quarter. Still, he found designing OpenType fonts rather challenging. "At first there was very little clear documentation on how to create Open-Type fonts," says Ray. "The FontLab documentation was not useful and the specs were too technical. It was a very steep learning curve for me." However, he now embraces the new font format. "Now that I've got it all figured out, I love it. I can't understand why people are still buying TrueType and Postscript formats unless they're still using old software," he states.

Ray believes it is easier than ever before to start your own type designing business. "All you need is FontLab and a good foundry name," he explains. "I think it's funny that we're still calling them foundries. My font manufacturing facility consists of a desk and a laptop. It doesn't feel like a foundry." These days, Ray finds the most difficult part of his work is answering emails and preparing the fonts for release. "Making sure multiple formats perform identically is no fun," says Ray.

He gives this advice to students when selecting a typeface for their work, "Don't get hung up on 'favorite fonts' but keep a few brand new ones on hand." He concludes by saying, "the Designer's Republic Japanese instruction manual style was interesting a decade ago... so enough with the Helvetica already. Don't be afraid of hand lettering: Jung Kwak created the Vice City logo using a marker and it looks more eighties than any font would have." ◄

institutions that have both platforms. Hundreds of these fonts are available from Adobe, Linotype, and other third-party manufacturers.

FONT MANAGEMENT SOFTWARE

It might be tempting to load all your fonts in the various font folders on your system; however, this can cause a number of difficulties. First of all, you may experience a slow down in the processing speed of your operating system as it constantly needs to read those fonts. Also, software will take longer to launch as it usually needs to optimize font menu performance when first launched. And you will find it frustrating selecting fonts in your page layout programs like Quark as your type menu will be incredibly long. An easier way to load fonts in your system is to use font management software that activates fonts as you require them. Although there are a number of font management software systems available for use on OS X and earlier systems, one that is reasonable and runs smoothly without many crashes is Font Reserve.

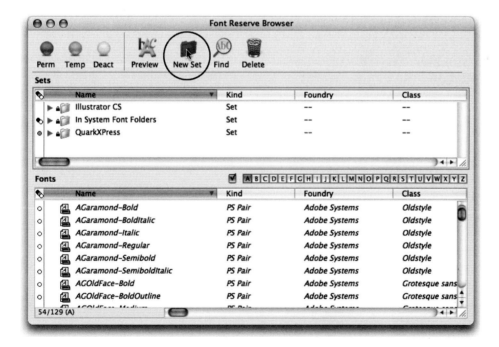

figure | 7 – 15 |

The specimen window gives you a preview of each font.

figure | 7 – 16 |

Try using your own name for a font set.

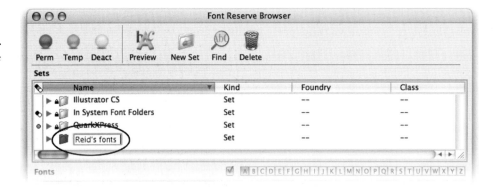

figure | 7 – 17 |

Find a font by using a keyword search.

figure | 7 – 18 |

Click on the Preview button to see how a font looks.

figure | 7 – 19 |

You can see a number of views of each font in the Specimen window.

Font Reserve

Font Reserve is a very useful application for loading fonts into your system. It is made by Extensis and has a user-friendly interface. It locates all the places where you have fonts on your system and automatically activates each one when you open the application for the first time. It also lets you create new sets (see figure 7 – 15). Once you have created the set, you can give it a personal name (see figure 7 – 16). Font Reserve can find fonts in your system using a keyword finder (see figure 7 – 17). Clicking on the Preview button gives you a preview of each font (see figure 7 – 18). You can alter the format the font is shown in by clicking on the icons to the left of the preview.

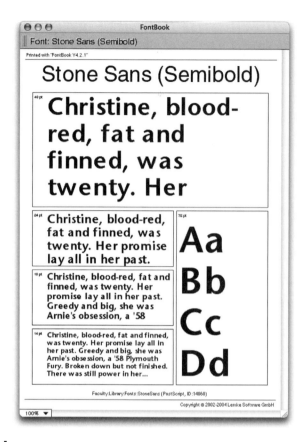

figure | 7 – 20 |

The Preview window in FontBook nicely displays the font.

If this is not enough, a Specimen window lets you look at a font in a number of views (see figure 7 – 19). You can scroll through your fonts by clicking on the arrows at the top of this window. And you can print out the specimen to your printer. If you are looking for font management software that is reasonably priced, try out the demo version of Font Reserve included on the CD with this book.

FontBook

Have you ever had trouble deciding which font to use when designing a project? You may have applied a dozen or more to some text before deciding on one of them. Here is a better solution: FontBook allows you to view each font individually. It comes with later versions of OS X (10.3 and up). Once you launch it, the first font in your system appears in the FontBook window. The window shows the font in a number of sizes (see figure 7 – 20). To select a different view, try going

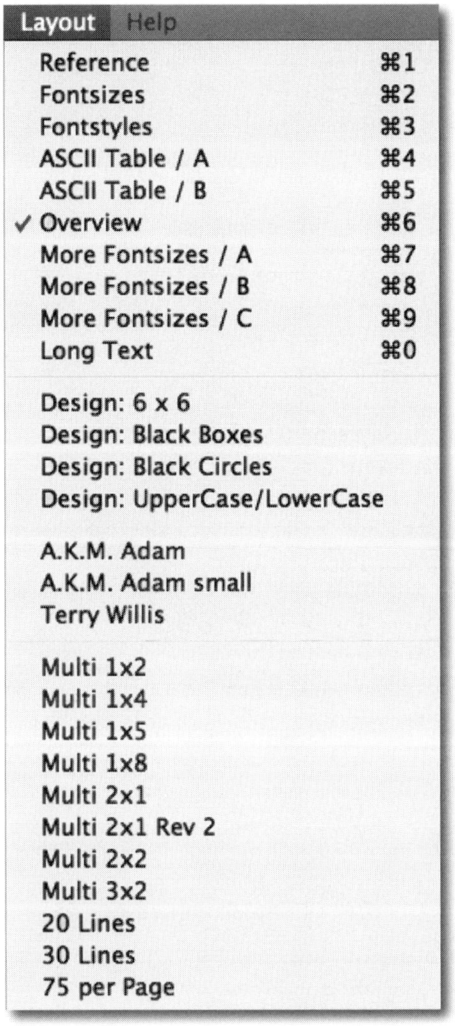

figure | 7 – 21 |

You can select a different view from the Layout menu.

under Layout in the top menu bar (see figure 7–21). You can select from 28 different views from this menu.

There are a couple of ways to select the font you want to view. First, you can go to Font in the top menu bar and select each font individually (see figure 7–22). Another way is to press the page down key on your keyboard, so you can quickly scroll through the fonts on your system until you find the right one. You can also print out a sample view of a font or go to File > MultiPrint (command/control-M) to print out a number of fonts (see figure 7–23). You can print from fonts installed on your system, a suitcase, or from a specific folder. Be careful not to try to print out too

figure | 7 – 22 |

FontBook lets you scroll through all the fonts in your system.

many at once or you could be waiting a while. If you are not connected to a printer, you can select to print either a PDF or PostScript file to the desktop.

FontBook is indeed a very handy piece of software and well worth the small shareware fee. It is a fast and easy way of selecting fonts before you load them onto your system. If you are one of those designers who cannot remember what each font looks like, then give FontBook a try.

SUMMARY

Typography has been around for more than 400 years and has gone through incredible changes during that time. Before computers, new typefaces were created by a small group of type designers. In the digital age of today, typographic design has

figure | 7 – 23 |

You can print fonts out individually or a several at a time.

become more commonplace than in the past thanks to new technology and software. There are many small independent type foundries, usually consisting of no more than one or two people. It is easy to become a type designer if you want to. Start by downloading trial software to create or modify your own fonts. You could become the next Herb Lubalin.

▶ *in review*

1. How many different folders are fonts kept in OS X?

2. What application allows you to load fonts into your system?

3. Name one type of font that is acceptable for prepress work?

4. What determines a font's point size?

5. What is the name of the first typesetting machine?

6. Why can't we use the style buttons in QuarkXPress when applying styles to text in a document from which we plan to make film?

7. Why isn't it wise to copy fonts from friends or other unauthorized sources?

8. What application allows us to preview fonts before applying them to text?

9. In what century was movable type invented?

10. How many possible characters are there in a font?

▶ *exercises*

1. This exercise will help you to become more familiar with fonts in your system. Open up your fonts folder and copy a few fonts to your desktop. Select one and double-click on the file. What application opens when you do this? Is there any data in the window? What type of font do you think it is?

2. Different software programs display fonts in different ways. Open up a Quark-XPress file. Go to the top menu bar and select Style > Fonts. Or if you are working in InDesign, go to the top menu bar and select Type > Fonts. Now open up a document in Microsoft Word and look under Fonts in the top menu bar. What differences do you notice in how various fonts are organized in a page layout program compared to a word processing application?

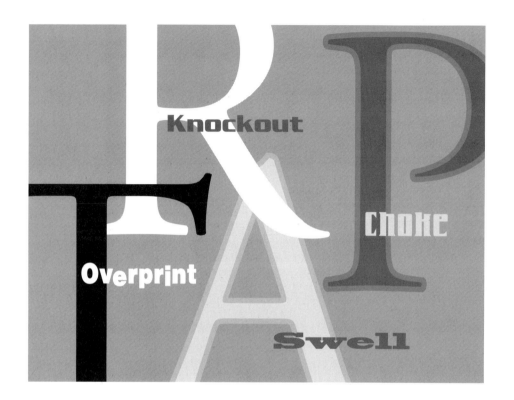

CHAPTER 8

objectives

- Explain trapping terms like overprint, knockout, spread, and choke
- Prepare QuarkXPress documents for trapping
- Prepare Adobe Illustrator documents for trapping
- Recognize the various trapping allowances for different printing methods
- Explore different trapping software

introduction

Trapping is an area of prepress that many designers try to avoid. They would rather pay someone to do it for them. However, when a document is built correctly using the right type of trap where it's required, trapping can be a snap! This crucial chapter will introduce you to the four trapping scenarios and explain why trapping is necessary in production of graphic artwork. As well, you will examine and see examples for trapping in the major software programs. In addition, you will understand how trapping can vary for various printing methods. Finally, you will be given an overview of how trapping software works.

WHY WE NEED TO TRAP

All artwork that is produced for commercial purposes or that will eventually be printed on a printing press needs to be trapped. Without trapping applied, the various colors in a document will have white spaces or edges between them. This is known as misregistration. Although misregistration can occur even with trapping applied to a document, it is less likely with proper trapping applied. When trapping is applied where two colors meet, they will slightly overlap. How much they need to overlap depends on three things: the printing method, the type of press, and the material being printed on. You will find more information on this later in the chapter.

How Misregistration Occurs

As the material or substrate moves through the press, various plates that hold the ink place an impression onto its surface. Although the person operating the press does their best to align the plates before the job is run and adjust them during the run, there will always be a small amount of movement in the position of the plates or stretching of the substrate. If the artwork is not trapped, there will be some misalignment at the edges where two colors meet (see figure 8 – 1). This produces the misregistration—every printer and designer's nightmare.

The Four Trapping Instances

Every instance where two separate colors meet must be trapped to make sure the colors align properly. Each situation may be different depending on the colors and

figure | 8 – 1 |

An example of how two colors can misregister when printed without trapping. See color insert.

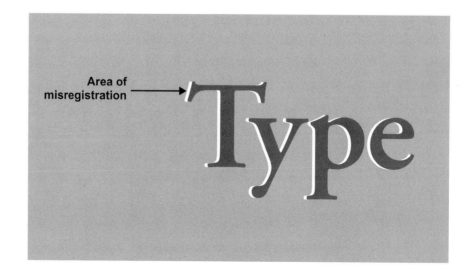

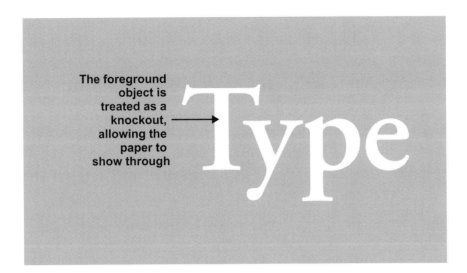

The foreground object is treated as a knockout, allowing the paper to show through

figure | 8–2 |

An example of a knockout with the paper showing through. See color insert.

printing method involved. For instance, in some types of printing where black is dense enough, it does not need to trap against the color it is next to, but can be printed right over the other color, since the secondary color will not show through. Now, let's explore the four different trapping instances.

Knockout

The name of this trapping scenario is appropriate since it essentially does what it says. It occurs when the substrate shows through another color when it is printed. Usually type is knocked out of other colors, but any object can be knocked out. If the substrate is a white paper stock, then the knockout will appear white otherwise it will be whatever the color of the paper is. This is not a true trap as only one color of ink is involved. However, it is important to specify it as such, in case the software program tries to apply a different type of a trap to the object.

Some designers mistakenly believe that white is always a knockout, but this is not necessarily true. White is always treated as a knockout in letterpress and offset printing; however, it is usually a printed ink in other printing methods like Screen printing and needs to be trapped against other colors beside it. If you are using white as a color in your document you need to apply a different trap than a knockout.

Overprint

This is where some designers become confused as to what constitutes an overprint. Basically, an overprint occurs when an area of one color completely overlaps another one below it. In this case, the two inks will mix and you will wind up with a color that is a combination of the two. However, it is rare for a designer to entirely overprint two objects as they have little control over how the colors will mix together.

Overprinting happens in the printing process even when a designer does not use trapping. Overprinting regularly occurs when you make up a color using screen percentages of two process colors. The laser dots of each process color will overlap to some extent. It also occurs when an image is separated into four process colors or a duotone (see figure 5 – 7). In this instance, particularly in AM screening, the halftone dots will slightly overlap. Overprinting also occurs when a stroke of one color is overprinted against a background. This is a different kind of trap that we will talk about soon.

Overprinting is primarily used when the density and darkness of one ink allows it to completely cover the other. Since black is the darkest color in the spectrum, it is usually dense enough to cover any other printed inks. For most offset printing then, black is treated as an overprint (see figure 8 – 3). In some cases, a printer may wish to trap black against another color, if they believe the other color may show through.

Spread

A spread refers to an instance where a lighter color has to be trapped against a darker background. In this scenario, the edges of the lighter color are expanded to "spread" into the darker color behind it (see figure 8 – 4). The reason that the lighter color expands into the darker one is that because it is lighter, the amount that it overlaps will not be noticeable. In a spread, only the part of an object that overlaps the color underneath it is trapped. The color of the paper stock is behind the rest of the lighter color.

figure | 8 – 3 |

An example of a black colored object overprinting a different background color. See color insert.

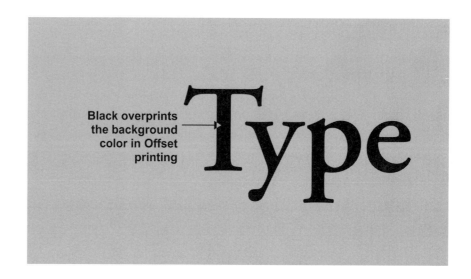

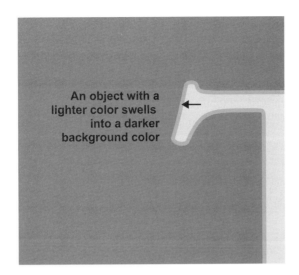

figure | 8 – 4 |

A spread occurs when a lighter object is placed over a darker background. See color insert.

Sometimes it is difficult to tell if the object color is lighter than the underneath color. In this case a densitometer would be handy, but since few graphic designers have one, you may have to take your best guess. There is another way to determine this, which you will discover shortly.

Choke

A choke is basically the opposite of a spread. In this instance, you have a darker color on top of a lighter color. In a choke, the lighter background color expands into the darker foreground. This way, the lighter color is not noticeable under the darker one (see figure 8 – 5). The darker color cannot spread because the overlap will be notice-

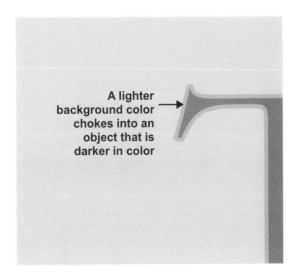

figure | 8 – 5 |

A choke is the opposite of a spread. Here darker text is placed over a lighter background. See color insert.

> ## Choke or Spread: How to Tell
>
> When you are trapping colors and you are not sure whether the two colors should be treated as a choke or a spread, there is an easy rule to remember that helps to determine it. The rule is: **The lighter color always does the action.** So if you are trapping a lighter colored object against a darker background, it should be treated as a spread as the lighter color will spread into the darker one. If you have a dark object on a lighter background, then it has to be a choke, as the lighter color surrounds the darker one and expands into the foreground object.

able and produce a larger object. You might not think this matters, but if you are trapping a small line of text and you spread it instead of choking it, then your type is going to look heavier.

TRAPPING DIGITAL ARTWORK FILES

You should now have a basic understanding of how trapping works in prepress. Before computer graphics applications, trapping was done by spreading or shrinking parts of the negative film when it was exposed through the camera that produced it. Luckily, digital artwork is much simpler and faster. Still, you have to know how to apply trapping in the software program you are using. Some software programs do not have trapping capabilities, so you may need to use third-party software in order to properly prepare your artwork for the press. Many manufacturers of PostScript Level 3 software include in-RIP trapping options, so ask your service provider if their RIP has trapping capabilities.

Let's now look at the various page layout and drawing software that allows you to trap and see how each one works.

Trapping in Quark

As you have seen, many designers use Quark for producing artwork for magazines, books, brochures, etc. Aside from the reasons you have read about in previous chapters, one of the other main reasons is that Quark makes trapping of objects and text you create simple and easy. Even if you forget to trap your Quark document, your artwork will probably be correct as Quark has a default trapping feature. Although, it might seem that this makes trapping in Quark unnecessary, the truth is that it is better not to leave the trapping on default. The reason for this will become clear as we go along.

The Default Trap Feature

The default trap feature is not reliable enough to properly trap a Quark document with. This is because the default trap feature has many limitations. For instance, you may have a situation where three colors may overlap, and since Quark is only reading two, the objects are not trapped correctly against each other. If you want to see what type of trap Quark has applied, then go to the top menu bar and select Window > Show Trap Information (see figure 8–6). When the Trap Information window appears, select an object and the trapping information for the object will appear in the window (see figure 8–7).

The default trap feature is handy if you are in a hurry and do not have any complex trap situations in your artwork. It can also be used to quickly determine what type of trap situation should be used. Unfortunately, the default trap feature has its limitations. Occasionally, you may have a situation where three colors may overlap, and since Quark is only reading two, the objects are not trapped correctly against each other. Or you may be trapping against a gradient, in which case Quark cannot read both colors you have used in your gradient, so it will only trap against one. In these

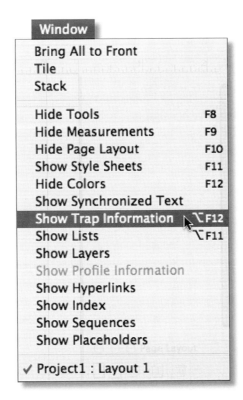

figure | 8–6 |

Opening the Trap Information window lets you see how items will be trapped.

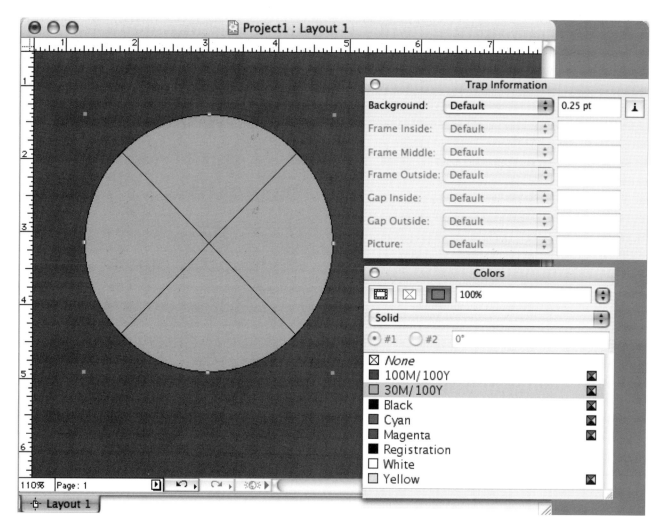

figure | 8 – 7 |

Select an object to see the default trap information on it.

situations, leaving the trapping on default can lead to improper trapping of your document and ultimately misregistration problems upon printing. There is a better way to ensure your document is properly trapped.

Item-by-Item Trapping

One of the great features of Quark is that it allows you to use an item-by-item method for trapping colors against each other. Although it is too time consuming for large projects, it can be used for documents that are four pages or less. The item-by-item method is much more reliable than leaving them on default. It prevents many errors that can occur when the default trap in Quark is reading a multi-colored

The Industry Standard

Each time you trap in Quark, you need to specify the trap allowance in your document. The trap allowance is the amount of overlap that will occur when two colors are trapped against one another. Quark has a default setting of 0.144 points. This is insufficient even for the most precise offset press. Check with your printer on what value they use for their press. If you cannot find this information, then use the industry standard for trapping on an offset press, which is 0.25 points. You can change this in Quark by opening up your document's Preferences (command-option-shift/control-alt-shift-Y). Select Trapping from the menu on the left and change the value in both the Auto Amount and Indeterminate to 0.25 points. Also make sure that the Ignore White and Process Trapping boxes are selected.

background. To trap item-by-item in Quark, you use the same Trap Information window as in the default method. Only instead of leaving the trapping on default, you will select the type of trap you want. For instance, if you have a white object against a red background, then select Knockout from the pop-up menu in the window (see figure 8–9).

If you have a black object on a red background, then you would select Overprint from the menu (see figure 8–10). A yellow object against a red background will be a spread. In this case, Auto Amount (+) is selected so the edges of the top object spread or spread into the background color (figure 8–11). If you have a red object on a yellow background, then you need to apply a choke. Select Auto Amount (−) from the menu to choke the background color into the object (figure 8–12).

Object or Underneath Color?

Before you manually apply trapping in Quark, you can quickly tell which is the object or foreground color and which is the underneath or background color. Click on the item to select it and then look at the Trap Information window. Click on the icon beside the box where the trap information is. A palette appears that displays the object and underneath color as well as the source of the trap values and the properties (see figure 8–8). You can use this box to determine what type of trap you require for each instance.

figure | 8–8 |

Click on the icon beside the trap information to see which is the object or underneath color.

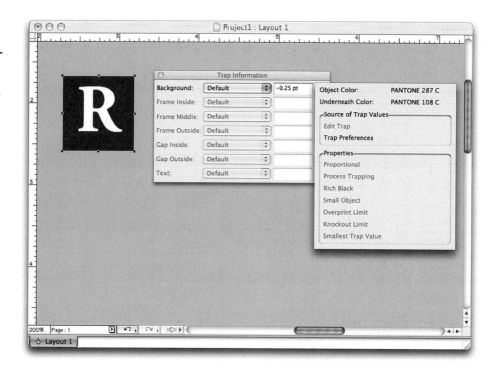

figure | 8–9 |

By selecting knockout from the pop-up menu, you ensure this white object traps correctly.

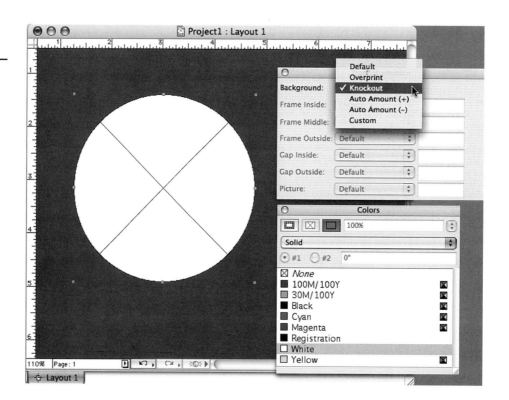

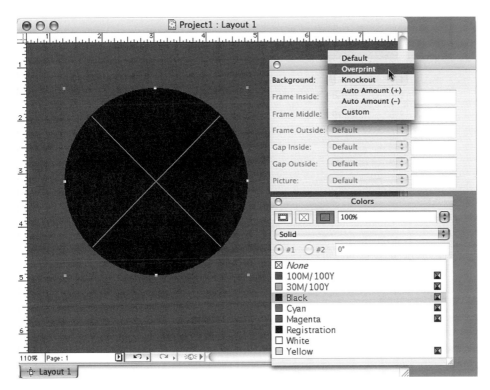

figure | 8 – 10 |

Select Overprint for black objects on a lighter background.

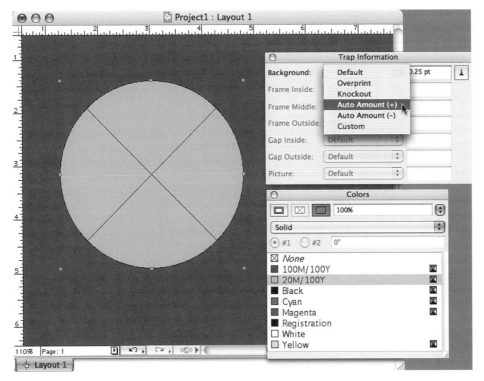

figure | 8 – 11 |

Auto Amount (+) needs to be selected in the Trap Information window for a spread.

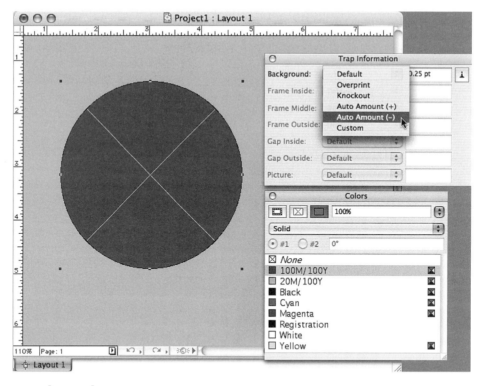

figure |8–12|

Select Auto Amount (−) so the foreground object will be choked by the lighter background.

Trapping Text

In Quark, trapping text is done the same way as any other object, the only difference being that the text must be selected with the Type Tool before any trapping can be applied to it (see figure 8–13). Any trap scenario can be applied to the text you have selected. It is also necessary to trap it when it is placed over four-color process images that you have imported into Quark.

Custom Trapping

Occasionally you may have a situation where more than two objects with different colors meet in Quark. For instance, if you have a text box that has another text box behind it acting as a drop shadow over a lighter background. In this case, it may be necessary to apply a custom trap to one of the objects. Usually the top object will have the custom trap. In this example (see figure 8–14), the top text box has a custom spread of 0.1 points. This is to allow the red text to trap against both the black shadow and the yellow background. If the red text is treated as a choke, then the black text will choke into the red along with the yellow, distorting

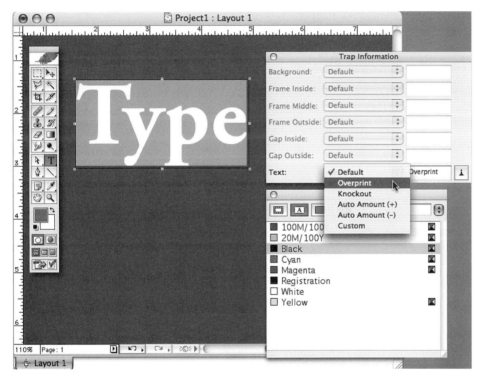

figure | 8 – 13 |

Select your text in Quark before applying any trap information to it.

the letterforms. This low trapping tolerance is acceptable if you only use it on one or two instances in your document.

Trapping Frames

When you apply a frame to an object in Quark, you notice that there is a pop-up menu in the Trap Information window for the inside and outside of the frame. This is to allow you to trap the frame against both the underneath colors beside it. In this example, a yellow ellipse with a red frame is against a blue background (see figure 8 – 15). Red

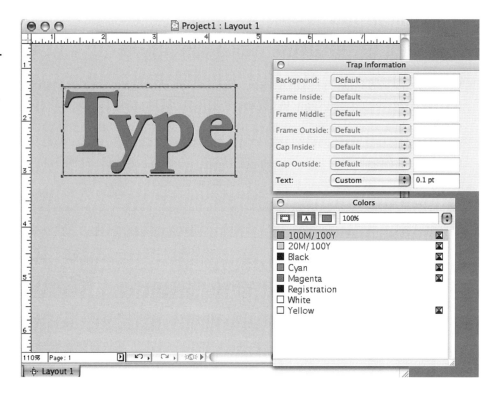

figure | 8 – 14 |

Creating a custom trap
lets you properly trap
three overlapping objects.
See color insert.

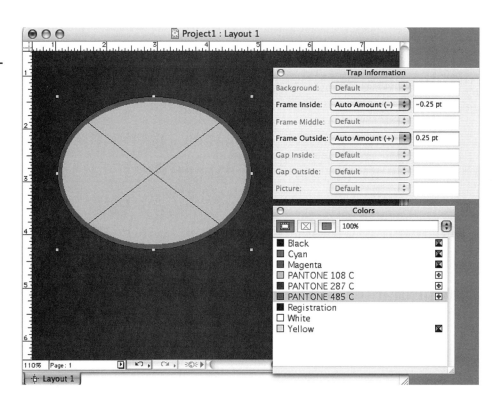

figure | 8 – 15 |

The frame on the inside
and outside of the ellipse
calls for two different
types of traps to be used.

is the object or foreground color since it is against the yellow and the blue. For the inside of the frame, the yellow ellipse chokes against the darker red. On the outside of the frame, the red spreads into the blue background. Be careful not to be fooled by the shape of the object, but make sure that you have applied the correct trap instance. Once again, it is important to remember the lighter colors must perform the trapping action.

Color-specific Trapping

You can use another method to apply trapping to colors in Quark. The color-specific method takes longer, especially if you are using a lot of colors, so it is not commonly used, but it does the trick nevertheless. Go under the top menu bar to Edit > Colors. Click on the object's color in the dialogue box and then click on the Edit Trap button. In the dialogue box that appears, you can select how the object color will trap against every other color in your document. Select a background color and then choose a trapping type from the pop-up menu (see figure 8 – 16). Repeat the same step for each background color. You need to perform this task for each color in your palette.

You have now seen how to go about trapping colors in Quark for both items and text. However, this is only half the puzzle. Unfortunately, Quark does not trap placed EPS files from Illustrator. You can only trap items that were created directly in Quark. In order to trap logos, illustrations, and other artwork from Illustrator, you must do so in their native program.

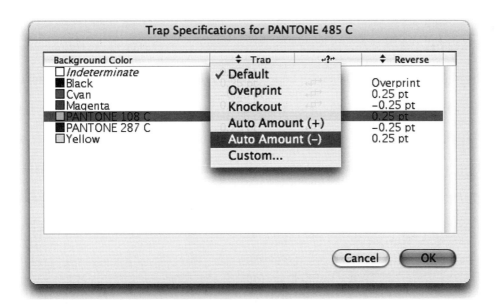

figure | 8 – 16 |

A pop-up menu in the trap specifications window allows you to specify how one color will trap against another.

Trapping in Illustrator

It would be nice to say that Illustrator also has a default trap feature, but that is not the case. Any items you create in Illustrator must be individually trapped. No matter what colors you use, no trapping will be applied unless you do it manually. Another stumbling block is that there is no Trap Information window in which to enter values, so trapping must be done manually. The trapping instances are the same of course, so let's start there.

Knockouts in Illustrator

This one is simple. Whenever you place an object over another in Illustrator, the top object will knockout whatever part of the lower object is underneath it. Therefore, no trapping needs to be applied to objects or text that is white when trapping for offset printing, as white is the color of the paper stock.

Creating an Overprint

As in Quark, black is usually treated as an overprint. Creating an overprint in Illustrator is relatively simple as well.

1. First select the object with a fill of black.

2. Open up your Attributes palette by going to Window > Attributes.

3. Now click on the Overprint Fill box (see figure 8 – 17). Again, this isn't recommended as a way to mix colors together as the results are unpredictable.

Spread the News

Creating a spread is also relatively easy in Illustrator. Follow the simple steps below.

1. Select the object by clicking on it once.

2. Apply a stroke of the background color by dragging the fill color into the stroke box in the toolbar.

figure 8 – 17

Click on the Overprint Fill box in the Attributes palette to make an object overprint another.

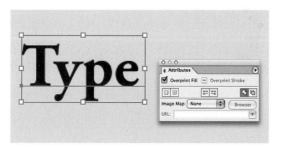

3. Set the stroke weight to twice the amount of your trap allowance. The reason for this is that the stroke runs on the inside and outside perimeter of an object. If you do not know the trap allowance, set the stroke weight to 0.5 points.

4. Finally, click on the Overprint Stroke box in the Attributes palette (see figure 8 – 18).

Chokes in Illustrator

This is where trapping in Illustrator becomes tricky. After trying this, it might seem easier to spread all your objects, but that will not produce artwork that is of acceptable quality. Following several steps carefully will produce the correct results.

1. Select the object to which you want to apply a choke.

2. Place a copy of the object in front of it by selecting Edit > Copy (command/control-C) and then Edit > Place in Front (command/control-F) (see figure 8 – 19).

3. Hide the copy of the object in front (command/control-3).

4. Select the original object and change the fill color to white (see figure 8 – 20).

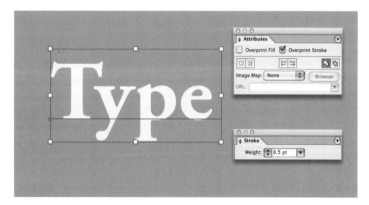

figure | 8 – 18 |

Stroke the object and select Overprint Stroke in the Attributes palette to create a spread.

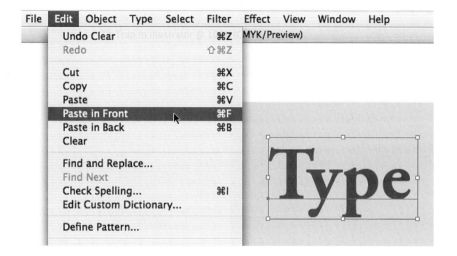

figure | 8 – 19 |

Place a copy in front of the object you are going to trap with a choke.

figure | 8 – 20 |

Fill the original, behind the copy you just hid, with white.

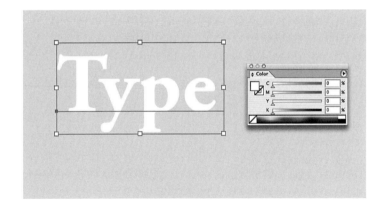

5. Set the stroke to the same color as the background object. Use the eyedropper tool and hold down the shift key to assign the color to the stroke and not the fill. Set the stroke weight to double the value of your trap allowance (see figure 8 – 21).

6. Bring back the copy of the top object by going to Edit > Show All (command-option/control-alt-3).

7. With the very top object selected, click on Overprint Fill in the Attributes window (see figure 8 – 22).

When You Don't Need to Trap in Illustrator

If you are creating artwork that uses only the four process colors, you may be able to save yourself some time by selecting one of the four process inks as a common color to run through all the objects in your document. If all your objects possess at least a 20 percent screen of two of the process inks, then trapping is not necessary. The reason for this is that all of the objects will appear on one of the plates when printed, so they use a common color. This technique is useful when you are creating complex illustrations with many objects overlapping one another. There may be filters applied as well as other complex Postscript features such as gradient meshes. In this case, trapping can be simplified by following this method.

figure | 8 – 21 |

Stroke the original with the background color and set the stroke to 0.5 points.

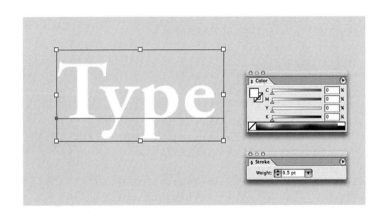

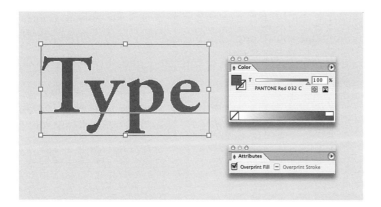

figure | 8 – 22 |

Show the copied object in front and apply an overprint fill to it.

Trapping a Stroke

You may have noticed you cannot apply a trap to a stroke that is over a background in Illustrator. There is a way to get around this though.

1. Select the object with the stroke.

2. Go under the top menu to Object > Path > Outline Stroke (see figure 8 – 23).

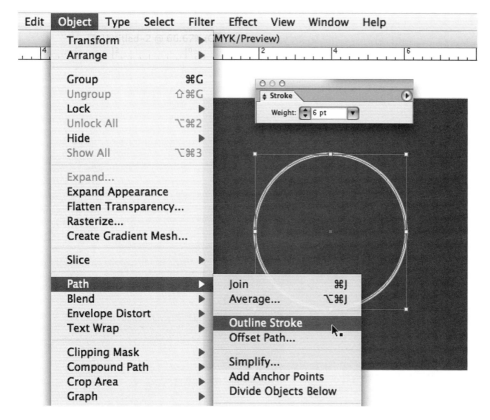

figure | 8 – 23 |

Outline the stroke in an object to create a separate object that can be trapped.

3. Once you have outlined the stroke, it becomes an object. Ungroup the two objects (command-shift/control-shift-G) and select the outermost object.

4. Apply a stroke to the object using the same color of the fill inside this outer object (see figure 8–24).

5. Set the stroke weight to 0.5 points and click on the Overprint Stroke box in the Attributes window (see figure 8–25). Now the stroke will trap against the original object and the background.

figure | 8–24 |

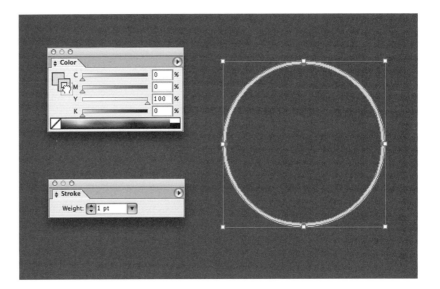

Stroke the newly created object with its fill color.

figure | 8–25 |

Change the stroke weight and overprint the stroke you just made.

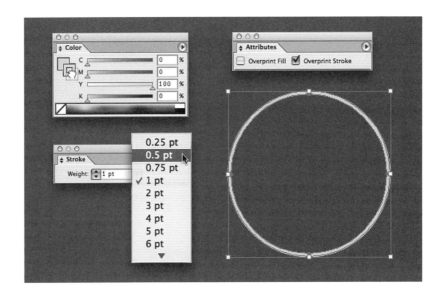

> ## Forget the Trap Filter
>
> A few years ago, Illustrator introduced a filter in the Pathfinder feature that allowed you to trap two objects by selecting them and then applying a trap. The trap filter works by creating a third object between the two colors that is a blend of those colors. The results of this filter are not always consistent. At times, no trapping object is created between the two objects, or a screen of only one of the colors is applied. This method also increases the number of objects in your document, so your file will be larger. Instead, use the methods outlined in this book, which are more reliable.

TRAPPING ALLOWANCES FOR DIFFERENT PRINTING METHODS

The trap allowance or registration tolerance you set in your artwork depends on what type of press the job is going to be run on. Applying the correct trapping depends upon the material or substrate on which the job is being printed. Offset and rotogravure printing is more precise than flexography or silk screening, so they require the plates to be positioned more accurately. Also, both the aforementioned methods are printed on materials that stretch and expand easily. It is always a good idea to check with your printer on their requirements before applying any trapping to your document.

Trapping for Offset

For the most part, artwork that you will be producing will be printed on an offset press. The trapping allowance for offset can vary depending on whether the press is sheet-fed or web offset. As explained earlier in the chapter, the standard trap allowance for a sheet-fed offset press is 0.25 points. This may not be sufficient for a web offset press, as they run at much higher speeds and print on large newsprint rolls which stretch more easily than single sheets. So most web offset presses require a trap allowance of 0.35 points.

Rotogravure

Gravure presses run at very high speeds. The material on which they print ranges from paper to plastics and foil. They use copper plates that are even more durable than offset plates, and are made from a zinc alloy. The registration tolerance can sometimes vary depending on the material and press used. A tolerance of 0.72 points is standard when trapping a document for a gravure press.

> ## Get the Right Specs
>
> The tolerances mentioned in this chapter are only rough guidelines for you as a designer to follow. They may not be accurate depending on the type of press, conditions in the printing plant, and the material on which you are printing. Always check with your printer before performing any trapping on your document particularly if you are using printing methods you are not familiar with. Or better yet, let your printer handle the trapping when they image the plates using their own equipment and software.

Flexography

Trapping allowances for registration in flexographic printing can also vary greatly. This is mostly due to the nature of the various materials on which flexography prints, but also that the plates are high-density rubber or photopolymer. For printing on plastics, a trap allowance of 2.5 points is common. However, the trap allowance may need to be increased proportionately if the printed area is larger than five inches. When printing on corrugated carton board, which has a softer surface, the rule of thumb is to have a trap allowance of 4.5 points on all elements. Since this printing process is used mostly for packaging, it may be wise to let an expert at your service provider do the trapping, rather than deal with misregistration problems at press time.

Screen printing

In this printing method, a fine screen is used to print on different substrates including cloth, ceramics, metal, and plastic. The size of a screen press can vary greatly. Some that print on clothing can be quite small (a couple of feet) while others that print flags and banners are very large (a hundred feet or more). Because of this and the different type of materials printed on, registration tolerances in screen printing vary greatly. The tolerances can range anywhere from 4.5 points up to 20 points depending on the material being printed on. If you are preparing digital files for screen printing, it is imperative that your printer performs any trapping necessary.

Third-party Trap Software

A number of software companies have developed trapping software that can save you time when applying trapping to a document. Creo leads the way with TrapWise (for OS 9.0 only) and Extensis offers Prinergy Evo for OS X users. Both of these programs possess complex interfaces, so a user manual is required. For Quark users, Dynagram offers an extension called INposition that allows trapping and imposition to be applied right in a Quark document. The cost of these applications is considerable, so unless you have a heavy workflow, it may not be worth purchasing them. As mentioned in the beginning of the chapter, your print provider may have in-RIP trapping capabilities in their Postscript software, so it is cheaper in the long-run to allow them to perform the trapping of your files.

Trapping software can save time on a large project, for example a brochure that is 84 pages. Trapping a project of this size item-by-item would take too long and your client would certainly not want to pay for it. So for those designers who are not so ambitious, or who want to spend their money on other things, it is often better to let the experts handle it.

SUMMARY

Even if you are not doing the actual trapping of your output document, being familiar with it is key to fully understanding the print production process. No matter what type of project you take on, it will become an issue at some point when you go to have it printed. Now that you have become familiar with trapping terminology, you can converse comfortably about trapping with prepress and print service providers and ask for the information you need. If you understand the basic principles in this chapter, you can make sure you never see misregistration lines in your printed piece.

▶ *in review*

1. Which color is usually overprinted in offset printing?

2. Where can you find out which color is the object and which is the underneath in Quark?

3. Explain the difference between a spread and a choke.

4. What do you need to do to create a knockout in Illustrator?

5. Where can you change the default trap allowance in Quark?

6. Which printing method has the largest trap tolerance?

7. What is the primary advantage of trapping software?

8. Which printing method often requires proportional trapping?

▶ *exercises*

1. To see the difference between the default and automatic trap setting in Quark, try this exercise. Open up a new QuarkXPress document. Open the Trapping Preferences and change the Auto Amount to 0.33 points. Click OK. Create two new Pantone® colors in the Colors dialogue box. Draw a square using the rectangle tool. Fill the box with the darker color. Inside the square, draw a circle and fill it with the lighter color. Open up the Trap Information palette. Select the circle and look at the default setting. What type of trap is it? Now take the trap off the default and set it manually to whatever the default trap was. Look at the number beside the information. What has changed?

2. Open up a new Illustrator document. Draw two objects with one of the drawing tools. Make the first color a mixture of process cyan and magenta and the second one a mixture of magenta and yellow. Place the first object over the second one. What's the common color in both objects? What type of trapping instance needs to be applied?

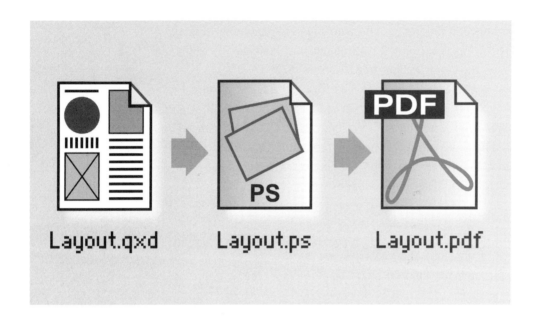

Layout.qxd   Layout.ps   Layout.pdf

CHAPTER 9

objectives

- Become familiar with Adobe Acrobat and the PDF format
- Produce a press-ready PDF file from Quark with Acrobat Distiller
- Produce a web or print-ready PDF file in Quark, InDesign, and Illustrator
- Discover how Pit Stop can edit a PDF file

introduction

The PDF file is a recent development in prepress that has revolutionized the way files are being imaged to film or directly to plate. Instead of simply being a method to send files across the internet, PDF has developed into a way to create a single file that contains all necessary output data. This chapter will examine the benefits and difficulties the prepress professional faces using PDF technology, as well as demonstrating the various ways of producing PDF files.

THE PDF REVOLUTION BEGINS

Adobe Systems created the technology behind the PDF in the early 1990s. You might remember from Chapter 1, PDF stands for portable document format. It was developed in response to a demand for a cross-platform file format. It was intended as a way that electronic documents would match the way they were imaged when printed. You can open a PDF file on a number of systems because all the fonts, images, color profiles, and other essential information are held within one file. Still, when the first version of Acrobat Reader came out, not everyone was quick to embrace it. For the most part, only business and government organizations purchased it, probably due to its expensive price tag. They saw it as a way to eliminate excessive use of paper from photocopiers and fax machines.

Adobe, however, recognized the potential for the graphics industry, and began distributing Acrobat Reader for free. They also started to incorporate PDF technology into their graphic design software, namely PageMaker. At the same time, Internet giants like Netscape and Microsoft began to integrate Acrobat plug-ins into their web browsers. Then Adobe introduced the PDF/X-1 standard in 1998, which caused the prepress industry to sit up and take notice. This format ensured that all graphic elements including fonts, high-resolution images, ICC color profiles, trims, bleeds, and trapping were consistently produced. The PDF revolution was gathering speed.

However, there were some drawbacks. Some of the Acrobat software like Distiller that created PDF files had not been perfected, so there was still some reluctance among design studios. Finally, when Illustrator 9.0 was launched in the first year of this century, Adobe decided to support PDF in this latest version of its popular drawing program. That decision paved the way for other software manufacturers to follow suit. When Quark introduced version 6.0 a few years ago, users could save print-ready PDF files directly in QuarkXPress without using Distiller.

Nowadays, the latest version of Acrobat has even better features such as preflighting capabilities, creation of separated files, layers, transparencies, a searchable database, better integration with workflow systems, and tools for editing RGB color definitions, hairlines and printer's mark, and much more. All these features have enormous implications for direct-to-plate imaging. Some day soon, imagesetters and film output may be extinct.

CREATING PRESS-QUALITY PDF FILES

If you plan on sending PDF files to print, the information they contain must be of a certain quality for press applications. Press-quality PDF files possess much higher resolution for printing purposes as well as embedded images. Acrobat Distiller is ideal for creating press-quality PDF files. However, you first need to print a Post-script version of your artwork file, since distiller will not generate a PDF file from a document created in a native application. The reason the term print is used is that you will set up your artwork document as if you were printing your file to an imagesetter. However, instead of an imagesetter, you will use the Adobe PDF printer description file.

Although you can print a postscript file from almost any program to run through Distiller, you will find that few of them produce a file that will image properly. In fact, a postscript file that is printed from Illustrator will not generate a press-quality PDF file from Distiller. It is not necessary to do this anyway. Later on, you will see how to create this type of file directly from Illustrator. For now, let's focus on the one program that does produce a postscript file that can be used.

Printing a PostScript File from Quark

QuarkXPress is an ideal program for printing PostScript files. As you know from Chapter 6, Quark has more options and flexibility for printing to output devices. The PostScript file you create must contain all the necessary data to allow Distiller to generate a press-quality PDF file. It is important that you set the print settings in Quark correctly, or Distiller will not properly image the PDF file. Follow the steps below to print a composite PostScript file from Quark.

1. Open the Quark file from which you want to create a PDF document.

2. Open the Print dialogue box (command/control-P).

3. In the Layout section of the Print window, select Registration On Centered from the Registration pop-up menu if you want registration and crop marks to appear at the edges of your PDF file (see figure 9 – 1).

4. Proceed to the next tab, which is Setup, and choose Adobe PDF for the printer description, with the correct page size and orientation. Do not reduce the document unless you have increased its size proportionally. Page positioning should be on Center (see figure 9 – 2).

5. In the Ouput section, leave the Print Colors on Composite and Halftoning on Conventional. Select the correct resolution for printing and the line screen frequency. In this example, 2400 dpi and 150 lpi are used (see figure 9 – 3).

6. In the Options tab, click on both the Quark Postscript Error Handler and the Full Resolution TIFF Output button. Make sure Data is set to binary if you are working on a MacIntosh (see figure 9 – 4).

7. Add the necessary bleeds into your document (see figure 9 – 5).

8. Click on the Page Setup button and in the window and in the Format For: pop-up menu choose Adobe PDF. Make sure you have the proper paper size (see figure 9–6). Leave the scaling at 100%.

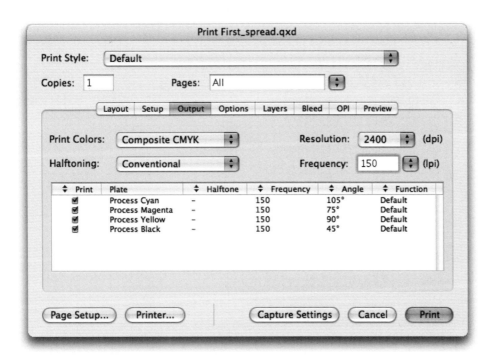

figure | 9 – 3 |

Set the resolution for imaging your film output.

9. Open the Print window by clicking on the Printer button and select Adobe PDF from the pop-up menu under Printer (see figure 9 – 7). Leave all other information the same unless your document requires it.

figure | 9 – 4 |

Data for working on a MacIntosh is always set to binary.

figure | 9–5 |

Don't forget to put bleeds in your artwork and set them for imaging the PDF.

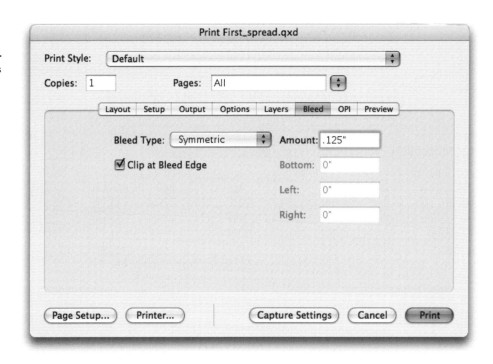

10. In the lower pop-up menu select Output Options and click on the Save File As button. Save the file as a postscript file (see figure 9–8).

11. Select PDF Options from the same pop-up menu as in step 10 and for Adobe PDF Settings choose Press Quality (see figure 9–9).

figure | 9–6 |

Select the proper paper size in the Page Setup window.

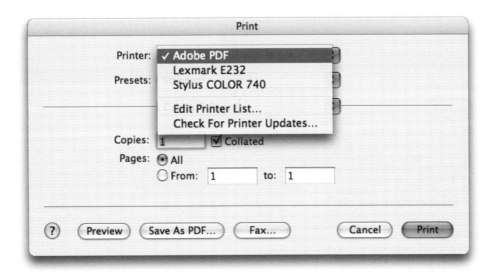

figure | 9 – 7 |

Choose Adobe PDF printer in the Print window.

12. In the pop-up menu select Printer Features and set the output resolution to the same value as in step 5. In this case it will be 2400 dpi (see figure 9 – 10).

13. Click on the Save button and save the postscript file to the desktop. Check to make sure the file is a proper postscript file. It should have a .ps extension at the end.

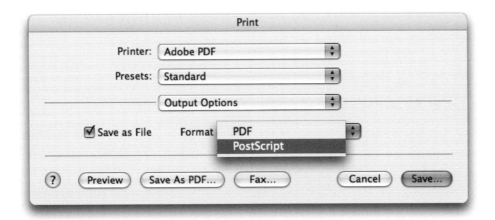

figure | 9 – 8 |

Click on the Save File As button under Output Options and choose Postscript from the pop-up menu.

figure | 9 – 9 |

Go to PDF options and
choose Press Quality.

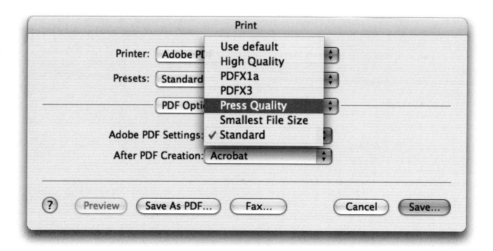

figure | 9 – 10 |

Set the output resolution
under Printer Features.

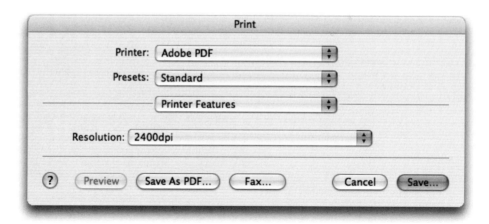

Generating a Press-ready PDF File in Distiller

Once you have printed the postscript file, the next step is to edit or create new PDF
settings in Distiller. These settings determine the complexity of the information that
will be enclosed in the PDF file. They also format the PDF file, so it can be imaged to
film or plates. Normally, you set these settings before you create your postscript file. It
is only if you are using the default settings in Distiller that this step is not necessary.

1. Launch Acrobat Distiller. Once the Distiller window appears, go under to the
   pop-up menu where it says Default Settings and choose Press Quality (figure 9 – 11).

If you wish to use the default settings, then you do not have to go any further in these steps.

2. Now go to the top menu bar and under Settings select Edit Adobe PDF settings (command/control-E) (figure 9 – 12).

3. In the window that appears under File Options, select the General tab and input the following settings (figure 9 – 13):

   a. Compatibility: **Acrobat 6.0 (PDF 1.4)**

   b. Object-Level Compression: **Tags Only**

   c. Auto-Rotate Pages: **Off**

   d. Binding: **Left**

   e. Change the settings in the Resolution field to whatever your laser dot output will be. It can be between 72 and 4000. In this example 2400 dpi is used.

   f. Deselect the Optimize for fast Web View box.

   g. Set the default page size large enough to accommodate your document.

4. Select the Images tab and input the following (figure 9 – 14):

   a. Color Images and Grayscale Images: Bicubic Downsampling to: **300** dpi for images above: **450** dpi

   b. Compression: **Automatic JPEG**

   c. Quality: **Maximum**

   d. Monochrome Bitmap Images: Bicubic Downsampling to: **1200** dpi for images above: **1800** dpi

   e. Compression: **CCITT Group 4**

   f. Anti-Alias to Gray: **Off**

5. In the Fonts section perform the following actions (figure 9 – 15):

   a. Click on the Embed All Fonts box.

   b. Subset Embedded Fonts When Percentage Of Characters Used Is Less Than: **100**%

   c. When Embedding Fails: **Cancel Job**

   d. For Embedding: Select **System** > **Library** > **Fonts** or another folder you want Distiller to read from. You can also choose to Always Embed or Never Embed fonts individually.

6. Select the Color tab (figure 9 – 16) and choose the following from the pop-up menus under Adobe Color Settings:

   a. Settings File: **U.S. Prepress Defaults**

   b. Color Management Policies: **Grayed Out**

   c. Working Spaces: **Grayed Out**

> ## Custom PDF Settings from a Printer
>
> If you are sending PDF files to a printing plant on a regular basis, you may ask the prepress manager if they have a settings file that is custom-made for the specification requirements of their presses. Most printers have such a file on an FTP server that can be readily downloaded. Once you have the file on your desktop, simply drag it into the Distiller window and the custom settings will appear in the Default Settings pop-up menu. Now you can use them at anytime to create a PDF file you are planning to send to your printer.

7. In the Device Dependent Data area, select the following:

    a. Preserve Under Color Removal and Black Generation: **On**

    b. When Transfer Functions are Found: **Apply**

    c. Preserve Halftone Information: **Off**

8. Leave the settings in the Advanced section unchanged unless you are an expert.

9. Also leave settings in the PDF/X section unchanged.

10. Click on the Save As or OK button and type in a custom name. Then click on Save (figure 9–17). The new name will appear in the Distiller window.

11. Locate the postscript file you want to distill and drag it into the Distiller window. A PDF file with the same name as your postscript file will be generated and placed on the desktop.

Creating Web and Print-ready PDF Files

Although Distiller is primarily used for creating press-quality PDF files, it can also be used to create web and print-quality files. It has a Smallest File Size and a Standard setting for this purpose. Print- and web-quality files contain images that are lower in resolution than press-quality files, normally 150 and 100 ppi respectively. Print-quality files usually have color management profiles for specific printers applied. The fonts are also embedded into these files. As well, the print resolution for a print-quality file is set at 1200 dpi. Web-quality files do not have fonts embedded and are not intended to be printed, so a resolution of 600 or even 300 is acceptable.

Manic Compression

The different types of compression in Distiller's PDF settings serve different purposes. If you want to apply compression to press-quality PDFs, use only JPEG with maximum quality for color and grayscale images. Although a lossy compression format, the compression ratio is low for this setting, so less color detail will be lost. Zip compression is also lossy, but Distiller does not allow you to alter the level of compression. This setting can be used if you have large areas of color or texture, but it's not recommended if you have high-resolution images as the loss in quality is too great. CCITT compression is used for one-bit images such as line art or maps. Since these elements are scanned in at four times the normal resolution, the bicubic downsampling must be between 1200 and 1800 dpi.

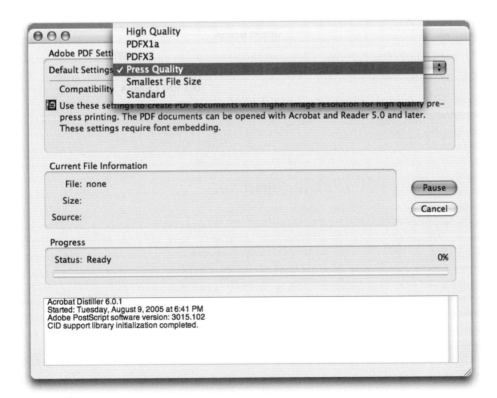

figure | 9 – 11 |

Choose Press Quality from the pop-up menu in the Distiller window.

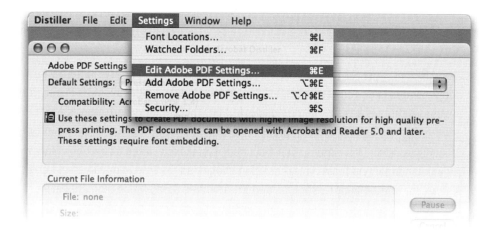

figure | 9 – 12 |

Open the Edit Adobe PDF settings window.

The procedure for creating files for these purposes is the same. However, it takes time to do it this way. A simpler way is to save them from within the application you are working in. Illustrator offers this option in the Save As window, while Quark and InDesign have a feature that allows a file to be exported to a PDF.

Print-quality PDF Files in Illustrator

It is quite easy to produce a standard print quality file in Illustrator. The steps below can also be used for a web- or press-quality file, with the settings adjusted accordingly.

1. Open an Illustrator document Go to File > Save As.

2. In the Save As window, choose Adobe PDF (pdf) from the pop-up menu (figure 9 – 18).

3. In the Adobe PDF Options window, select the General section and choose the latest version of Acrobat from the pop-up menu. Also select the boxes for Preserve Illustrator Editing Capabilities and Embed Page Thumbnails (figure 9 – 19).

figure | 9 – 13 |

Input these settings in the General section.

4. Go to the Compression section and set the resolution of the images to the following (figure 9 – 20):

   a. Color Images and Grayscale Images: Bicubic Downsampling to: **150** dpi for images above: **225** dpi

   b. Compression: **Automatic JPEG**

   c. Quality: **Medium**

   d. Monochrome Bitmap Images: Bicubic Downsampling to: **600** dpi for images above: **900** dpi

   e. Compression: **CCITT Group 4**

   f. Compress Text and Line Art: **On**

figure | 9 – 14 |

Input the correct
resolution for all your
images.

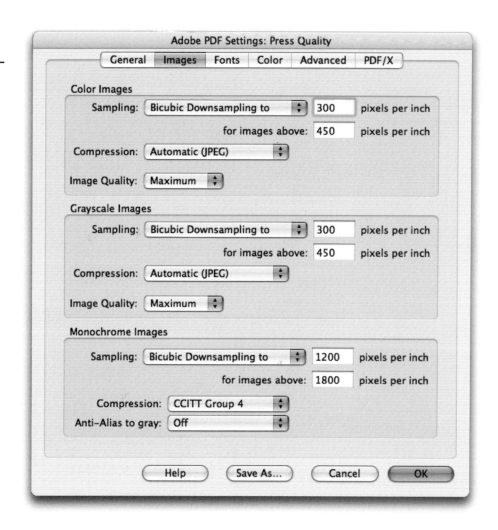

5. In the next section, Marks and Bleeds, select All Printers Marks only if you require them, otherwise, leave them off. The same goes for bleeds. Only put in values for top, bottom, left, or right if you need them.

6. Now click on the Save PDF button and save the file to a destination that is easy to find.

Press-ready PDF Files from InDesign

InDesign is another graphics software that allows you to create press-quality PDF files from within the application. Because the software is manufactured by Adobe, the steps are similar to those for creating these types of files in Illustrator.

1. Open an InDesign file. Go under the top menu to File > PDF Export Presets > [Press] (figure 9 – 21).

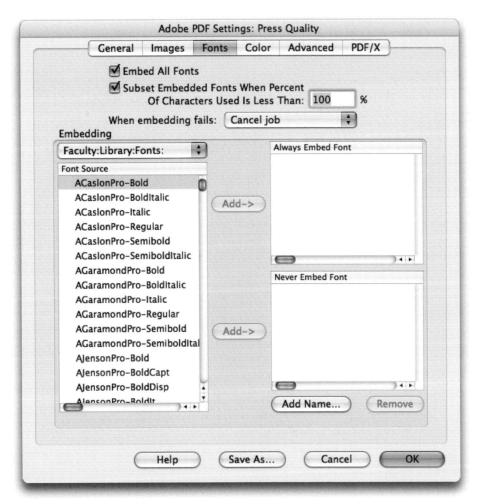

figure | 9 – 15 |

Make sure to select the correct font folder when embedding fonts.

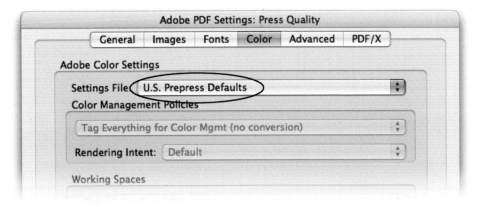

figure | 9 – 16 |

Make sure you select U.S. Prepress defaults for the setting.

Where Did the PDF File Go?

If you drop the postscript file into Distiller and you get an error message in the Distiller window that says that no PDF file was created, it is most likely due to a Postscript error in the file or a font did not embed. Common causes of Postscript errors in Quark are rotated picture or text boxes, embedded images, and horizontally or vertically flipped images. Remember, it is better to perform these tasks in the image's native program. Fonts do not embed if they are not activated on your system, or they are missing, or you haven't selected the right font folder in Distiller. If you get an error message in Distiller, then check these problems out and try again.

figure | 9 – 17 |

Name the PDF settings file you saved with a name that reflects its purpose.

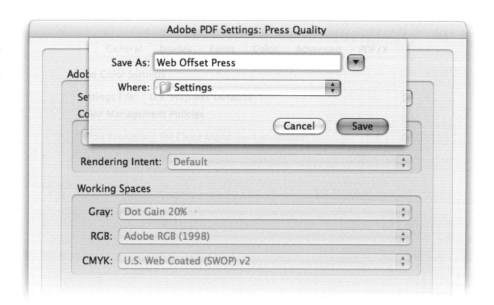

2. In the Export window, name the PDF file and click Save (figure 9 – 22).

3. A new window called Export PDF appears. In the General section, select the page range and click on spreads if you are printing more than one page. Under Options set the Compatibility to the latest version of Acrobat (figure 9 – 23).

4. In the Compression section, set the compression for the images the same as you did for the prepress-quality settings in Distiller (see figure 9 – 24).

5. Turn on Printer's Marks and input the necessary bleeds in the Marks and Bleeds section (figure 9 – 25).

figure | 9 – 18 |

Select Adobe PDF in the pop-up menu.

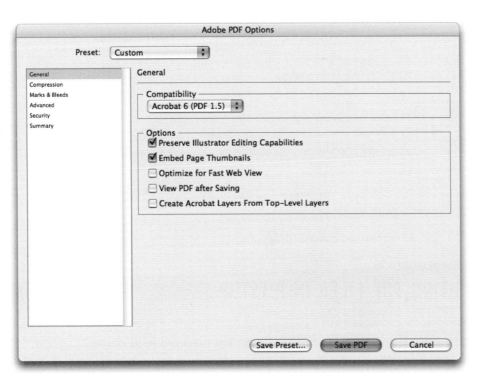

figure | 9 – 19 |

The Adobe PDF Options settings for print quality.

▶ **Editing a PDF File in Illustrator**

Illustrator is the only application that lets you make changes to a PDF file you create from the application. When you are saving a file as a PDF in Illustrator, simply click on the Preserve Illustrator Editing Capabilities box in the General section of the Adobe PDF Options window. You will then be able to open the file in Illustrator at any time and make changes to your artwork.

figure | 9 – 20 |

The Compression tab lets you determine the resolution of images and text.

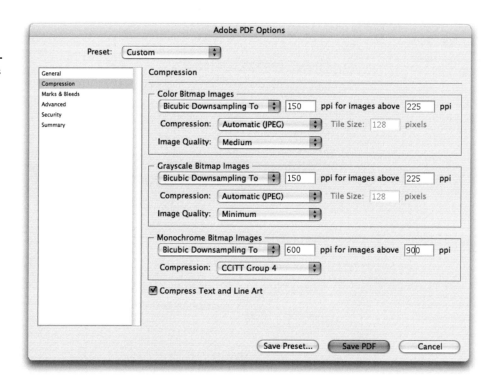

6. Select the CMYK for the color you are using in your PDF file in the Advanced section (figure 9 – 26).

7. Click the Export button when finished.

EDITING PDF FILES IN PITSTOP

After you have created your PDF file, you may want to edit afterward, particularly if you receive changes from a client. Although you can do limited editing of text and images in Acrobat thanks to an advance toolbox, you cannot create new objects or

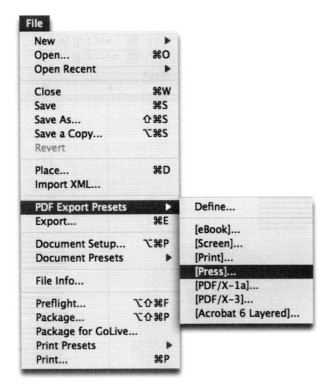

Choose [Press] from the PDF Export Presets.

modify existing ones. Luckily, Enfocus Software has a solution. PitStop is a very useful plug-in that allows you to perform sophisticated editing of your PDF files. The number of features, tools, and capabilities that it has are too numerous to mention here, so let's have a look at a few of them.

Name your PDF file.

PitStop Tools

The tools that let you create and manipulate objects are similar to those found in Illustrator. There is a Select Objects tool that permits you to select any object in your PDF file (see figure 9 – 27). The Select Similar Objects tool lets you choose multiple objects that possess the same attributes. Beside that tool, there is the Select Rectangular Area tool, which aids in selecting parts of objects (see figure 9 – 28). Select Polygon Area does much the same thing. Once you have an object or area selected, you can move, scale, rotate, and shear it using the tools in the Move Selection button (see figure 9 – 29). Under the same button menu, there is the Create New Rectangle and Create New Ellipse tool.

As far as adding or editing text goes, PitStop provides many options. You can edit text as a single line (vertically and horizontally), or in a paragraph using the Edit Text Line tool (see figure 9 – 30). You can also alter paths around objects using the Edit Path tools (see figure 9 – 31). With this tool you can add and remove anchor points

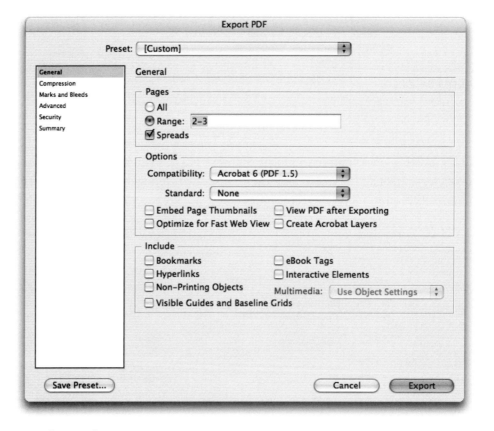

figure | 9 – 23 |

Input the pages you want to image. Click on Spreads if you want them to appear side-by-side.

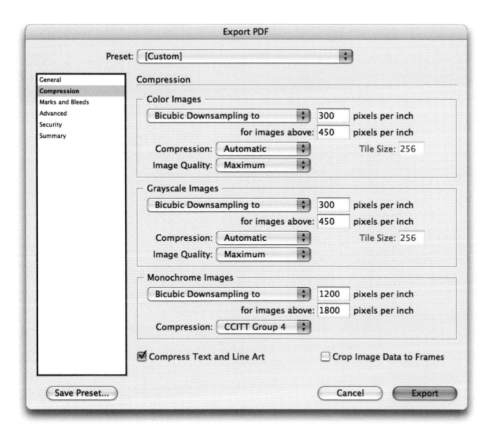

figure | 9 – 24 |

Ensure the compression and resolution of images is for press quality.

and create new paths. Beside that tool are the Eye Dropper tools, where you can select colors, copy and paste attributes, place guides, and measure objects (see figure 9 – 32). Each time you select one of these tools, a window appears that will give you specific information on each of these. Click on the tool icon on the page and the information appears. Like Illustrator, PitStop also lets you view your document in Page Boxes and Wireframe mode. If you are an accomplished Illustrator user, you will find the tools in PitStop a breeze to master.

PDF Preflight Panel

One of the most attractive features of PitStop is that it has its own preflight capabilities. You can check your document using the various print profiles by going to Window > Show PitStop Preflight. Besides editing profiles, you can add new ones, remove old ones, duplicate, and even password lock them. When you click

figure | 9 – 25 |

Turn on printer's marks and set bleeds.

on the Create Report button, a PDF file of all aspects and possible errors is generated (more on this in the next chapter). This feature will ensure your PDF file is correct before you output it to film.

Action Lists

A quick way to modify the way your PDF file will image when output is to use action lists. These are used to apply automated changes to color profiles, inks, and the format of your document. They are found under the top menu bar. Go to Window>Action List Control Panel. You can also add or remove lists, import and export them, and create reports.

There are many more features and tools in PitStop that can save you time and money. The last few pages should have provided a short overview of this valuable application. The demo version on the CD included with this book will show you how easy it is to modify your PDF documents using this convenient software.

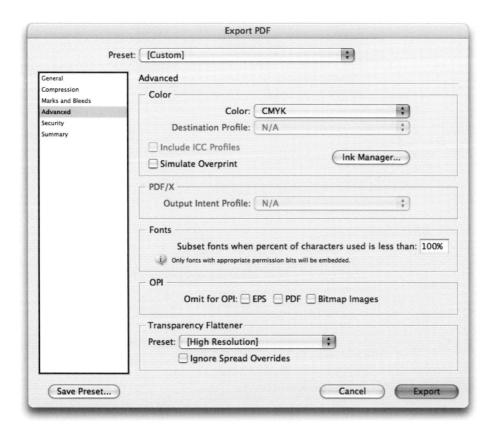

figure | 9 – 26 |

Choose CMYK for the color mode of your document.

figure | 9 – 27 |

Choose any object using the Select Object tool.

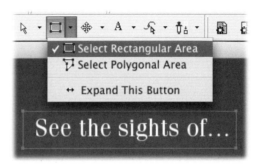

figure | 9 – 28 |

Select an area whose boundaries can be any shape.

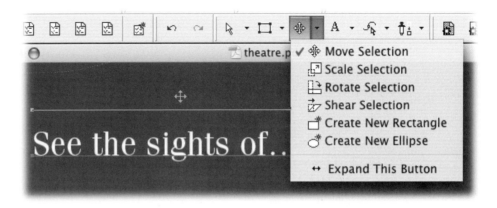

figure | 9 – 29 |

These tools allow you to modify that selection.

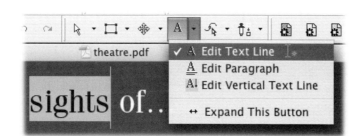

figure | 9 – 30 |

Edit or add text to your PDF document.

figure | 9 – 31 |

Create or alter a path around an object.

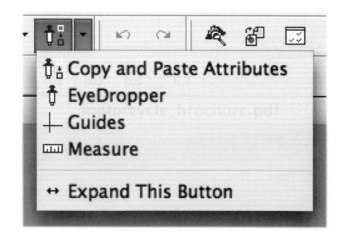

figure | 9 – 32 |

The eyedropper button has tools to change colors in an object, measure, or make guides.

SUMMARY

Twenty years ago no computer graphic artist would have believed you if you had told them that there would come a day when they would only send one file to be output to film. But there is no denying that PDF technology has become the norm. Printers are using it more and more to image plates with, recognizing the potential to accelerate their workflow. The new software that is being developed along with it makes it even more attractive to prepress professionals. Try the exercises at the end of this chapter to see for yourself how PDF files can benefit your workflow.

▶ *in review*

1. Which software programs now support Adobe Acrobat within the application?

2. What window lets you create a print-quality PDF in Illustrator?

3. What printer should you select when saving a postscript file in Quark?

4. What resolution do your CMYK and grayscale images have to be set at in a press-ready PDF file?

5. Where can you specify that you want your document printed out in seperations in InDesign?

6. What isn't embedded in a PDF file on the lowest quality setting?

7. Name the software that allows you to create a PDF file from a Postscript document.

8. Name three tools in PitStop that are similar to those found in Illustrator.

exercises

1. This exercise will help you see the difference in quality between a press-ready PDF file and one that is for web viewing, Open up an InDesign document. Go to File > PDF Export Presets > [Press]. In the Export window click Save. Look through the various sections of the Export PDF window. Click Cancel. Now go to File > PDF Export Presets > [Screen]. In the Export window click Save once again. Look through the sections of the Export PDF window once more. What differences do you notice?

2. Try this exercise to compare how information is saved differently in PDF files that are for different printers. Open up an Illustrator document. In the Presets pop-up menu, select [Illustrator Default] and choose the latest version of Acrobat in the General section. Now click Save PDF and save to your desktop. Open the original Illustrator document again and repeat the steps over again, but select [Press] from the Presets pop-up menu and change the name slightly. Make sure you select Printer's Marks from the Marks & Bleeds section. Click on both files and get the information for them (Command-I). Which file is larger in size? Do you know why?

3. Now try generating a PDF file from a Quark document. Open a Quark document that is prepared for print production. Follow the steps outlined in this chapter to save the file as a postscript file. Now open Distiller and change the default settings to press quality. Drop the postscript file into the Distiller window to generate the PDF file. Open the file after it appears on the desktop and check each plate carefully. Open the demo version of FlightCheck from the CD, and open the PDF file in FlightCheck and review the information contained in the various window. Are there many erors showing? How can you fix these errors?

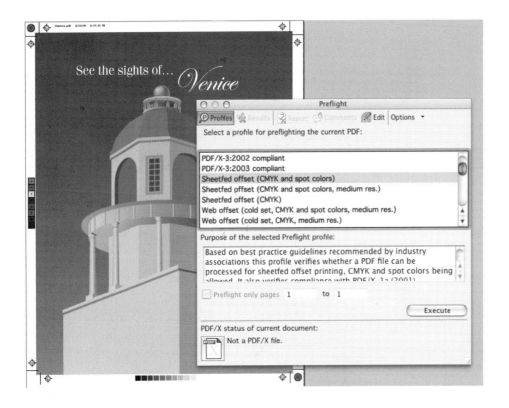

CHAPTER 10

objectives

- Recognize the importance of preflighting documents
- Examine documents carefully before sending them out for imaging to plates or film
- Discover how FlightCheck can speed up the checking of your documents
- Explore preflighting documents in Acrobat Reader using FlightCheck and PitStop

introduction

There are many components to each output file and the supporting files that go along with it. Each one is crucial to the film work being imaged correctly. As you have seen, formats and specifications for each file must be exact, otherwise your film will end up in the recycle bin. With all the information that a designer is required to know as well as the procedures they must take, the potential for errors to occur is enormous. Preflighting your artwork allows you to find these errors before going to the expense of making film or plates. Preflighting a file means that you are examining it to determine if it is ready for print. If you use preflight software to do this, it can give you specific information about the file, including the document's size, page setup, the number of and types of colors, fonts, resolution, and formats of all supporting files. This chapter will explain the necessary steps required to ensure files are output correctly.

SEEING IS BELIEVING: ENSURING YOUR FILES OUTPUT CORRECTLY

The last nine chapters have covered a lot of ground on the theoretical aspects of prepress as well as workflow systems and procedures. While this information will help you use your graphics software in a more productive way, it still leaves you wondering what steps you need to take to ensure your files will print out the way you want them to. Even if you are not using preflight software, you can manually check your document and supporting files to ensure your artwork is imaged correctly.

Once you begin working in the industry, you will quickly learn that plates and film work are expensive, and errors can cost you or your studio considerable dollars. However, if you carefully check your digital files, you will save yourself a lot of time, grief, and money. Here is a list that summarizes the steps you can take when preparing to output your files.

Manually Preflighting Your Artwork

Building Your Output File

When you are constructing the document you will use for outputting to final film, always use a layout program like QuarkXPress or InDesign. As you have seen, these documents interact better with imagesetters, filmsetters, and other output devices. They process through faster and have more functionality in terms of being able to define how you want your film imaged.

Confirm the Document Size is Correct

Make sure your document size equals the trim size of the printed piece you are producing. This way you can print with crop and registration marks turned on. Manual registration and crop marks are time consuming and unnecessary in most cases. The printer will also easily be able to tell where to trim the final printed piece.

Check the Color Model

Check your colors in the Edit Colors window. Make sure all the colors in your document are in a model that is suitable for prepress (i.e. CMYK or Pantone®, and not RGB, HSB, or LAB mode). Also check that all of the colors are set to different screen angles, especially if you have used Pantone® or spot colors.

Examine Your Fonts

Check the font usage and delete any fonts that are not applied to any text in your document. Unused fonts add additional memory to your document. Replace any missing fonts as well.

Check Your Pictures

Check the picture usage and click on the More Information box to ensure there are no missing or modified images. Also check thar they are in the proper mode (CMYK), in addition to being saved in the correct format (EPS or TIFF). Replace or update any images that are still in RGB mode.

Eliminate Embedded Images

Make sure your imported Illustrator EPS files do not contain placed images that will be embedded when imported into Quark (this includes templates you used to redraw items such as a logo). Embedded images often cause postscript crashes in imagesetters.

Apply Trapping

Trap all items in your layout and drawing programs using the methods outlined in Chapter 8. Make sure that items are not left on default trap unless you are having your service provider trap your document.

Proper Page Order

Check all the pages of your document carefully to make sure they are in proper order and there are no blank pages in the middle of your document. If you are producing a magazine, then leave the pages in reader spreads unless the service provider specifies otherwise.

Collect all Elements for Output

Use the Collect for Output feature in Quark or the Package feature in InDesign to ensure all supporting files, color profiles, and fonts are sent for film output.

Proof Your Document

Print laser separations of your file as well as a color proof. Proofread and spell-check each page carefully. It is a good idea to show the client a proof from the film work before going to press (see the next chapter).

> ## The Proof is in the Reading
>
> Proofread your document throughout each stage of the design phase through to the final prepress phase. It is easier to catch errors along the way than all at once. When you have proofread your final copy and are ready to send the files out for a proof to show the client, give it to a colleague or friend and have them proofread it again. A second pair of eyes may catch errors that you have overlooked. This will keep your boss happy and the studio's clients even happier.

By checking your files manually, you ensure that they are correctly prepared for the printing press. You can also rest easy knowing that the end product will come out the way you had envisioned it. As a designer starting out in the industry this is important. Your employers and their clients will soon see that you understand the prepress process and will entrust you to work on larger, more elaborate projects.

PREFLIGHTING DOCUMENTS BEFORE PRESS

If you feel the steps you have read seem like a lot of effort, especially if you have many documents to print, you can save yourself some time by using software to preflight them before sending them for film. In order to electronically preflight your files, you need to open them through a software program that will analyze them and report any errors. The report can vary in the amount of detail it provides, but the main areas that are checked are page formatting, colors, fonts, and images. To better see how this process works, take a look at one software program that can preflight files before the press stage.

FLIGHTCHECK

FlightCheck is a software program that can provide you with an accurate analysis of your native and supporting files, so errors can be corrected before valuable time and money is squandered. It is available from Markzware. This preflight application works with the major graphics software including QuarkXPress, Adobe InDesign, Illustrator, Acrobat, Photoshop, Macromedia Freehand, Microsoft Publisher and Word, and CorelDraw. It will even check postscript files.

When you open a file through FlightCheck, it generates an analysis of your document that shows information on the document's format, page setup, images, colors, fonts, profiles, trapping, and print specifications (see figure 10–1). Go to File > Open or click on the Open icon in the top menu bar and select the file you want to preflight. When the file is processed a Results window appears showing the data from the analysis of the file. Any area that has a green checkmark beside it is correctly set up for print production, while any area that has a red "X" beside it has at least one error that could cause the film to be imaged incorrectly. You can click on the triangles beside each area to see exactly where the error is occurring in the document.

An Overview window appears behind the Results window that gives more detailed information on color, fonts, and images used in your native file (see figure 10–2). Looking at the different components of a document that FlightCheck analyzes will assist you in recognizing what errors could occur in your own files.

Page Setup

In this area you can check to make sure the page size, orientation, and setup is correct (see figure 10–3). It will also warn you if the size of your document is being reduced in the Page Setup section. As mentioned previously, film must be imaged size at 100 percent, unless you have deliberately enlarged or reduced it and are scaling it back to be output at full size.

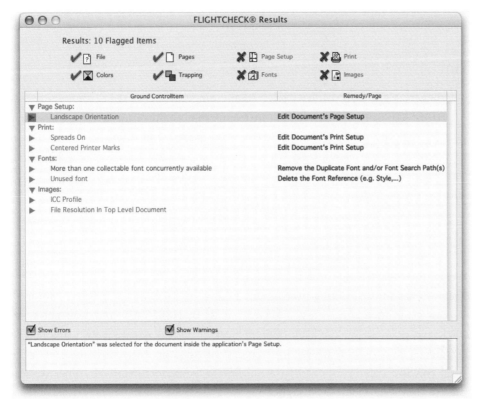

figure | 10–1 |

The FlightCheck Results window provides an overview of your document.

figure | 10 – 2 |

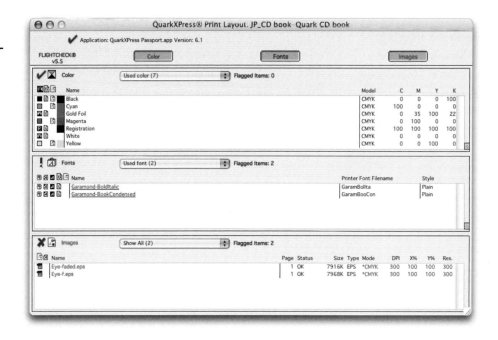

The Overview window shows more specific information on colors, fonts, and images.

figure | 10 – 3 |

Errors in page size, orientation, and setup can be viewed here.

Print

You will get a warning if you have selected anything unusual in your print window of your native application. Some of the problems that could occur are printing single pages as spreads, printing only odd or even pages, and tiling your document (see figure 10 – 4). In some cases these errors can be ignored, especially if you are planning to have a service provider print out the document and you have already indicated the format in your Output Request Form.

Colors

An error message will appear here if you have chosen to use color models that cannot be reproduced in the printing process (see figure 10 – 5). Only CMYK and Pantone® inks can be printed on a press. Convert all RGB, HSB, LAB, and web colors to CMYK and preflight the file again. FlightCheck also gives warnings for unnamed or mismatched colors (i.e. two Pantone® colors with slightly different names). As well, it tells you if a color is applied to a hairline in your document. Hairlines do not image to film well and often disappear.

Use the FlightCheck Shortcut Buttons

Rather than always using the top menu bar to perform certain functions in FlightCheck use the shortcut buttons underneath it. The buttons are there to give you faster access to common operations such as opening a document to check it for errors, adding documents to ones you have already checked, altering your settings and preferences, printing results, or performing a Collect for Output. This can save you a considerable amount of time if you have multiple documents to check.

figure | 10 – 4 |

The Print area of FlightCheck gives warnings on incorrect print descriptions.

figure | 10 – 5 |

Make sure your colors are in the CMYK or Pantone® model.

Fonts

This area displays warnings if there are problems with fonts in your document (see figure 10 – 6). An error message will appear if there are fonts missing from the system and therefore they are not being displayed correctly in your document, or if a font is applied to a space or cursor mark and not being used on any text. FlightCheck can also give you a warning message if you have used TrueType or system fonts instead of Postscript or OpenType. Go back to the native file and replace the font that is missing or remove the font that is not in use. This can be done through Font Usage in Quark.

Images

By looking through this area of the Results window, you can see a number of possible errors made when importing images into your layout document (see figure 10 – 7). FlightCheck gives a warning for the following image errors:

figure | 10 – 6 |

Replace any missing or unused fonts.

figure | 10 – 7 |

Errors in image format, mode, resolution, and color profile can be seen in this section.

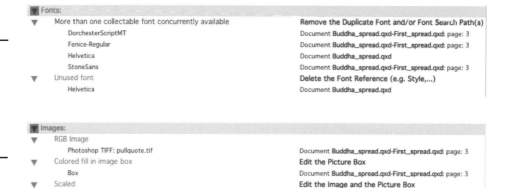

- If an image is left in either RGB, Index, or LAB mode
- When a color fill is used for the background of an image box instead of white
- If an image is scaled or rotated in the output document instead of its native program
- If any image files are missing or modified within the document
- When an image is saved in a format not suitable for prepress (i.e. JPEG, GIF, PICT, etc.)
- When the resolution of an image is too low for print production
- If an incorrect color profile is applied to the image.

These are all serious production errors that will affect the quality of your film. Remember to go back to the native program to effect any changes. In some cases where the image resolution is too low for instance, you will have to rescan the original continuous tone image.

After you have made changes to the image, you can rescan your document by going to the top menu and selecting Preflight > Show Image Folder. Select the folder where the images are located and open the supporting file. FlightCheck will rescan the output file and update the Overview window accordingly.

FlightCheck Preferences

You can alter the way FlightCheck displays information as well as the amount of information it shows you in the Preferences window. In the top menu bar, go to FlightCheck > Preferences or click on the Preferences icon. In the Preferences window (see figure 10 – 8), you can select or deselect buttons to get more information on images and fonts or add extended features. You can also add to a list of relative search paths for images and fonts or add to a list of file types that can be preflighted.

figure | 10 – 8 |

Use preferences to change the way FlightCheck displays the results.

Collect for Output

Once you are satisfied that your document is free of errors, you can use FlightCheck to collect all the various components in your document and save it to a folder on the desktop, in a similar way that Quark and InDesign do. After you have checked your file, go to the top menu bar and select Collect > Collect Job (command/control–J). In the Collect window (see figure 10 – 9), you can select if you want the files compressed, the type of files to be collected, and specifically which files you want to collect.

figure | 10 – 9 |

The Collect feature can place all your files for a job together so outputting is easier.

Choosing the Right Version

There are different variations of FlightCheck you can use depending on what your needs are. FlightCheck Professional is perhaps the most widely used by prepress professionals in the graphic arts industry. FlightCheck Designer is a lighter version that provides the same information as the professional one using less technical terminology. The program is mostly used by freelance designers, smaller studios, and service providers when they preflight files. FlightCheck Studio is perfect for larger studios and agencies where a standardized policy can be implemented and given to all the designers so that the results from the analysis are consistent with every job. For those companies, like publishers or printing firms, with much greater workflow requirements and those who wish to do batch processing of files, there is FlightCheck Workflow and FlightCheck Online.

If you plan to freelance and will be outputting your files for film, it is well worth your while to invest in the designer version of FlightCheck. There is a demo version on the CD included with this book for you to try out for 15 days. After trying the demo, you will soon be wondering how you ever got by without it.

PREFLIGHTING PDF FILES IN ACROBAT

As PDF technology is becoming more commonplace among printers and service providers for imaging digital files directly to plates, there is less emphasis on checking native documents and more emphasis on ensuring the PDF file is properly imaged. So it comes as no surprise that Adobe included a preflight function in the sixth version of Acrobat, which can provide a detailed report on your PDF document using a specific profile that matches the way your file was built.

When you open a press-quality PDF file in Acrobat, you can check the press quality of the document by using this pre-flight feature. Like FlightCheck, it checks the status of many aspects of your document including image resolution, fonts, and colors or plates that are being used. Open the PDF file you want to check and go to Advanced > Preflight. The Preflight feature uses a number of built-in profiles to do this (see figure 10 – 10). You can edit these profiles by clicking on the Edit button in the PreFlight window (see figure 10 – 11).

The Results Window

To obtain a general analysis of your document for an offset press, select the Sheetfed Offset (CMYK and spot colors) profile from the top and click on the Execute button. This will bring up a Results window that provides information on the PDF file (see figure 10 – 12). The window also provides an overview of the document in terms of how it is constructed, whether it contains embedded files, the color spaces used, type

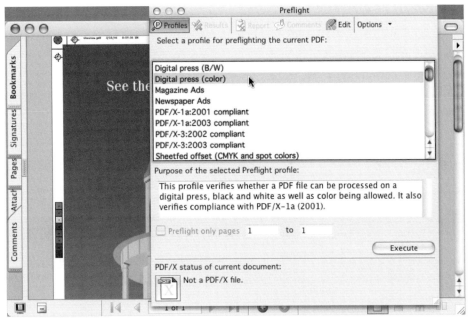

figure | 10 – 10 |

Obtain a complete preflight overview of your document by selecting the appropriate profile.

figure | 10 – 11 |

You may edit a particular profile to reflect certain criteria in your PDF document.

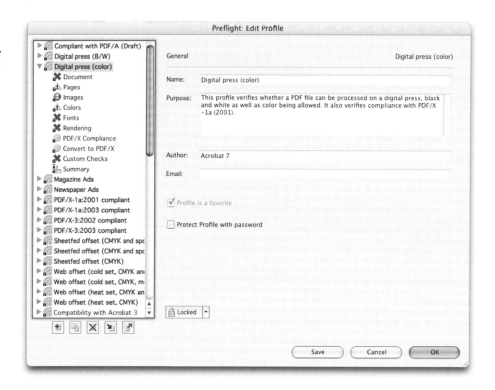

of fonts, information on images, and graphic properties (which includes trapping). Select Overview at the bottom of the Results window to see how it describes the information in the file.

Document Information

This area of the Preflight Results window shows you detailed information on your document including the version of PDF the file was created with, the name of the file, file size, title, author, the native program that created it, which program generated the PDF file, the date it was created and modified, and if trapping is applied. It also shows whether you have used layers or placed embedded files in it (see figure 10 – 13).

Color Spaces

Color spaces provides important data on the color components and profiles used in your PDF file (see figure 10 – 14). It shows the number of components (in this case four), the type of color space used by the data (CMYK), and the technical details of whatever color profile was applied to the document. Some aspects of the technical data for the color space include the profile version number, color space of data, the manufacturer and platform for which it was created, the profile creator, and creation

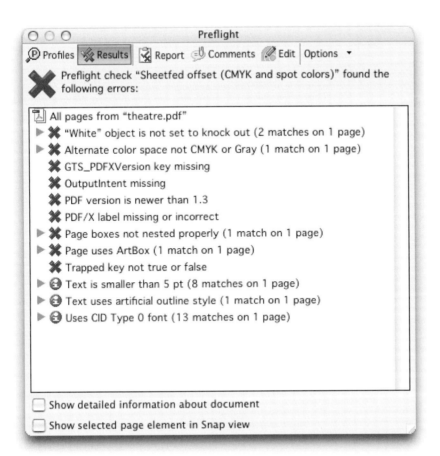

figure | 10 – 12 |

The Results window contains all pertinent information about your document.

figure | 10 – 13 |

Look under Document to see specific information on the construction of your PDF file.

figure | 10 – 14 |

Color spaces provides specific information on color profiles.

date. The Default Rendering Intent for most color profiles is set to Perceptual, which is calibrated for general reproduction of photographic images using standard printing methods. The Profile Illuminant refers to the profile's white point that is plotted using an *X, Y, Z* axis in the CIE L*A*B color model. In addition, there is a profile description that shows for what type of printing it is calibrated.

Fonts

You can see what type of fonts you are using in your system in this section of the Results window. Look at the font icons to determine this (see figure 10 – 15). In this case, they are Postscript type 1 fonts.

> ## Previewing Plates in Acrobat
>
> Like InDesign, Acrobat allows you to preview your separations when you have created a composite PDF file. Go under the top menu bar to Advanced > Separation Preview. The Separation Preview window opens allowing you to see each plate individually. Click off the button in the left side of any of the ink plates you do not want to see. This method if useful if you have spot or Pantone® colors you want to preview to ensure they are in the document.

▼ 魚 Fonts
    ▶ 魚 Type 1 font
    ▶ 魚 Type 1 font
    ▶ 魚 Type 1 font

figure | 10 – 15 |

Look at the font icon to see what type of font is embedded in your PDF file.

Images

In this section you can view details on the configuration of the images embedded in the PDF document (see figure 10 – 16). The results include width and height of the image, bit-depth, whether there is a mask, or if the image has been scaled (interpolated). It also shows the color profile information for that specific image using the same criteria discussed previously under color spaces.

Graphic State Properties

Graphic state properties apply to any object contained in the PDF document. This part of the Results window shows you if any of your objects have an overprint fill or stroke applied to them, which indicates if a trapping instance is applied (see figure 10 – 17). It also provides information on blends you may have used on the objects in your PDF document and if there are any clipping masks. There is a separate graphic state property for each type of object within your document.

Page Information

This area provides information on how your document is constructed. It shows you the size of the document in terms of page size, trim size of document, bleed area, and also shows the number of individual plates (see figure 10 – 18).

Flattening Transparencies

Occasionally you may have a vector image that is not printing properly in Acrobat. This may be because it has a transparency applied to one or more objects in the vector image. Using transparencies can often cause problems when a native document is saved as a postscript file and used to generate the PDF file. In order for it to print correctly, you need to flatten the image. This will change it into a raster image that can be printed. Select Advance > Preview Transparency from the top menu bar. Click on the Refresh button when the Flattener Preview window appears. Slide the arrow in the Flattener Settings toward the left (raster) until the image is flattened enough to print correctly.

▼ Images
   ▼ Images
      ◇ Width: 1446
      ◇ Height: 938
      ◇ Bits per color component: 8
      ◇ Treated as a mask: False
      ◇ Perform interpolation: False
    ▶ ◇ Encoder/Decoder filters
    ▼ ICC based color space
      ▶ ◇ Components range
      ◇ Number of color components: 4
      ▼ ◇ Alternate color space
         DeviceCMYK color space
      ▼ ◇ ICC profile data
         ◇ Profile version number: "2.1.0"
         ◇ Color Management Module (CMM) type: "ADBE"
         ◇ Profile/Device class signature: "Output Device profile (prtr)"
         ◇ Color space of data: "cmyk data (CMYK)"
         ◇ Profile Connection Space (PCS): "Lab data (Lab)"
         ◇ Magic number: "acsp"
         ◇ Primary Platform: "Apple Computer, Inc. (APPL)"
         ◇ Device manufacturer: "Adobe Systems Incorporated (ADBE)"
         ◇ Device model: ""
         ◇ Profile creator: "Adobe Systems Incorporated (ADBE)"
         ◇ Creation date: "07/26/2000, 05:41:53"
         ◇ Default rendering intent: Perceptual
       ▶ ◇ Profile illuminant
         ◇ Copyright information: "Copyright 2000 Adobe Systems, Inc."
         ◇ Profile description: "U.S. Web Coated (SWOP) v2"

figure | 10 – 16 |

The Images section will show you relevant data on how your images are configured.

▼ 🖳 Graphic state properties
   ▼ 🖳 Graphic state properties
      ◇ Stroke adjustment: False
      ◇ Smoothness: 0.020004
      ◇ Overprint mode: 1
      ◇ Overprint for stroke: True
      ◇ Overprint for fill: True
   ▼ 🖳 Graphic state properties
      ◇ Stroke adjustment: False
      ◇ Smoothness: 0.020004
      ◇ Overprint mode: 1
      ◇ Overprint for stroke: False
      ◇ Overprint for fill: False

figure | 10 – 17 |

Graphic state properties check for trapping on objects in your PDF file.

▼ 📄 **Pages**
  ▼ 📄 Page : 1
    ▼ 📑 Page information
      ▼ ◇ MediaBox (assumed media size)
        ◇ 0.000000
        ◇ 0.000000
        ◇ 612.000000
        ◇ 792.000000
      ▼ ◇ CropBox (Clipping region in viewer): inherited from MediaBox
        ◇ 0.000000
        ◇ 0.000000
        ◇ 612.000000
        ◇ 792.000000
      ▼ ◇ ArtBox (Partial page area for positioning): Inherited from CropBox
        ◇ 0.000000
        ◇ 0.000000
        ◇ 612.000000
        ◇ 792.000000
      ▼ ◇ TrimBox (Size of trimmed page): Present
        ◇ 136.512009
        ◇ 56.484009
        ◇ 475.488037
        ◇ 735.516052
      ▼ ◇ BleedBox (Bleed area): Present
        ◇ 130.512009
        ◇ 50.484009
        ◇ 481.488037
        ◇ 741.516052
      ◇ Page rotation value: 0
      ◇ Thumbnail: Not present
      ◇ Annotations: Not present
      ◇ Additional actions: Not present
      ◇ Page is a separated plate: No
      ▼ ◇ Plates
        ◇ Number of plates: 4
        ◇ Names of plates: "(Cyan) (Magenta) (Yellow) (Black) "

figure | 10 – 18 |

The Pages section shows how the document is built.

Preflight Information

This last section shows you when the preflight took place. It also shows on what system the original file was created, and which version of Acrobat was used in creating the preflight report (see figure 10 – 19).

▼ Preflight information
  Preflight, 7.0.5 (106)
  Date: 2/15/06 8:46 PM
  User name: Reid Anderson
  Computer name: Faculty Computer
  Operating system: Mac OS X 10.3.9
  Acrobat version: 7.05
  Duration of Preflight analysis: "00:00:01"

figure | 10 – 19 |

The Preflight Information section shows where and when the check took place.

Although FlightCheck can give you an analysis of your PDF document, you might as well save yourself some time and perform the check using the Preflight feature in Acrobat. When you start to work in the graphics industry, you may have a job that requires you to make a lot of PDF files. In that case, you will be grateful for this feature.

Comments

Another way to view preflight information on your PDF file is to click on the Comments button in the Results window. This places markers with comments around your document where there are problem areas. Just click on one of these markers to open a Comments palette and view the comments for that part of your document (see figure 10 – 20). You can see all the comments for your PDF file by clicking on the Options Arrow in the Comments palette and select Show Comments List. In the Comments List window, you can review each comment one-by-one.

PREFLIGHT WITH PITSTOP

If you have PitStop installed on your system, then you can also use it to preflight your PDF files before outputting them. The Enfocus PDF Profile Control Panel will create a report of your PDF file outlining any potential problems with fonts, colors, image resolution, bleeds, page layout requirements, etc. (see figure 10 – 21). Open this panel by going to Window > PitStop Preflight Panel.

When the window first opens, select a profile that reflects how your document was built (i.e. how many colors it has and how it will be printed or published) from the menu on the left (see figure 10 – 22). In the Checking tab, click on the Regular Preflight button or click on the Certified Preflight button if you want. Then select the pages you want to check, or the entire document. The next tab is the Managing

figure | 10 – 20 |

A Comments palette allows you to review comments relating to specific parts of your PDF document.

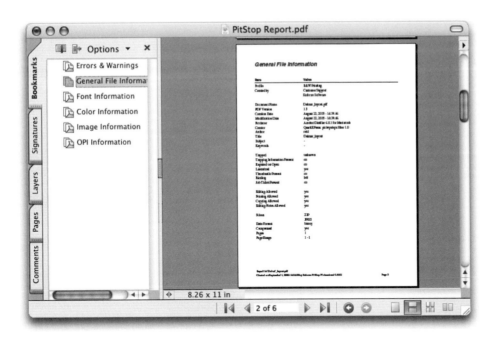

figure | 10 – 21 |

A PitStop Report lets you check various components in your PDF file.

section, which lets you create a new profile or edit an existing one, and import or export a profile. As well, you can enter a profile name along with the author's name, and lock the profile with a password (see figure 10 – 23). Lastly, in the description tab section, you can view the PDF profile description (see figure 10 – 24).

figure | 10 – 22 |

Select a profile that describes the way your document is constructed.

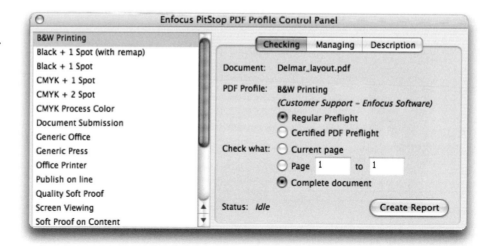

figure | 10 – 23 |

The Managing section allows you to make changes to the profiles.

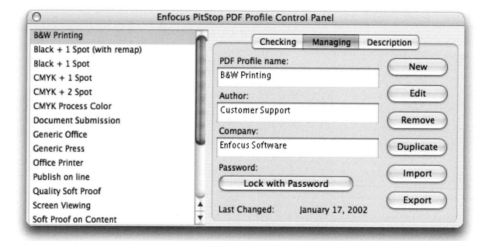

figure | 10 – 24 |

View details of your profile in the Description section.

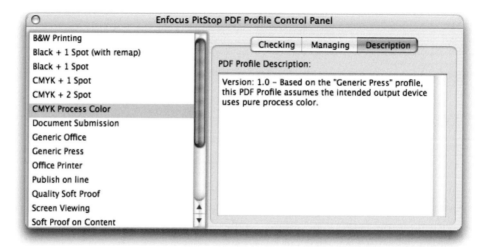

SUMMARY

Preflighting is a necessity if you are producing artwork for printing. Every file that is going to press requires careful checking before being sent to a service provider for imaging to film or plates. You can use the manual method outlined in the beginning of this chapter or purchase software that can perform the check for you. Either way, get in the habit of routinely preflighting your digital files. Once you become accustomed to the steps necessary to ensure artwork is imaged correctly, you will be able to do it in your sleep.

▶ *in review*

1. Why do we preflight files in the first place?

2. Under what menu do you need to go to preview separations in Adobe Acrobat?

3. Name three parts of your digital file you would check when manually preflighting it before it is sent out for imaging to film or plates.

4. What other function does FlightCheck do besides preflighting a file?

5. What are the main areas of an output document that preflight software performs an analysis of?

6. How can you flatten vector images with transparencies applied in a PDF file?

7. Which other type of software performs a check of your PDF files?

8. When is the best time to proofread your document?

▶ exercises

1. Try performing a manual preflight on a document. Open up a Quark document that you are planning to send for output. Go to Utilities > Usage. Click on the tab for Pictures. Click the More Information box and then select one of the images. What type of information is displayed? Now repeat the steps for the Fonts tab. What is different about the information displayed for this section of the Usage window?

2. Now try the Preflight feature in Acrobat Professional. Open up the press-quality Acrobat PDF file that you created from Illustrator in Exercise 2 from the previous Chapter. Go to Advanced > Preflight to open the Preflight Profiles window. Select the List Images not CMYK profile and click the Execute button. Did any errors show up in the Results window? What can you do to correct these errors?

CHAPTER 11

objectives

- Examine the difference between analog and digital proofing methods
- Explore soft proofing of digital artwork files
- Recognize the difference between dylux, color keys, laminates, and digital proofs
- Discover the advantages of digital proofing in direct-to-plate printing

introduction

As far back as the early years of the graphic design industry, agencies and studios became aware of the importance of proofing artwork before running a job on press. The need to show clients how their project would look became more apparent as four-color artwork began to appear in magazines in the late 1800s. Although early proofing methods were not as precise as today's, they were still a necessary step in the approval of artwork.

Seeing is Believing

As we discussed in Chapter 2, once you have preflighted your artwork and have received your film work back from the service provider, you are ready to have the client sign off on a proof of the film work. This step is necessary before going to press since the client has only seen a comprehensive presentation so far and needs to know that the printed piece will be what they are expecting. Having the client sign-off on the proof limits your liability if there are errors in the artwork.

There are a number of methods of producing a proof that you can use depending on the color accuracy required, budget allowance, and type of job. These methods fall into two basic categories: analog and digital. This chapter will explain the various proofing methods and discuss the advantages and disadvantages of each. In addition, some alternatives to proofing from film will be looked at including soft proofing and inkjet or color laser proofs.

ANALOG PROOFING METHODS

All these types of proofing methods use actual film work to image the proof. Because of this, analog proofing is also referred to as contact proofing. In most cases, the film must be placed against the proofing material inside a vacuum frame and exposed to light, so each method requires a certain amount of set up time. If you have many film negatives in your artwork these types of proofs can be expensive. Let's review some of the analog methods that are still in use today.

Dylux or Bluelines

These types of proofs go by many different names, but blueline and dylux are the most common. It is the least expensive proof available, which is probably why it is so popular. A dylux proof is produced by exposing photosensitive paper to ultraviolet light (see figure 11–1). The paper itself is yellowish in color, and will turn blue when exposed to the light source. To create the image on the paper, the film negative is placed on top of it in the bed of a vacuum frame and then exposed to light for about fifteen seconds. After one film plate has been exposed, another one is placed over the paper. This plate must be properly registered with the previous plate, and given a longer exposure. By varying the exposure times for each plate, the different inks become noticeable in the proof, as the tones on the paper get darker with more exposure to light.

Dylux proofs are best for proofing jobs that don't have many plates, like two- or three-color jobs. They are infrequently used to proof artwork that will be printed in four-color process. This is mostly due to the monochromatic nature of this type of proof. In a dylux, the difference between the inks becomes less noticeable as the number of plates increases. Another disadvantage is that they can fade over time, particularly if the room they are kept in has fluorescent lights. If you can plan to keep dylux proofs around for a while, then place them in a safe dry environment away from light. Otherwise they will turn completely blue very quickly.

Dyluxes are useful for proofreading, checking color breaks, and binding of signatures. Obviously, they are not practical for proofing colors, so soft proof your artwork to make sure your colors are correct (more about this later on in the chapter). Also bear in mind that your client may not be accustomed to viewing artwork in a monochromatic way, so they might not notice errors as easily as if the proof was in color. Still, for the cost-conscious client, bluelines provide a reasonable facsimile of the final printed piece.

figure | 11 – 1 |

A dylux is a monochromatic proof from film negatives.

Color Keys

When you want to show your client a proof that depicts differences in color and that looks closer to the printed piece, then a color key is an economical alternative.

figure | 11 – 2 |

A color key uses four acetates in each of the process colors to produce a color proof.

A color key proof is made by taping four CMYK acetate gels onto a white backing stock. The acetates must be aligned so they are in registration (see figure 11 – 2). Each acetate gel is imaged from one of the four-color process plates using a vacuum frame and exposing it to UV light. They are then run through a processor that removes the ink on the surface of the acetate that was not exposed.

> ▶ # Proofing Your Trapping
>
> Using a color key to proof your artwork allows you to check the trapping on your document as well. Since color keys use transparent acetates overlaid on top of one another, they are ideally suited for this purpose. By separating an acetate away from the others, it is easy to determine whether a swell, choke, knockout, or overprint of black has been used where two colors meet.

Although this method is accurate for checking the position of elements and overall color definition, it is not good if you want to show your client accurate color corrections. The thickness of the gel acetates makes any images you have in your artwork appear darker than they actually are. As well, the processing of the gels sometimes leaves too much or too little of the color on the gel, affecting the balance of the process colors. Another drawback of color key proofs is that Pantone® or spot colors cannot be shown in a color key, as there are no gels available in these colors. This can be a problem if you use any special inks in your artwork. An acetate for these inks can be imaged from one of the four process colors, but then your proof will not be accurate when you show it to your client.

Color keys are considered to be a medium-priced proof. If you are looking for more precise color matching or have special colors in your piece, then it is probably better to go with a more expensive and elaborate proof.

Laminates

These types of proofs are also imaged from film negatives and are made by laminating micro thin gels together onto a thick paper sheet (see figure 11–3). They are used when you require a more accurate representation of the color in your artwork. They can include Pantone® or special inks, but only by converting them to CMYK first. This can sometimes pose a problem if you are using metallic or fluorescent inks in your design. Laminates tend to be mostly used by designers when a job is being printed with more than two ink systems, usually a job that is in four-color process with one or two special inks.

Like other analog proofs, they do not show dot gain, so images will appear clearer than in the final press proof. However, the colors in a laminate proof are considered to be the closest to press quality as they are laminated onto a glossy paper. Laminates are also called PressMatch proofs, which is Agfa's trade name for their lamination process.

figure | 11 – 3 |

A laminate is a contact proof where gels are attached to a white backing card. See color insert.

The types of machines that produce laminates vary in terms of resolution and accuracy, so it's a good idea to check with your service provider about what type of equipment they are using before ordering a laminate proof. Certain laminating machines can also print onto special stock, so your proof will look even closer to the printed piece. They can also be useful for three-dimensional mock-ups for packaging and other prototypes where the proof sheet may need to be folded. Make sure you score the back of the sheet first, so the gels will not crack when the sheet is bent. Laminate proofs are more expensive than color keys.

> ## The Right Proof
>
> Consider all aspects of a job when determining what type of proof you want to order. Cost is an important factor, but do not sacrifice quality for it. The proof must represent the artwork clearly, so the client is aware of what they are getting. Still, if you are producing a one-color job and show the client an expensive laminate, be prepared to absorb some of the cost if they complain about your bill. Follow the suggestions made in the description of each type of proof as a guideline if you are unsure.

Cromalins

Cromalins are also known as dry powder proofs as they use inks in the form of powders to create an image. A photopolymer substance is laminated onto a thin white cardboard sheet and exposed to light through negative film. The exposed areas will harden so the laminate can be peeled back. The uncovered areas are tacky and any ink applied to these areas will adhere to the surface of the paper. The process is repeated over again for each color. Once all the colors have been applied, a final laminate is used to protect the underlying inks. One drawback of cromalins was that the top laminate tended to dry out and crack over time if it was not stored properly. This could prove to be frustrating to a design studio as cromalins cost more than laminates. They are the most expensive type of proof.

The primary advantage that cromalins have over other analog methods is that the inks come in different models including Pantone® and Toyo®. You can also print metallic or florescent inks using this method. They used to be very popular with designers for this reason, as well as the fact that the cardboard stock was ideal for making mockups for packaging. Nowadays, cromalins are not frequently used due to the nature of the ink powders and the increasing popularity of digital proofs.

DIGITAL PROOFING METHODS

As clients are demanding faster turnaround times, computer-to-plate printing has become the norm for most design studios and agencies. Hence, the traditional analog methods of proofing are gradually becoming obsolete. Many service providers do not even carry the materials to make color keys anymore. If you are using CTP technology, then you will need to use a digital proofing method rather than the analog ones described in the last few pages.

Digital proofs are made directly from the electronic file, without film or plate separations. If you have ever printed out your files to a color laser printer or inkjet, then you have already seen an example of a digital proof. However, some of these proofs are considered to be acceptable only for presentation, and do not always have colors that are accurate enough for press-quality comparison. The majority of inkjet printers compose images using continuous tones of color instead of halftone screens. Also, inkjet printers compose images using continuous tones of color instead of halftone screens. This can be problematic since many of the colors they print will be out of the normal gamut range for printing inks (see Chapter 2). If you want more exact color representation as well as exact halftone screening, then more complex proofing equipment must be used as well as color profiles that exactly match the output device. Having a look at the different types will assist you in selecting a method that best suits your needs.

Digital Plotters

Digital plotters fall into two categories: inkjet and raster. The first type operates in the same way that smaller inkjet printers do. Inkjet plotters can produce up to eight colors in a proof using a similar process to inkjets, where solid bars of process colors are melted into a well and sprayed through a nozzle onto the surface of the paper (see figure 11–4). Raster plotters print artwork by means of plotted dots with a medium resolution. They can be imaged either in color or as a monochromatic proof, which bear similarity to a dylux proof.

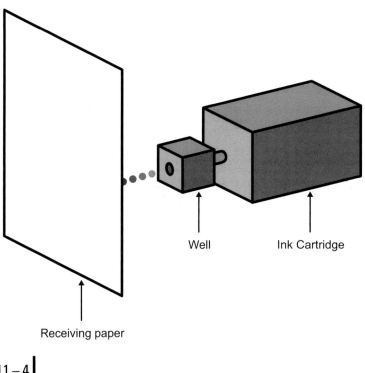

Well   Ink Cartridge

Receiving paper

figure | 11 – 4 |

Inkjet printers use a spray process to transfer ink onto paper.

Many of these plotters are capable of printing on two sides of a large roll of paper up to 42 inches wide. This makes them ideal for checking file imposition on signatures with a number of spreads on them and ensuring that they are collated properly for binding. Advances in inkjet technology also allow the inkjet proofs to be used for checking color quality as the manufacturers have integrated color management into software used to RIP files through the digital plotter.

Dye-sublimations

This type of proofing equipment has become very popular with designers who want a quick proof of how their artwork will look. Dye-subs produce an image on paper by way of transparent rolls of film that embed the various colored dyes onto the paper by way of a heating process. The dye for each color is heated to a certain temperature, turns gaseous, and then spreads onto the surface of the paper. The higher the temperature, the more dye adheres to the surface of the paper.

Unfortunately, dye-subs also use a continuous tone process to reproduce images in the artwork, which does not give close enough color matching for press conditions. They also do not reproduce images in sufficient resolution compared to that of digital proofers. However, they are relatively inexpensive and print the proofs very quickly, hence their popularity.

In the last few years, laser sublimation proofers, a close cousin of dye-subs, have appeared on the market and are considered to reproduce colors close to those of analog proofing systems. They print colors in much the same way as the dye sublimation system, but use a dot screen pattern that simulates the rosette screen pattern produced by the traditional film process. Because of this, laser sublimation proofers RIP files much slower than dye-subs, yet produce results that are far closer to press quality. Most service providers will offer their customers this type of sublimation proofing because of the superior quality.

Both kinds of sublimation proofers have color management capabilities that allow them to accurately print files with ICC color profiles applied to them. This makes them advantageous compared to many other types of proofing systems.

Thermal Wax

Like laser printers, thermal wax printers also use halftone dot screens to reproduce a photographic image. The inner mechanics of these printers contain a colored wax ribbon for each of the process inks. As the paper is fed through the printer, a heated printer head melts the ink onto the paper. The process colors must be printed one at a time to produce a full-color proof. They are generally faster then inkjet printers, and produce results that are closer to press standards. Like dye-subs, they can also print on different stocks of paper so are ideal for jobs where you want to show your client a proof that closely resembles the final printed piece.

Laser Printers

Although many of the early laser printer models did not have PostScript capabilities, currently nearly all laser printers are PostScript enabled. As you know from reading the first chapter, this means that they possess built-in translators that are capable of rendering complex graphics, including EPS image files, from a digital artwork file. However, they are limited in the way they reproduce halftone images as the line screen for this type of printer ranges from 60 to 106 lpi.

Laser printers work by creating an electrostatic image on the surface of the paper and then adhering toner onto it. In the case of a color laser printer, this process is repeated four times for each of the four process colors. Most laser printers print a four-color image to a separate plate before placing it onto the paper. However, the more complex ones have a separate drum head and toner cartridge for each color.

The price range for these types of printers differs greatly, mainly because there are a variety of models and some are more complex than others. On one hand, there are simple black and white lasers, and on the other there are high-end color laser printers with separate RIP software. Most color laser printers are considered acceptable for proofing text and overall position of elements on a page, but are not reliable for color proofing. Laser printers do not interpret Pantone® or special inks accurately as they simulate them with process colors in much the same way laminates do. Still, laser printers are helpful for creating presentations and print much faster than inkjet printers. The ink cartridges are also cheaper than the ones used for inkjets.

One type of proof that is very useful in determining if colors and inks are ascribed correctly to various elements in your artwork is a black and white separated laser proof. To print a separated proof from InDesign, perform the following:

1. Open your artwork document file and select File > Print from the top menu bar.
2. In the Output section of the Print window, select Separations from the pop-up menu (see figure 11 – 5).
3. Set the line screen frequency to the highest level for the printer you have selected.
4. Go to the Marks and Bleed section and click on All Printer's Marks box (see figure 11 – 6). Add any necessary bleeds if you have them in your document.
5. Click on the Print button.

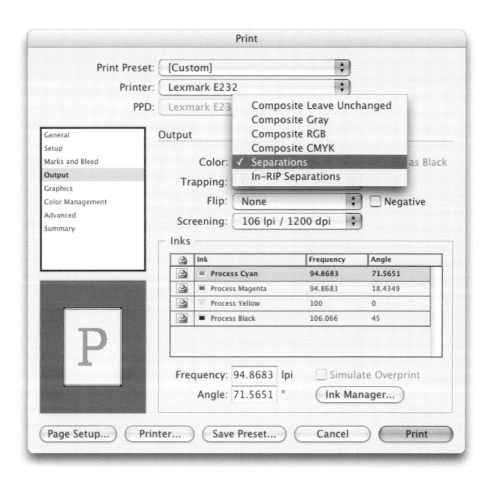

figure | 11 – 5 |

Select Separations from the pop-up menu to print a laser separation proof.

Laser printers can provide a good overview of page layout, color definition, and image resolution. However, they should not be used for proofing for accuracy of color, or if trapping is present, and do not show imperfections such as moiré patterns.

CHECKING YOUR PROOFS

Like press approvals, it is a good idea to look your proofs over before showing them to your client. This helps to avoid costly changes to the printing plates. It is also necessary to ensure that the press run will not be interrupted if errors are noticed at this stage.

1. Check the proof against any laser prints you made to make sure all elements such as text, images, lines, and other objects are showing up and are correctly placed (i.e. no images are missing, no fonts have defaulted to Courier, etc.).

2. Proofread all copy one more time to make sure there are no errors before showing it to your client.

figure | 11 – 6 |

Add printer's marks to the printout of your document such as crop marks and registration marks. Make sure you allow for bleeds if they are in your document.

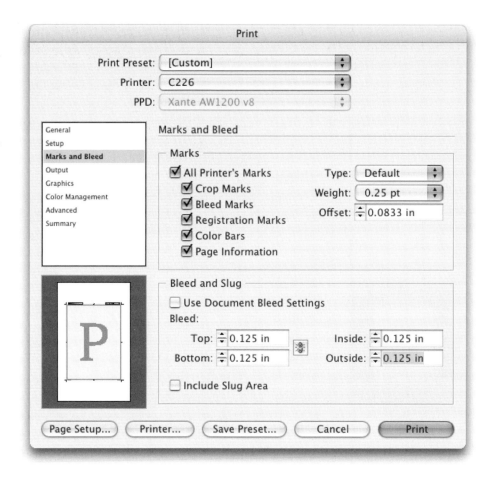

3. Check the trim size of the artwork to make sure it is correct. Occasionally, proofs are accidentally enlarged or reduced in size when output. Because of the configuration of the line screens for the halftone images, film cannot be enlarged or reduced once it has been output.

4. If it is an analog proof, check the color bars on the proof. Make sure the colors are correct and in the proper mode. Also check the trapping of colors, which will be visible on this type of proof.

5. Examine the proof to see if there are scratches or dust marks. If it is an analog proof, then check to make sure these imperfections are not on the film itself. You will want to reprint the proof if the marks detract from the quality of the proof.

SOFT PROOFING

There are times when you may want to preview how the color and images in your artwork will print while you are still working on it. This could be a PDF file

> ## Loading a Custom Profile
>
> Ask your printer if they have a custom profile that is calibrated for their presses. If they do, then simply have them e-mail it to you and drop it into the Profile folder. Apply it as you would with any other custom profile. This way you can soft proof your images so you know what they will look like when printed on their presses.

that you are planning to send to a client, or even a Photoshop file placed in a program like InDesign. If you don't preview the file using the correct profile before making a proof, you may end up wasting time and paper. By following a few simple steps, you can achieve color results that are close to those that will be realized when the job is printed.

Soft Proofing in Photoshop

When Adobe introduced Photoshop 6.0, there was a sigh of relief from designers and prepress experts across the continent. It was the first time that they could preview their Photoshop images with specific profiles. This made life easier for many who found it frustrating that the way their color printouts looked varied depending on what type of peripheral device they used. These days, all peripheral devices such as digital cameras, monitors, scanners, and printers come with software that allows you to apply a profile that is synchronized with the device itself.

Apple has also come a long way in providing numerous built-in color profiles for different presses printing on a variety of paper, as well as profiles for various output devices in the OS X library folder. These are used for most of the hardware that comes with the OS X operating system. A drag and drop approach can also be used to add new profiles to this folder.

However, even applying the correct profile will not ensure that your colors are displaying correctly. Actually, the first step in soft proofing documents on your system is to calibrate your monitor (see Chapter 3). Without a correctly calibrated monitor, the colors in your images will still look different than when you print the document out. The target white point of your calibration should be set for standard graphics work, so it should be set at 5,000 K. If you use the quick calibration method, then you would select D50 in the Target White Point area of the Display Calibrator Assistant window. Once you have done this, you are ready to preview the soft proof of the artwork on your monitor.

figure | 11 – 7 |

Choose View > Proof
Setup > Working CMYK
to quickly soft proof how
RGB colors will translate
into CMYK.

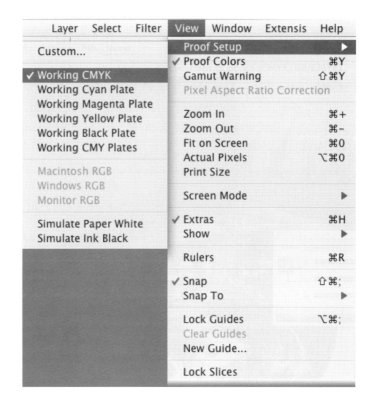

Proof Setup

Photoshop makes it easy for you to soft proof colors using profiles that are made for
different press conditions and devices. You can soft proof using one of the built-in profiles
that comes with OS X, such as working CMYK (see figure 11 – 7), or choose a custom one.

1. Launch the Photoshop application.

2. Go to View > Proof Colors (command/control-Y).

3. Now go to View > Proof Setup and select Custom. You can select a profile for an
   RGB or CMYK or grayscale device, a color printer, your monitor, or a specific press.

4. In the Proof Setup window, select a custom profile that matches the device to
   which you will be outputting your document (see figure 11 – 8a). If you cannot
   find a profile that matches your printer, then select the one that matches your
   monitor (see figure 11 – 8b).

5. Click on the Preserve Color Numbers checkbox (see figure 11 – 9). This lets you see
   how your document will look if you send the document to the output device
   without converting it. It also shows you how different profiles will appear when
   they are sent to different output devices. However, in order for it to work, both your
   document and your output profile have to be in the same color mode. Deselect the
   Preserve Color Numbers checkbox once you have finished previewing your image.

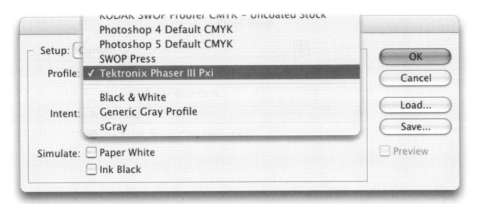

figure | 11 – 8a |

Select a profile for the printer that will be outputting your document in the Proof Setup window.

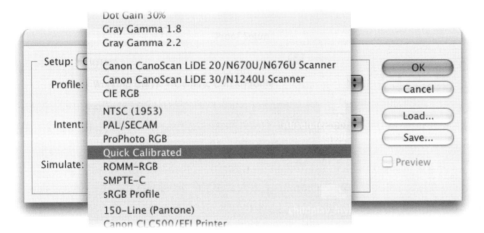

figure | 11 – 8b |

Choose View > Proof Setup > Working CMYK to quickly soft proof how RGB colors will translate into CMYK.

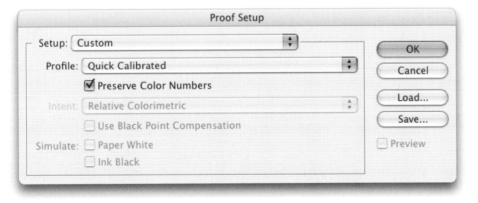

figure | 11 – 9 |

Click on the Preserve Color Numbers box to see how the document will look if it is printed without the new custom profile applied. Deselect the box after previewing.

6. In the Intent pop-up menu, select either Relative Colorimetric or Perceptual (see figure 11 – 10). If you want your printer to produce all the colors it is capable of, then select the first one. However, if there are colors in your image that do not fall into the range of gamut for your printer, banding may begin

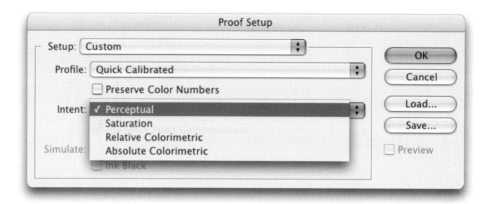

Different Rendering Intents affect the gamut range of colors that can be produced on the selected printer.

to appear when you print them out. Perceptual rendering compresses the gamut of the image, so if there are colors that are not within your printer's range, the printer will substitute the next closest color. This eliminates any banding showing up in your printout.

7. Click on the Black Point Compensation if you want the density of black in an image you see on your monitor to match the black when it is printed on your output device (see figure 11 – 11). The black you see on your monitor is usually darker than what you see in a print due to the screen's luminosity. Some professionals recommend leaving this button unchecked, although most graphic

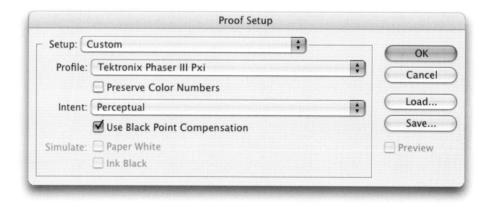

Black Point Compensation matches the density of black shown on a monitor with the color printout.

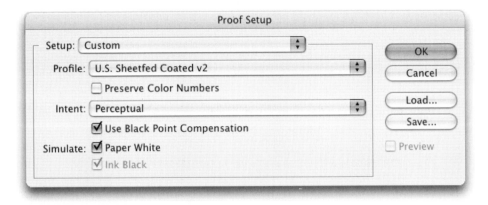

figure | 11 – 12 |

The Paper White checkbox will show you on your monitor how black will look when printed.

artists leave the Black Point Compensation turned on. Try printing out some test sheets from your printer and decide for yourself.

8. Checking the Paper White box will change the rendering intent to Absolute Colorimetric (see figure 11 – 12). This matches the density of the black ink to what you see on your monitor. Be aware that selecting this box causes the black in the image to dim somewhat to match the print on the output device.

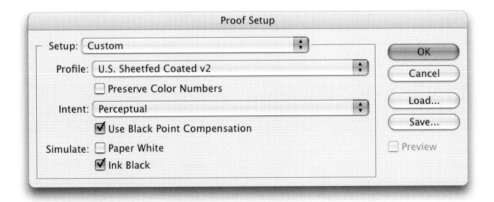

figure | 11 – 13 |

The Ink Black checkbox indicates how dense the black will appear on the paper stock on which it is being printed.

What's Your Intent?

When choosing a profile in the Proof Setup window, try different rendering intents to see which one works best for each profile you select. Absolute Colorimetric or Relative Colorimetric work best when you want the proof to match a specific output device or working space. Relative Colorimetric and Perceptual usually produce better results when you are converting images from RGB to CMYK.

9. The Ink Black box shows you how dense the black will appear on the type of paper on which you are printing (see figure 11–13). However, if you select the Paper White box, then the Ink Black box will be grayed out. There are only a few profiles that can render both of these at the same time.

10. If you want to save your profile, then click on the Save button on the right hand side of the Proof Setup window.

Soft Proofing in Acrobat

Adobe Acrobat also allows you to soft proof your artwork in much the same way as you would in Photoshop. You might recall that when you create a PDF file, you embed color profiles in your document. These profiles will be used to manage color when the PDF file is RIPped through the platesetter. However, these profiles may not display those colors correctly on screen, particularly if you send them to someone whose monitor is calibrated differently than yours. You should always check the colors in your PDF file before sending it for printing. After you have created your PDF document, open it up and follow these steps:

1. In the top menu bar, select Advanced > Output Preview (see figure 11–14).

2. In the Simulation Profile pop-up menu, choose the profile that matches how the artwork will be printed (see figure 11–15).

3. Click on either the Simulate Ink Black (see figure 11–16a) or Simulate Paper White (see figure 11–16b). The effects of these settings are described earlier in the section on soft proofing Photoshop images.

4. Clicking on the Ink Manager button will bring up a window that allows you to change the densities of the various inks used in your PDF document (see figure 11–17). This affects the inks in both the profile preview and in the separation process.

figure | 11 – 14 |

The Output Preview function lets you soft proof Acrobat files.

5. You can select which types of colors you want to preview in your document by clicking on the Show pop-up menu and scrolling down the list (see figure 11 – 18).

6. Select Color Warnings and click on the Show Overprinting button to see which colors in your document may be overprinting. This includes blended colors and transparency effects. Click on the Rich Black button if you want to check areas where black may be mixed with other inks (see figure 11 – 19). This shows problem areas where the total coverage of all the inks exceeds 400 percent and will become oversaturated when printed.

7. The Total Area Coverage box allows you to see what effects will take place if you change your ink coverage limit for all the plates in your PDF document. The pop-up menu lets you select from a number of preset numbers (see figure 11 – 20).

Soft proofing in Acrobat is easy and well worth the time spent. If your printer uses a workflow that applies color profiles to PDF files before RIPping them through their platesetter, then you may not need to worry about embedding color profiles in Acrobat documents. Still, you should preview the colors to make sure they meet your design criteria.

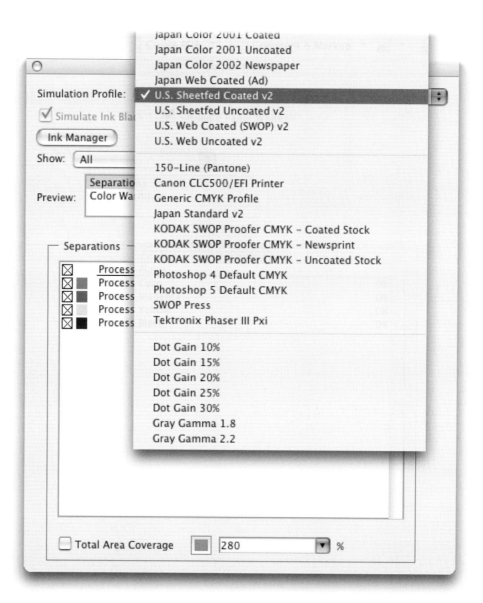

figure | 11 – 15 |

Select a profile that matches how the PDF file will be output.

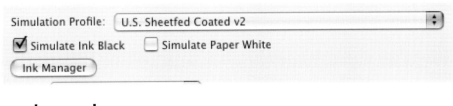

figure | 11 – 16a |

Click on Simulate Ink Black to see how the black ink will look as defined by the profile.

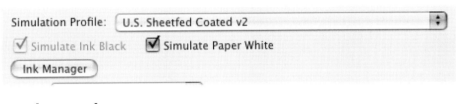

figure | 11 – 16b |

Simulate Paper White shows how ink will look on the paper stock associated with the profile.

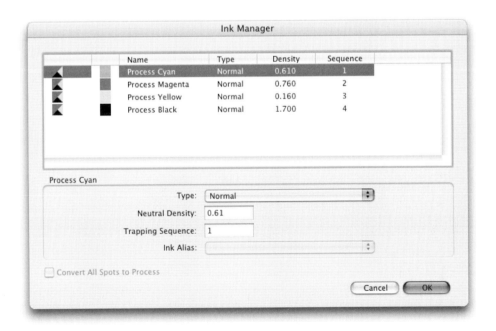

figure | 11 – 17 |

The Ink Manager window lets you change how inks are viewed and how they will print out in separations.

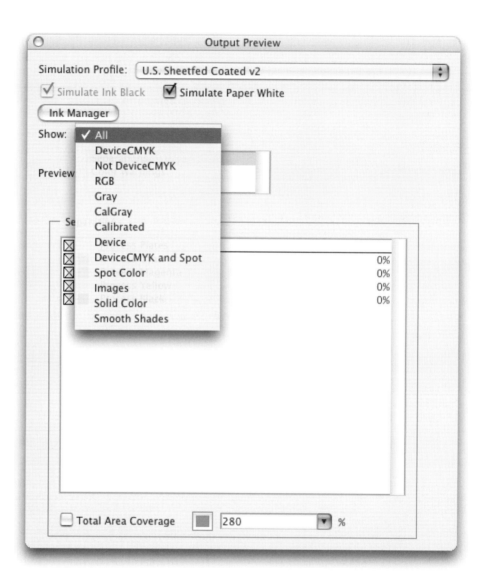

figure | 11 – 18 |

Select specific color models you want to preview.

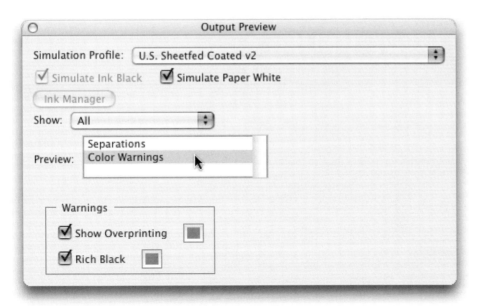

figure | 11 – 19 |

Color warnings alert you to possible overprinting of colors and over-saturation errors.

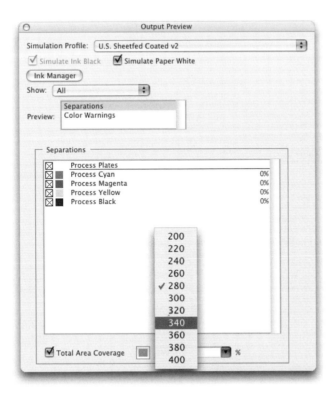

figure | 11 – 20 |

Total Area Coverage lets you change the amount of total ink limit in the PDF file.

THE *professional* PROFILE *David Hunter*

THE PROOF IS IN THE PROFILE

David Hunter began his career working for Aldus Corporation as a Regional Manager before starting his own consulting firm, Pilot Marketing, in 1994. As an expert in color management, David has worked with a number of high profile clients such as Ford, Apple Cupertino, Radius Corporation, Xerox, Imation, LightSource, and Ameritech. He provides his clients with training and software solutions to achieve outstanding color from their printers and proofing devices. He is also an instructor at the Graphic Arts Technical Foundation in Pittsburgh.

David is a firm believer in using a variety of applications as well as color profiles to achieve accurate results when proofing from various output devices. "A user needs multiple additional software programs to achieve better color accuracy. For instance, a user needs profiling software to create ICC Profiles that define how their devices reproduce color," he states. "Depending upon their workflow software, they may need a RIP to drive their inkjet proofing device, and the RIP provides the 'proofing conversion' that makes the inkjet simulate the actual printing condition. They may also want to consider proof verification software that verifies that the proof is matching the color that it is supposed to be matching," he concludes.

As for which proofers are the ideal for the small design shop, David believes that Epson is the leader, although Canon and HP also make very good devices for high-end digital proofing. He recommends embedding Apple's Color-Sync profile into each document and also using third-party calibration software like Monaco Optix Pro or GretagMacBeth EyeOne Display2 to properly calibrate your monitor before soft proofing your work. David advises his clients to always use a target when creating a profile for a specific device. "The idea behind a profile is to define the gamut or range of color for a given device. To do this, we must test how the device handles color. The target determines this," he explains. "The targets for a scanner, digital camera, monitor, and printer are all different, and there are reasons to use certain targets in specific combinations." He offers free profile targets for downloading on Pilot Marketing's web site.

Graphic designers who want to gain a complete understanding of color management can take a course, such as ColorSync Management, which he co-teaches at the GATF in Pennsylvania. There are also a number of courses offered at other community colleges and universities across the U.S. and Canada. He offers this advice to designers who are beginning their careers: "Learn everything you can about the print production process, because the industry has been compressing over the past ten years, and that trend will continue. The more a designer understands how to take advantage of the print process, the better their jobs will turn out, and it will make for happier customers." ◄

SUMMARY

You now have all the information you need to produce superior proofs. There are many options available for proofing your artwork before the film and plate making stage. Each one has its benefits and drawbacks, so choose carefully. Remember that your client will be expecting to see a printed piece that closely matches the proof they signed off on. So the proof must be imaged to reflect the actual press conditions. Make sure the text on the proof is clear and easy to read. This will help the client proofread it and give the signoff more credibility in case of errors.

▶ *in review*

1. What is the difference between an analog and digital proof?

2. Explain the process behind the making of a color key.

3. Name three types of digital proofs and list an advantage for each one.

4. Name one reason you should soft proof your files.

5. How do you soft proof an image in Photoshop?

6. How do inkjet printers create an image on paper?

7. What does the Black Point Compensation box show you in the Proof Setup window of Photoshop?

8. List four things you need to check in an analog proof.

▶ *exercises*

1. Let's see how different color profiles affect the output quality of an image. Open up a Photoshop document that you have color corrected in RGB. Go to View > Proof Colors (command/control-Y). Next open up the Proof Setup window by going to View > Proof Setup > Custom. Under the Profile pop-up menu, try selecting various profiles for different printers, presses, and working spaces. What changes do you notice in the image when the different profiles are applied?

2. Now, try soft proofing colors in Acrobat. Open up the press-quality Acrobat PDF file that you created from Illustrator in Chapter 9. Go to Advanced > Output Preview. Select the U.S. Sheetfed Coated v2 profile form the Simulation Profile pop-up menu. Now click on the Simulate Paper White box. What changes do you notice in the white clipboard area surrounding your artwork?

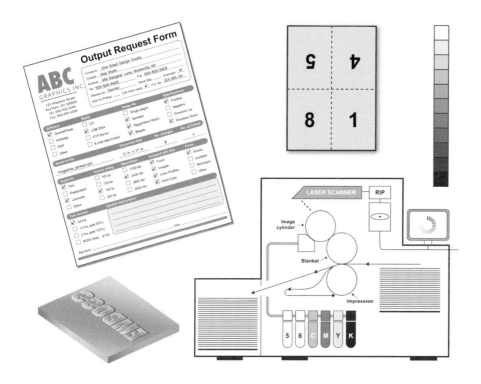

CHAPTER 12

objectives

- Describe the traditional methods of printing
- Explain how digital printing works
- Prepare an output request form
- Discover what to look for at the press approval stage

introduction

If you have been paying close attention and taking notes over the last eleven chapters, then you must be wondering, "If I do everything I am supposed to, then it should all turn out correctly on the press, right?" Well, theoretically yes, but there is still a possibility for errors to occur. There are many variables that occur during the press run that can affect the quality of your artwork. Besides human error, and press operators are only human, there is the actual press machinery, the inks used in printing, the environment in the plant itself, as well as the stock on which you are printing. Any variance or change in these factors could alter the finished piece. The prepress-savvy designer recognizes this and takes steps to ensure the final outcome is what they were expecting. A designer who is knowledgeable about printing has a definite edge. They can foresee problems arising while they are constructing their document as well as knowing which printing process, or combination of printing processes, will give them the look they are after. This chapter will help to demystify the printing process and help you achieve the best results possible.

THE PRINTING PROCESS

Once you have your film work completed, you are ready to hand it over to your printer. At this point, you will probably be asking yourself, "What happens after I receive the film back from my service provider? What am I still responsible for? Is it okay to leave it all up to my printer once the film or plates are done?" These are good questions that really depend on the printer and the type of press used to run your job. So to start answering them, let's begin by looking at different printing processes.

Letterpress

Letterpress printing is based upon the same mechanics as Guttenberg's movable type press. Originally, metal letterforms and other graphics were affixed to one side of a platen-type press, which was like an oversized clapboard. The letterforms were inked and then brought together with the other side of the press carrying the paper. Eventually, the press was modified so that the paper was placed on a flat bed cylinder and transferred to a revolving impression cylinder that carried the paper. The press bed carrying the inked letterforms would move back and forth and the pressure would leave an impression from the ink (see figure 12–1). Aside from some

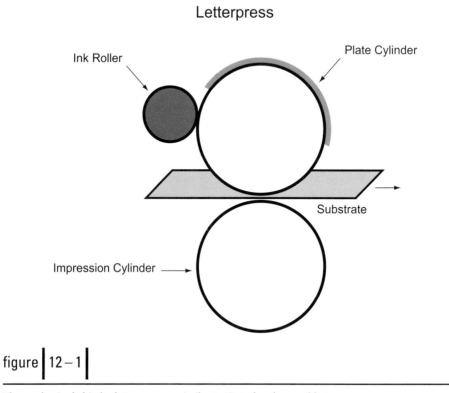

Letterpress

figure | 12–1 |

The mechanics behind a letterpress are similar to Gutenberg's movable type press.

museums and independent printers, letterpress printing is rarely used these days. It has been replaced by a much faster and more precise method.

Offset Printing

An offset press uses a similar method of printing as letterpress with one distinct difference. The basic principle behind offset printing is the same as lithography, which was invented sometime in the late 1500s. In early lithography, an artist drew an image onto a smooth wet limestone surface with something that resembled a greased pencil. A piece of paper was applied evenly to the surface. The image had to be in reverse (wrong reading) so that when it is applied to the paper it would be correct. That is right reading. The idea is that water and oil don't mix, so the stone transferred the image to the paper. Offset works in a similar way in that ink is transferred from the plates on a roller onto an impression cylinder and then back onto a sheet of paper or cardboard (see figure 12–2). However, offset printing no longer requires a water process. Ultra thin metal plates have made this unnecessary.

There are two types of offset presses. The first is a sheet-fed press and the other is a web offset press. The first one is used for printing single sheets of paper such as letterhead, cartons, or brochures. The second one is used for larger runs where large rolls of paper are required, for instance newspapers, catalogs, or magazines. Web offset presses run at very high speeds, so registration allowances for traps and bleeds are greater. However, dot gain is less on an offset press, due to the thinner plates. Most graphic arts work is printed on these types of presses.

SWOP

If you have applied color profiles to your documents while reading this book, then you have probably come across this term. It stands for Specifications for Web Offset Publications. It represents standard printing conditions used in the graphic arts industry. The different SWOP profiles you select when color managing a document (such as SWOP coated, uncoated, and newsprint) reflect the various papers used in offset printing. Each specification is configured differently due to four factors: the tolerances of the press (sheet-fed or web), the amount of dot gain, whether UCR or GCR is used, and the total ink limit. A SWOP profile is useful in proofing files before going to press; however, most print providers like to apply a profile that is custom made for their presses.

Flexography

This type of printing is often used for packaging, specifically corrugated board, foil, and plastics. Originally, a high-density rubber plate was attached to a cylinder with

figure | 12 – 2 |

The image is transferred onto a blanket cylinder first and then to an impression cylinder in offset printing.

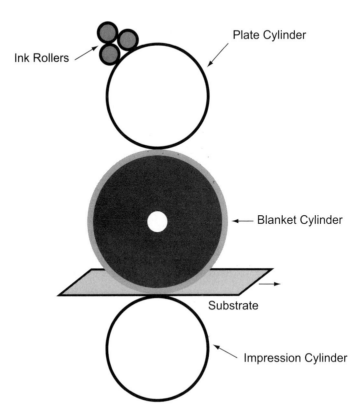

Offset Press

Plate Cylinder

Ink Rollers

Blanket Cylinder

Substrate

Impression Cylinder

the substrate material fed through an impression cylinder (see figure 12 – 3). An Anilox and Fountain roller carry the ink to the rubber plate cylinder. After the substrate passes through the plate and impression cylinders, a dryer then dries the ink. The ink contains a solvent that allows for immediate drying. These days, a photopolymer plate has replaced the rubber plate and water-based inks are used since they are more environmentally friendly. Due to the flexibility of the photopolymer plate, flexographic printing is not as precise as other printing methods, so trap and bleed allowances are greater. Four-color process is infrequently used in flexography for this reason.

Rotogravure

A rotogravure press is the most precise type of printing as it uses copper plates with recessed cells to carry the ink. These cells are chemically etched and are incredibly fine (5,000 cells per square inch). As a result, this type of printing produces excellent quality proofs. Gravure presses run at speeds of up to 3,000 feet per minute. And like

Flexographic Press

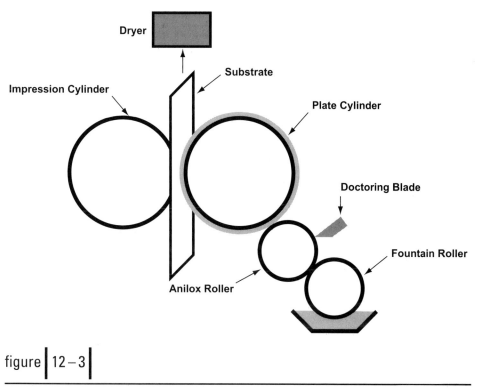

figure | 12 – 3 |

Flexographic printing is not as precise as other printing methods.

flexography, the inks contain a solvent and are dried nearly instantly after going through each roller (see figure 12 – 4).

Gravure printing used to be very expensive and was only used for runs in the millions. Nowadays, it has become more economical and so it is used more frequently. It is mostly used for plastic or foil packaging, although some designers prefer it for printing high-quality art books, as halftone images are of better quality with gravure printing.

OTHER PRINTING METHODS

Occasionally, you may be working on a project that uses a printing method that is not one of the ones mentioned above. It is wise to become familiar with these methods as they can add value and interest to your work. Here then, is a short description of each one, what material they print on, and when the method could be used.

Rotogravure Press

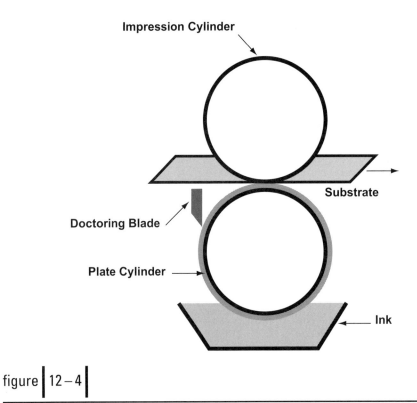

figure | 12 – 4 |

Paper and other substrates move rapidly through a gravure press.

Screen Printing

Although many graphic designers are not familiar with screen printing, it is frequently used to print large posters or banners for sporting events or for signage. It is also used to print on many promotional items such as coffee mugs, clothing, and decals for automobiles. The production of artwork for this type of printing requires precise specifications, especially for trapping (see Chapter 8), so it may be better to leave this to an expert.

The actual size of a screen press can vary, depending on what type of material the printing plant specializes in. For instance, if the printer specializes in flags, the press would have to be very large. In screen printing, there are no plates but rather a light-sensitive screen that carries a cutout of the image to be printed, almost like a stencil. Originally, the screen was made of silk, and was originally called silk screening. However, these days a synthetic nylon mesh is used.

Four-color printing is not common in screen printing because of the absorbency of the fabric and problems with registration. The viscosity of the ink must also be carefully monitored. If it is too low, it will soak into the fabric. If it is too high, it will clog the screen. Screen presses vary greatly in size and can be no larger than a bread box or several feet in length.

Thermography

You may have seen older business cards that are printed with ink that looks raised or embossed. It is very shiny and looks almost plastic. This is thermographic printing. It used to be a very common method of printing business cards, but is used less frequently today. It involves a combination of both a powdered resin as well as wet ink. As the paper moves through the press, the wet ink is applied where the image is and then the resin powder is placed over the entire surface. A vacuum takes away the resin that has not stuck to the paper and it moves through an oven that melts the ink onto its surface.

Thermography is often used in combination with letterpress and offset printing. Some designers have achieved very interesting effects using a combination of these two methods. Rather than making part of the artwork embossed, which requires a separate printing process anyway, a designer may decide to produce the same effect using this specialized printing method. Thermographic inks come in a variety of finishes, which can enhance your finished piece even more.

SPECIAL FINISHES

Although special finishes are not really a true printing process, they still play an important role in the creation of exquisite looking graphics. By using these in conjunction with the aforementioned printing methods, you can achieve a more sophisticated and luxurious appearance to your work. A brief overview of each process will give you an idea of how they can enhance your designs.

Foil Stamping

Foil stamping is used on very expensive packaging and specialty materials. Instead of printing with gold or silver ink, actual metal foil is applied to the surface of the paper using a hot foil press (see figure 12 – 5). The metal foil has a special backing behind it, and is heat stamped using a die onto the surface of the paper leaving the design of the die imprinted onto the paper. Foil stamping is frequently used with embossing to create a three-dimensional look to the finished piece.

figure | 12 – 5 |

An older model of a hot foil press. (Courtesy of Don Black Linecasting Service Limited, Toronto.)

Embossing

This type of finish helps to create a three-dimensional look to your printed piece. A separate plate is created for the embossed part of the artwork and a die is then cast using this plate (see figure 12 – 6). The printed piece is placed in position onto an embossing press and compressed with heat into the die to raise that part of the

figure | 12–6 |

An illustration of a die used for embossing.

artwork. Another type of finish similar to embossing is debossing (in this case the substrate is pushed down instead of being raised up).

Varnishes

Using a varnish on your artwork can protect the inks from smudging or fading. Most varnishing is done on an offset press. As with other printed finishes, a special plate is required. The last roller on the press is filled with the varnish instead of the ink. After all the inks are applied, a varnish is printed over all or part of the artwork. For most offset printing, only four-color images are varnished, however a varnish can also be applied to select areas of the piece as a design element to make it look more sophisticated. This is known as spot varnishing and it is usually used to repeat a pattern (such as a logo or symbol) throughout the artwork.

Die-cuts

A die-cut is used when the printed piece has a trim shape other than square or rectangular, or is cut out in a unique way. A die-cut machine literally punches out the shape from the printed piece, much the same way a cookie cutter would. A designer has to provide an outline of the die-shape to a die maker. This person then traces it onto a wooden board and uses a router to make a groove around the shape.

> ### Creating a Plate for a Die-cut
>
> If you want to use a die-cut in your artwork document, create the die-line in Illustrator first. It is best to draw it using a color that does not exist by itself anywhere in your artwork, like a Pantone® or spot color. Then import it into Quark or InDesign and place it on a separate layer. Now name the layer "die-cut" so the printer knows what the plate will be used for when the artwork is imaged to film. Create new layers for the other graphic elements, so you can print them separately from the die-cut layer.

Strips of metal are then hammered into the wood. The tops of these strips have a sharp edge, which serves to cut the die out of the printed piece (see figure 12–7). This process is commonly used in the production of packaging.

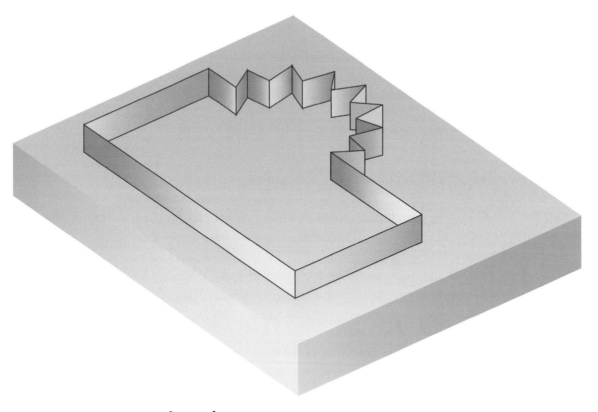

figure | 12–7 |

An illustration of a die board used to make a die-cut.

Digital Printing

Digital printing is becoming the norm for short print runs and where quick turn-around time is necessary. The printing process is faster because the usual film work is eliminated with this type of printing. The electronic files are RIPped directly through the printer where they are imaged onto paper using similar technology to that used in offset printing. The most common type of digital printer in use today is an Indigo press (see figure 12–8). This type of press can print up to 40 color pages per hour and can be used on runs of 500 to 10,000 copies. An Indigo press uses an electrically charged liquid toner rather than dry ink powder that is found in other types of digital printers like laser printers. The toner is brought into contact with the paper and adheres only in the areas not exposed to light. For this reason, each plate in a digital must be imaged each time a copy is produced. This may seem like a drawback, but the process actually offers greater flexibility.

The technology behind digital presses allows the print provider to make use of variable data, meaning that special text or imprints can be made for each individual copy. Content can be individualized for each copy printed. In traditional printing, the same plates are used for the entire press run. Many direct marketing companies

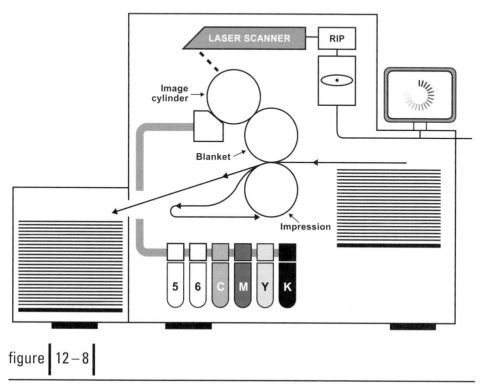

figure | 12–8 |

An Indigo press uses a process similar to offset printing.

are now making use of this technology to target their mailings to individuals within a specific audience.

You can also print on almost any type of paper stock with a digital press. And the quality of a proof from them is very close to those in offset. Although printing from a color laser or large format inkjet costs less per copy, they are not capable of printing large volumes of a job at the same speed as a digital press.

BINDING METHODS

Another area of printing and finishing that you will need to become familiar with is how the pages of your document will be bound together once the press run is over. For the most part, your print provider will offer suggestions based on their experience. Still, it is helpful to be familiar with the various types of binding processes, as different types of binding can affect the quality of the finished piece. An overview of each method will help you select the one that suits your piece.

Saddle-stitch Binding

Nearly every magazine you see on the newsstand uses this method of binding. Pages are printed together as spreads, collated and then the signatures are stapled together in the center of the publication, from the outside inwards. After the stapling is done, the signatures are trimmed out. The name is derived from the part of the machine that holds the signatures when they are stapled. Saddle-stitching is one of the most common and economical types of binding methods.

Case Binding

Hardcover books use this method of binding as it is much stronger and more durable than other ones. It is also the most expensive. The signatures are sewn on the left side of the page and then glue is applied to the outside edge. The pages are then glued to a cloth that is in turn glued to the hard cover, which is also called a case board, hence its name. The gluing of the cloth to the case board is known as backlining. This is what makes it so durable. You can see how this process works by opening a hardcover book and looking at it from its top. You will notice a gap between the pages and the cover.

Perfect Binding

Many large brochures, manuals, and annual reports are bound together using this method. Like case binding, it also uses a gluing process. Once the signatures are

> ## Beware of Creep
>
> When you are planning to use saddle-stitching to bind your document, ask your print provider for information on creep allowance. Creep occurs in saddle-stitching because the thickness of the paper makes the very inside signatures extend outside the normal trim size. In publications with more than 30 pages, this can mean the inside pages are much narrower than the ones on the outside. In most cases, you need to compensate for this by decreasing the margins on the inside pages.

placed together, they are flattened and ground down to a relatively smooth edge. The cover is then glued to the signatures and trimmed to size. It is a less expensive process than case, but also less durable.

Cerlox and Spiral Binding

These two methods are quite similar to each other. Cerlox uses a plastic comb spine on the left side of the document. The teeth in the comb are inserted into holes and hold the pages together. This way, the spine can be removed, making it easy to add or delete pages. Spiral binding also involves punching holes and then threading a spiral wire through to secure the pages.

As you begin to work in the graphics industry, you will find out there are more ways to bind your document; however, these are the most common. Many design schools teach students how to do their own binding for presentation mock ups. Once you learn them, you can bind your own booklets. Many designers find this valuable when creating a self-promotion piece or a portfolio.

Imposition

When a printer configures a number of pages together on a larger sheet of paper, it is called imposition. This is done because it is more cost effective than printing out one sheet at a time. For most magazines and brochures, four pages are placed together on one side of a single sheet. The individual pages that are printed together on the larger sheet are called a signature. Although the orientation of each page is often different, they will be in the correct order when assembled and bound together.

Reader and Printer Spreads

Depending on how your final piece is bound, you need to build your digital document using either printer or reader spreads. Reader spreads are basically pages in order of how you would normally read them. They are used for all the binding methods, except saddle-stitching. In programs like Quark and InDesign, you would select the Single Pages box when creating a new document. When saddle-stitching is used, you must create a document with pages side-by-side or in spreads. In this case, you need to select the Facing Pages box when a new document is created. However, your pages cannot be in numerical order, but must be organized by placing the fist page with the last page, then the second page with the second last page, and so on (see figure 12–9). This way, your pages will read correctly when the spreads are collated together.

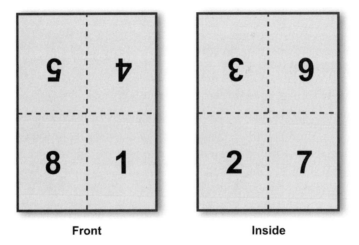

Front   **Inside**

figure | 12 – 9 |

A signature contains several pages on a large sheet of paper. In this case, the pages are arranged in printer spreads.

For instance, if you were producing a book or magazine, your printer would imposition several pages together in proper order on a large sheet (see figure 12–9 again). The size of the sheet can vary, depending on the press. When planning out the layout of the imposition sheet, a printer must allow room for crop and registration marks, bleeds, fold lines, and color bars. As a designer, you generally do not need to worry about imposition, as your printer takes care of the setup of the signatures.

SENDING YOUR FILES FOR OUTPUT

Sooner or later you will have to send the artwork files you have prepared to a service provider for film work to be completed. Although you may have properly prepared your document, collected all necessary supporting files and fonts, and printed laser separated proofs of your work to ensure all colors will separate properly into plates, you still have to indicate to your service provider how the film should be imaged. Providing incorrect information will only cause delays and result in wasted materials and ultimately, money.

Filling Out an Output Request Form

Nearly every service provider has its own customized Output Request Form. If we look at a representation of a generic form, you can determine what type of information they require for imaging your files (see figure 12–10). By systematically reviewing that information, you will see for yourself how to prepare one. The essential parts of an Output Request Form are:

- Client name, contact, address, and phone numbers
- Delivery information
- Job information (platform and applications used, what media was provided, if images, fonts, and a hard copy were supplied, etc.)
- Page and ink specifications (what size of page, bleeds, crop and registration marks, number of colors, etc.)
- What type of proof is required (dylux, color key, laminate, or digital)
- Specifications on how the job will be output (i.e. film or paper, negative or positive, emulsion down or up, etc.)
- Number of pages to be output and format (single sheets, spreads, etc.)
- Resolution of printed film (dpi)
- Halftone screen ruling (lpi)
- Turnaround (normal, rush, or emergency)
- Special instructions.

Although the Output Request Form may seem fairly straightforward, the information you enter for each job may vary depending on what application you use, what type of press on which it is being printed, and how you want the document formatted for the

Output Request Form

ABC GRAPHICS INC.

123 Prepress Street
AnyTown, NY 005556
Tel: 555-505-0056
Fax: 555-505-0556

Invoice to __One Great Design Studio__
Contact __Skip Monk__
Address __456 Designer Lane, Hucksville, NY__
Tel: __555-500-5600__ Fax: __555-500-5605__
Delivery by __Courier__ Same Day ____ Overnight __✔__
Hold for Pickup ____ Call when ready __✔__ P.O. No __123-456-06__

Software	Media	Image As	Specifications
☑ QuarkXPress	☐ CD	☐ Single pages	☑ Positive
☐ InDesign	☑ USB Stick	☑ Spreads	☐ Negative
☐ PDF	☐ FTP Server	☑ Registration Marks	☐ Emulsion Up
☐ Other	☐ E-mail attachment	☑ Bleeds	☑ Emulsion Down

Name of File	Document Size	No. of pages	No. of Colors
magazine_spread.qxd	11 in. x 17 in.	8	4

Ouput to	Screen ruling	Resolution	Included with files	Fonts
☑ Film	☐ 100 lpi	☐ 1200 dpi	☑ Fonts	☑ Adobe
☐ Pressmatch	☐ 133 lpi	☑ 2400 dpi	☑ Images	☐ Linotype
☑ Laminate	☑ 150 lpi	☐ 3600 dpi	☑ Color Profiles	☐ Monotype
☐ Dylux	☐ 200 lpi	☐ 4500 dpi	☑ Hard Copy	☐ Other

Turn around

☑ 24 hrs
☐ 12 hrs (add 50%)
☐ 2 hrs (add 100%)
☐ NOW! (beg... a lot)

Special Instructions:

Signature _____ Date _____

figure | 12 – 10 |

An example of an Output Request Form with information for a job that will run on a sheet-fed offset press.

film work. For instance, if you are outputting film for a business card, you may choose to combine several pages of your artwork documents together on a larger sheet. If you want your service provider to image more than one document per page, you will need to indicate this on the Output Request Form.

> ## Let it Bleed
>
> Make sure you have placed bleeds in your artwork document, as well as indicating crop marks, registration, and bleeds on your Output Request Form. Bleeds are applied to all items that run over the edge of the trim size of your document (see figure 12–11). Normally, they are set to one-eighth of an inch for a job that will be run on a sheet-fed offset press and one-quarter of an inch for a web offset press. Failure to allow for bleeds means that the printer must try to trim the printed piece exactly along the printed edge, an almost impossible task.
>
>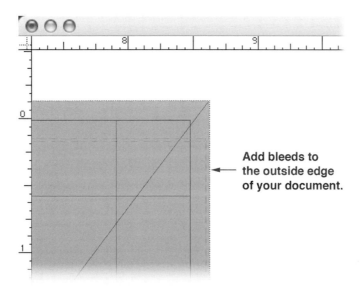
>
> **Add bleeds to the outside edge of your document.**
>
> figure | 12–11 |
>
> Apply bleeds over the page boundaries of your document.

The information on this mocked up version of an Output Request Form (see figure 12–9 again) was entered as if the job was being printed on a sheet-fed offset press with a medium clay coated stock. Look at the areas where job information is entered, as well as the resolution, page, and ink specifications. The information entered shows that the job will be imaged to the following specifications: negative film, emulsion down, four process colors, 11″ × 17″ spreads with crop, registration marks, and bleeds. The printer resolution is set at 2400 dpi and the line screen frequency is 150 lpi. A PressMatch or laminate proof is requested with a turnaround time of one day.

Lean, Mean Files

Remove any unused objects and their contents from your output document and supporting files before outputting to film. These elements will only cause your files to take longer to RIP through the output device. This includes items left on the pasteboard in these applications. Also, crop images in their native program rather than in the output document. The output device still has to read all the information for the Photoshop or Illustrator file whether it is showing or not. Fixing these will make sure your files print faster and avoid extra charges for long processing times by your service provider.

The information would change if you were printing on either an uncoated stock or a high gloss stock. It would also change if you were printing on another type of press, such as a gravure press. Always check the specifications for resolution and film specifications with your print provider before sending your files to the service provider.

Turnaround Time

You should allow at least two days for processing the film, in case unexpected problems occur. This way, you will still have time to fix the problem without incurring extra charges. Most errors that happen at the film stage are due to missing fonts or images. Once again, performing a Collect for Output of all your files is essential. Normal turnaround for most service providers is 24 hours. They add 50 percent to the price of the job if the turnaround time requested is less than 24 hours and 100 percent if less than 12 hours.

In case you don't have an Output Request Form from your service provider handy, Quark provides one for you. Look in the QuarkXPress application folder and go to Templates > English > Output Request Template.qxt. The information is more or

All Together Now...

Make sure you output every color plate in your film all at once. This is because text can reflow and other elements can change position when a document is opened on a different system or if changes are made to the original document that was sent for film. The same rule applies if one plate does not print correctly when you get your film back. Be sure to reprint **all** the plates in the film again to be on the safe side.

less the same as you have seen on the mock up earlier in this chapter. Once you open the template, you can fill the information in, save the file as a separate document, and print a copy for the service provider. It is a good idea to keep a copy for your own records in case they make an error. (These people are good, but not infallible.) This way, you have proof that you sent the correct information.

THE PRESS APPROVAL

Your responsibilities as a designer do not end as soon as you send the film to the printer. If you work for a design studio, or even freelance, you will be required to attend a press approval at some point in your career. It might seem like a rather trivial task, but in fact it is absolutely essential, particularly for large and expensive press runs. Sure, you might be able to skip a trip to the printer for a small one- or two-color job, especially if you have a good working relationship with the printer. However, you cannot afford to miss a press approval for work that is four or more colors. In fact, most printers demand that you check and approve a press proof.

The Press Proof

Once the press operator has prepared the presses by adjusting the ink flow, paper feed rates, tension of the cylinders, aligning the plates, compensating for vibration of the press, ensured proper registration, and adjusting for humidity levels, the press approval can begin. The press operator will run about 200 or so copies during this adjusting phase. Once the press operator is satisfied with the quality, a proof is pulled from the stack that meets the standards the printer has set for their work. It is up to the designer to find possible imperfections and color imbalances in the press proof.

Checking the Proof

It is easy to miss small defects if you are not paying close attention when checking a press proof. Scan the proof carefully and visually check the following areas:

- The alignment of the registration marks. You should only see one mark, not several that overlap. If you see more than one, the colors are not registered properly on the proof (see figure 12–12). A printer's loupe can aid in determining this.
- The color bars that run down the side of the paper. Look at the solid color bars and the tint bars (see figure 12–13). Check for ghosting and fading of the CMYK inks and also any spot colors you may be using. Ask the press operator to check any trouble areas with a densitometer.

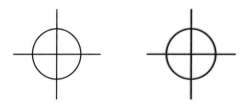

**registration marks
that are in alignment**

**misregistered
registration marks**

figure | 12 – 12 |

A printer's loupe (or magnifying glass) will help you determine if the registration marks on a press proof are correctly aligned.

- Check the trapping. Make sure there is no separation where two different colors meet.

- Look for imperfections in the proof caused by dust or scratches on the plates. These can include broken type, mottling, and hickeys. Hickeys are flecks of dust on the plate that causes the ink to pool in small spots on the printed sheet. They often show up in areas of high ink density.

- Check for color imbalance in the skin tones of people or objects in the images on the proof. At times, the tension of one of the cylinders can be set too high and the color becomes oversaturated. This usually occurs with cyan or magenta ink. If you notice a cast on the skin tones in the press proof, ask the press operator to ease off the tension on the roller for that plate.

- Make sure the stock is correct. Sometimes a press run is finished before someone notices that the stock was different than what was ordered. Bring along a sample of the stock to check the press proof against. Some paper stocks are so close that even the press operator may not see the difference.

- If you are using direct-to-plate printing, then look for any images or text that may be missing. If you are bypassing the film stage, there is a chance that elements may not show up on the plates. Make sure you get a digitally plotted proof before the press run begins.

- If you are checking a spread in a brochure, magazine, or annual report, then fold the paper along the fold lines to ensure that the pages are in the correct position and aligned properly.

Always remember that press time is very expensive and changes to plates after the print run has begun can be very costly. It is better to check your work carefully before you send the files out for film. If you are not sure you are correctly imaging your film to your printer's press specifications, then don't assume... ask for help! Taking the time to ensure your work will print out properly is well worth it.

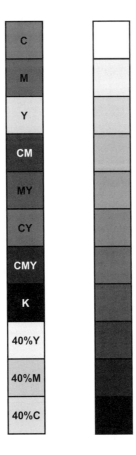

figure | 12–13 |

The color bars can assist in determining the density of the printed inks. See color insert.

Resources

Evans, P. and Thomas, M. (2004) Exploring the Elements of Design, Delmar/Thomson Learning

Rivard, P. (2006) Digital Color Correction, Delmar/Thomson Learning

Romano, F. (1996) Pocket Guide to Digital Prepress, Delmar/Thomson Learning

Sharma, A. (2004) Understanding Color Management, Delmar/Thomson Learning

Web Resources

http://www.donblack.ca

http://www.enfocus.com

http://www.pilotmarketing.com

http://www.typodermic.com

http://www.markzware.com

SUMMARY

The majority of information I have written in this book has been derived from more than quarter of a century of working and teaching in the graphic arts industry. I hope that after reading it, you have a clear understanding of prepress theories and procedures. This chapter in particular is important in that it provides a glimpse of what happens after the prepress phase when the job finally goes to press. The greatest satisfaction a graphic designer can experience is when they see that first piece they designed in printed form. Whether it is a packaged product, an annual report, a brand identity, or an editorial piece, there is a sense of pride in seeing your work in the real world.

If you have read this book through thoroughly and understood the content, then you can't go wrong when you reach this final yet crucial phase. Apply the teachings to the work you are doing now to prepare yourself for actual industry situations. Once you have mastered these methods, you will see for yourself that having a sound knowledge of prepress makes you a better designer. Success in any area of life depends on how you approach it. If you readily embrace prepress technology then you will soon become a more accomplished graphic designer.

▶ *in review*

1. What is a printer's loupe used for?

2. Name one printing method that uses polymer plates.

3. Name three things you should check at the press approval.

4. What print resolution (dpi) would you use for printing on a medium quality clay coated paper with a sheet-fed offset press?

5. Why is it necessary to output all your film plates at once?

6. Name three binding methods and briefly explain each one.

7. Which printing method creates an embossed appearance to your artwork?

8. What is the normal print run range for an Indigo press?

▶ *exercises*

1. Open up a Quark document where the page sizes are small. Go to File > Print. Set up the different sections the way you would for any other project you will print out. In the Print window, click on the Printer button and select Layout from the pop-up menu. Choose the maximum number of pages you can fit on one sheet of letter size paper. Now select how they will be orientated toward each other. Print the file out. What do you notice about the pages and the way the artwork is oriented?

2. Open up the press-quality Acrobat PDF file that you created from Illustrator in Chapter 9. Look at the color bars on the side and bottom of the document. What colors are represented? What other marks are there on the page? Do you know what they are called and why they are there?

glossary

Additive colors A color system whereby white light is achieved by adding together full values of red, green, and blue. Black is produced when the RGB values are at zero.

Analog proof A color proof that is imaged from negative film.

Average key A photographic image where the color is located mostly in the mid-tones.

Algorithms A programmed set of routines that certain software programs use to perform a particular function.

Bleed A graphic element that runs over the edge of a document or printed sheet.

Bit The smallest amount of information in computer language with a value of either 1 or 0.

Bit-depth The maximum number of bits contained within a pixel.

Camera-ready artwork A white art board with all the elements such as type, images, and line art pasted into position. It is used for making film negatives.

CIE Internationale de L'Eclairage (or the International Commission of Illumination), an organization that sets standards for measuring color.

CMYK An acronym for cyan, magenta, yellow, and black. They are printed inks that are used to represent graphics and images on a page. Also known as process colors.

Continuous-tone image A photographic image where all the colors blend into each other without separation by halftone dots.

DCS Desktop color separation. An image format that separates the channels into individual files with an additional file that is an 8-bit preview.

Densitometer A device that measures the consistency of color in a press run.

Dot gain The amount of ink saturation on the surface of paper during printing. Results in the increase of the size of the laser and halftone dots on a page.

Digital proof A color proof made from an electronic file that does not require film to produce it.

Emboss The raising of a paper's surface to create a three-dimensional effect.

Encapsulated PostScript (EPS) An image format that does not allow for editing except in the program in which the file was created. It allows output devices with postscript translators to reproduce graphics onto a printed sheet.

Font All the characters, numbers, and symbols in a typeface that is specified to a certain size and style.

Four-color process The printing of screen separations of CMYK inks to produce an image.

Gamma The amount of contrast in the mid-tones of a photographic image, based on a mathematical formula.

Gamut The range of colors that can be reproduced by either a system or a device.

GCR (gray component replacement) A process that removes high densities of cyan, magenta, and yellow in all tonal regions and replaces them with black.

Ghosting A faint duplicate of an image that appears on a press sheet in areas of dense ink coverage.

GIMP Gnu image manipulation program. An image-editing program created for the Linux operating system.

Halftone A grid pattern of dots that vary in size to create the appearance of a continuous tone image.

High key A photographic image where the color is mostly in the highlights and mid-tones.

High resolution An image where the number of pixels per inch is high, which results in better quality.

Highlights The lightest area in a photographic image.

HSB color system An acronym for hue, saturation, and brightness. The HSB model defines color in percentages of these three characteristics.

Imposition The configuration of pages on a press sheet so the pages will be in proper order when folded and trimmed.

Input device A device that collects information from the outside world and translates it into data that is stored electronically in a computer's operating system.

Imagesetter An output device that images graphic elements onto photosensitive paper or film.

JPEG An acronym for Joint Photographers Experts Group. This image format uses a high level of compression, resulting in loss of color.

Kelvin (degrees) A temperature reading that describes the color quality of light. If the temperature is lower, the light is warmer (yellow). If it is higher, it is cooler (blue).

L*A*B* A color system developed from the earlier CIE chromaticity model that uses three axes of luminance, blue to yellow, and red to green to describe color.

Laser dots   The smallest printable dot pattern used to represent text, colors, blends, and images on paper. Smaller laser dots combine to form the larger halftone dots.

Ligature   A combination of letters in a font that are combined into one character.

Line screen frequency   A term used to describe the resolution of halftone images (also known as lpi).

Low key   A photographic image where the color is mostly in the mid-tones and shadows.

Loupe   A small, rectangular magnifying glass that a press operator uses to check registration on a press sheet.

Mid-tones   Tonal values in a photographic image that are approximately halfway between the highlight and shadow tones.

Moiré pattern   A printing error that occurs when two colors are set to the same screen angle. Can also be caused by two screen patterns overlapping each other.

One-quarter tones   Tonal values in a photographic image that fall approximately halfway between the highlights and the mid-tones.

Open type   A cross-platform font format based on Unicode that supports any language and provides a wider range of features.

Output device   A device that translates data onto a printed page.

Pantone®   A color matching system that uses solid inks. It was developed by Pantone, Inc. and displays inks in coated, uncoated, matte, and metallic finishes.

PDF   A multi-platform file format in which all fonts, images, and color profiles are embedded into the file. It is necessary to have a copy of Acrobat Reader to open or view a file in this format.

Pica   A measurement system that is used to measure the point sizes of characters in a font. There are six picas in an inch.

Pixel   Small squares of color used to reproduce a photographic image on a monitor.

Phosphor dots   Small dots made with an electronically charged substance that emits red, green, or blue color on a monitor. The electronic charge can be varied to create different hues and saturation of color.

Photocomposition   A method of typesetting where light is first passed through a negative disc and then through a prism onto light-sensitive paper.

Photostat A black and white reproduction of a graphic imaged onto photosensitive paper using a photostat camera.

Photoshop A software program made by Adobe Systems, Inc. used to edit pixel-based images.

PostScript A page-description language invented by Adobe Systems, Inc. Output devices use the postscript data contained within each file to print elements from a graphics program.

PostScript fonts A font format where there are two components, a screen font and a printer font that is read by the output device. Also known as Type 1 fonts.

Press operator A person responsible for the setup and maintenance of a press during the printing process.

RAM Short-term random access memory that is stored in memory chips inside the CPU.

Register Ensuring that various plates align exactly with one another during the printing stage.

Reader spreads The pages of a document that are in sequence of how they will be read and numbered accordingly.

Right reading An image that is produced so that the viewer reads left to right.

RIP An acronym for raster image processor. It is the process by which the post-script language, contained in a graphic artwork file, is converted into printed dots.

Saturation The density of color in an image.

Screen angles The rotating of screens of the four process colors to create a rosette pattern. Also called traditional or AM screening.

Screen font Contains the bitmap metrics data that allows the software program to render it on a monitor.

Serif Short lines at the ends of the stroke in a character.

Service provider A business that supplies film separations from digital files.

Soft proof A proof where the colors are viewed on screen, instead of printed inks on paper. The proof simulates different color systems on various paper stocks.

Spot color A premixed ink that represents color on a page. The inks are solid and not made up of screen dots of CMYK.

Subtractive colors   A color system in which the colors that reach our eyes are from waves of light reflecting off printed dots of cyan, magenta, and yellow. In order to achieve white, the process inks must be removed or subtracted. In theory, 100 percent of cyan, magenta, and yellow should produce black, but lack of purity in the process inks requires the addition of black (K) to provide definition and detail.

SWOP   Specifications for web offset publications. The specifications used for standard printing conditions in the graphic arts industry.

TIFF   Tagged image file format. An editable image format that is used by output devices to reproduce graphics on a printed sheet. Unlike the EPS format, the output devices do not require postscript translators.

Trap   The overlapping of colors where two different inks meet.

Three-quarter tones   Tonal values in a photographic image that lie approximately halfway between the mid-tones and the shadows.

Thumbnail   A miniature sketch that represents a design or idea.

Trapping   The overlapping of inks to avoid misregistration in the printing process.

TrueType   A font format that is used mostly on computers with a Windows operating system.

Unicode   A 16-bit character code that includes character sets from every language.

UCR (under color removal)   A process that removes high densities of cyan, magenta, and yellow in the shadow regions of an image and replaces them with black.

Varnish   A protective coating applied to the surface of the paper during the press run.

Vector   Graphic elements that are comprised of plotted points connected by lines.

Wavelength   The distance between two corresponding points of equal amplitude on an electromagnetic wave of light. Measured in terms of nanometers.

White point   Full values of red, green, and blue in a monitor. It is measured in degrees kelvin, which represents the color temperature. This temperature ranges between 5000 and 9300 K.

Working space   The window displaying the information contained in your software document.

Wrong reading   An image that is horizontally flipped so it reads right to left, or backward.

index

figure |1|

Wavelengths of light reflecting off objects provide our eyes with color information that our mind translates into an image.

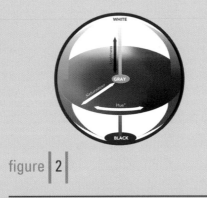

figure |2|

The HSB model defines color in attributes of hue, saturation, and brilliance.

Addititive Color System

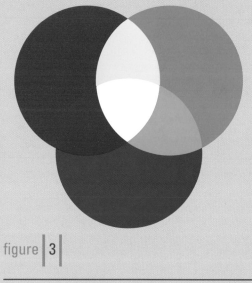

figure 3

Maximum values of RGB produce white in the additive system, while '0' values produce black.

Subtractive Color System

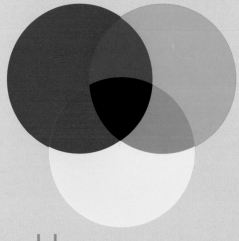

figure 4

All the subtractive colors combine to form black, while white is the absence of color. Note that combining different subtractive colors also produces red, green, and blue.

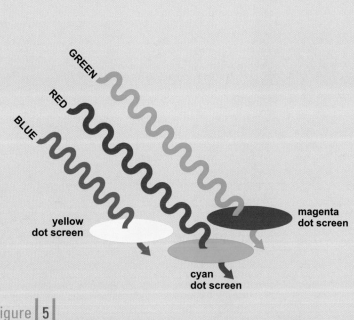

GREEN

RED

BLUE

yellow
dot screen

magenta
dot screen

cyan
dot screen

figure | 5 |

Process screen dots absorb one wavelength of light and reflect the others back to our eyes. The illustration shows which one of the RGB colors the yellow, cyan, and magenta screen dots absorb.

Before

After

figure | 6 |

Open and compare the before and after image to ensure your color corrections are accurate.

figure |7|

This photo has faded over time and taken on a yellowish cast.

figure |8|

Print the final file to ensure details in the highlights and shadows are visible, and the color balance is correct.

figure | 9

A high key image lacks color in the three-quarter and shadow areas, so there is very little contrast.

figure | 10

The final image has better color balance and contrast making it more dynamic.

figure | 11 |

This photo is too dark in the one-quarter and mid-tones.
This makes the person's features appear flat and not
clearly defined.

figure | 12 |

The final corrected image has better contrast and
definition between the shadows and the other tonal
areas. Notice the high percentage of yellow in the
man's face.

figure | 13 |

This photo is an average key image that has a definite reddish cast.

figure | 14 |

The final corrected image has a richer tonal quality than the original along with colors that are more realistic.

figure | 15 |

Halftone dots in CMYK form a rosette pattern in traditional (AM) screening.

figure | 16 |

Stochastic or FM screening produces a smoother, finer halftone image.

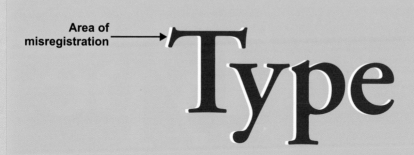

figure | 17 |

An example of how two colors can misregister when printed without trapping.

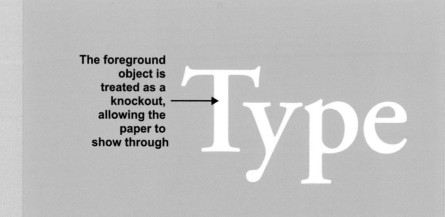

figure | 18 |

An example of a knockout trap with the paper showing through.

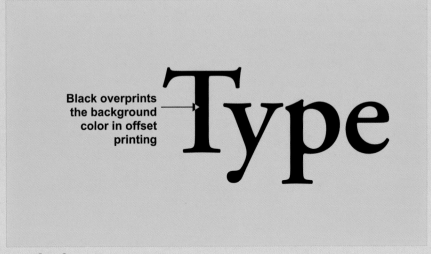

**Black overprints
the background
color in offset
printing** →Type

figure │ 19 │

An example of a black colored object overprinting a different background color.

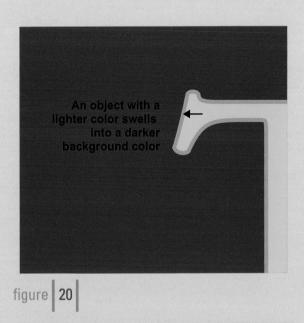

**An object with a
lighter color swells
into a darker
background color**

figure │ 20 │

A spread occurs when a lighter object is placed over a darker background.

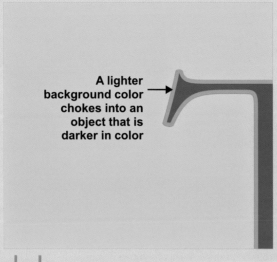

A lighter background color chokes into an object that is darker in color

figure | 21 |

A choke is the opposite of a spread. Here darker text is placed over a lighter background.

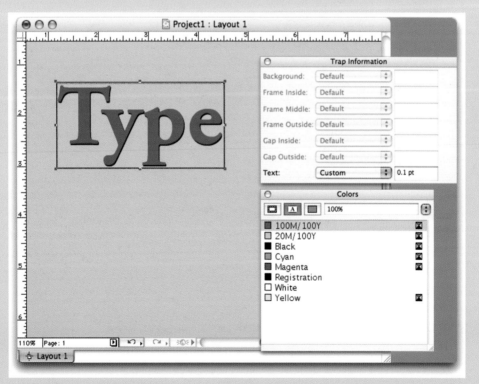

figure | 22 |

Creating a custom trap lets you properly trap three overlapping objects.

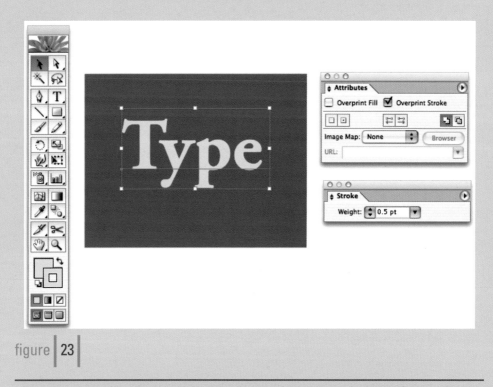

figure 23

In Illustrator, a spread is created by placing a stroke around the object and selecting Overprint Stroke in the Attribute palette. This technique can be used when importing an object into Quark or InDesign and placing it over a background or four-color image.

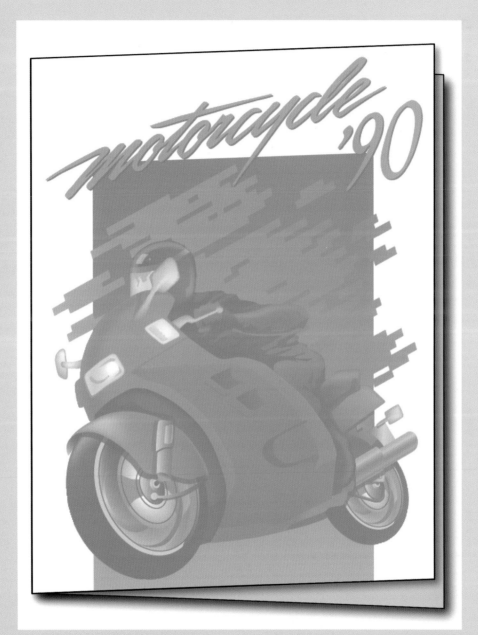

figure | 24 |

A dylux is a monochromatic proof made from film negatives. Each negative is given a different exposure time, which allows you to discern each color. A dylux is commonly used for artwork where only one or two colors are being printed. It is also referred to as a "blue."

figure | 25 |

A Color Key is made up of four acetates in CMYK. Each of the four process colors is on top of another, in register, to produce a color proof. Color Keys can be used to check trapping and whether colors are specified correctly, but does not accurate show how the colors will look after they are printed on a press.

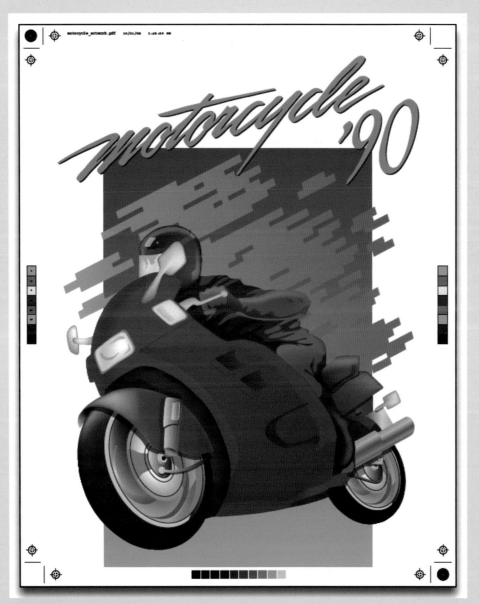

figure | 26 |

A laminate is a contact proof where gels are attached to a white backing card.

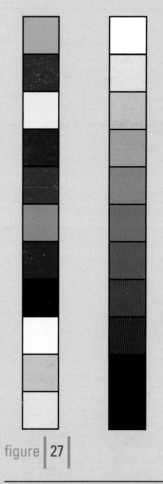

figure | 27 |

The color bars can assist in determining the density of the printed inks.